ONSTAGE WITH MARTHA GRAHAM

UNIVERSITY PRESS OF FLORIDA

Florida A&M University, Tallahassee
Florida Atlantic University, Boca Raton
Florida Gulf Coast University, Ft. Myers
Florida International University, Miami
Florida State University, Tallahassee
New College of Florida, Sarasota
University of Central Florida, Orlando
University of Florida, Gainesville
University of North Florida, Jacksonville
University of South Florida, Tampa
University of West Florida, Pensacola

ONSTAGE
with
MARTHA GRAHAM

· ·

STUART HODES

Foreword by Deborah Jowitt

University Press of Florida

Gainesville · Tallahassee · Tampa · Boca Raton

Pensacola · Orlando · Miami · Jacksonville · Ft. Myers · Sarasota

Frontis: Stuart Hodes dancing with Martha Graham in *Appalachian Spring* at the Alvin Theater, New York City, 1953. Photographer unknown; from the author's personal collection.

Many of the images in this book are from the author's personal collection. Readers with information on missing credit details are asked to contact the publisher.

26 25 24 23 22 21   6 5 4 3 2 1

ISBN 978-0-8130-6638-7
Library of Congress Control Number: 2019950418

The University Press of Florida is the scholarly publishing agency for the State University System of Florida, comprising Florida A&M University, Florida Atlantic University, Florida Gulf Coast University, Florida International University, Florida State University, New College of Florida, University of Central Florida, University of Florida, University of North Florida, University of South Florida, and University of West Florida.

University Press of Florida
2046 NE Waldo Road
Suite 2100
Gainesville, FL 32609
http://upress.ufl.edu

I imagined myself preparing for flight.

—Dorothy Bird on Graham floor moves

Contents

Foreword

When Stuart Hodes took his first dance lesson at the Martha Graham School at 66 Fifth Avenue, in New York City, he was almost twenty-one years old and had been de-mobbed after spending three years as a pilot in the U.S. Army Air Corps. It was 1946, and Graham had accustomed herself to losing male dancers to World War II and schooling late starters. Hodes had been dancing less than six months when she put him onstage.

You may guess from the first chapter of his *Onstage with Martha Graham* that motion exhilarated him. He was also—perhaps unbeknownst to him at that airborne time—on his way to becoming a writer.

Entering Martha Graham's company after active service in the military, he must have drawn on the discipline that had been drilled into him, as he trained his body to master such skills as turning out his legs and pointing his feet. Not surprisingly, the first solo that he choreographed, *FLAK* (1951), was based on his earlier bombing missions.

He found the bedrock of Graham's technique exhilarating: Contraction and Release—a fierce execution of the act of breathing—has the whole body responding in subtly complex ways to the impulse to cave in and then expand again. Being strong and tall, he fit well into her creative plans; almost every man she recruited in those days stood six feet in height or more. Paul Taylor, in his memoir *Private Domain*, wickedly offered this view of his role as a dancer in Graham's company during the 1950s: "We're usually stiff foils, or something large and naked for women to climb up on."

Hodes's memoir differs from many other books by those in the dance world, in that his career eventually pushed him onto several parallel, intersecting, or branching paths. As he explains in *Onstage with Martha Graham,* he discovered pretty quickly that not much money could be made performing in a modern dance company. The Martha Graham Dance Company usually had a week-long salaried season in a Broadway theater (maybe even a two-week or a three-week one), plus tours consisting mostly of one-night stands. Rehearsals, which most often took place at night, didn't involve money, and little if any came the dancers' way during the summers, when Graham taught at the American Dance Festival in New London, Connecticut.

Hodes got used to juggling his responsibilities to her with forays into Broadway musicals. Imagine him in 1958, for instance, no longer even in her company, naked but for a jockstrap and some feathers, performing Crazy Horse in a City Center revival of the musical *Annie Get Your Gun*—he'd danced the role in the 1957 TV show too—and months later slipping back into the character of the far-seeing Husbandman in Graham's *Appalachian Spring* for Nathan Kroll's film of it (when his wife Linda, née Margolies and also in the Graham Company, gave birth to their second daughter on the second day of shooting, they named her Martha).

For years, Hodes danced not only in musicals but also, as he writes in his memoir, in "nightclubs, cabaret shows, industrials, and TV." However, Martha—whose sudden and irrational fits of temper he coped with or counterattacked, whose genius could not be denied, and who could charm him with her wit and her generosity—remained a vital part of his artistic life, in a sense his lodestar. In 1954, for instance, he's performing in *Arabian Nights* at Jones Beach Marine Theater, enduring such unexpected events as sailing onstage for a number with three other dancers, just after one of the two elephants preceding them has let loose with a copious amount of urine. During the run of the musical, Graham needs him for her company's single performance in the Hollywood Bowl, so he threatens to quit the show unless he's allowed to yield a single performance to his understudy. Permission granted, he leaves for the opposite side of the country at dawn, checks the spacing of *Diversion of Angels* and *Appalachian Spring* on the huge outdoor stage, performs in the two works, and catches a red-eye flight back to Jones Beach and more Arabian delights.

For some Graham dancers, other skills beside artistry come in handy. In 1952, when Martha's great friend and discreet patroness Baroness Bethsabée de Rothschild bought a spacious old two-story building on East 63rd Street, Hodes and fellow Grahamite Robert Cohan spent a long day in the main studio with a sander and an edger scraping the old maple floor; the next day they applied sealer. Yet from October, 1955 into January 1956, he committed himself wholly to performing leading roles in Graham's repertory while the company toured Asia and the Middle East, sponsored by the U.S. State Department. He kept a diary. Astonishing sights and enthusiastic audiences made up for injuries, makeshift stages, and the occasional splintery floor. He took every theater and television job he could get in 1956, after the birth of his first daughter, Catherine, yet in his memoir he defined that period as "while waiting for Martha to start a project." And long after he stopped dancing in Graham's company, he still taught at her school.

In 1975, after three years on the job as head of the dance program of New York University's School of the Arts (now Tisch), Stuart invited me to teach some kind of thinking-about-dance course to the MFA students. They sat around on a studio floor while I perched on a chair and raised topics I thought relevant. That somewhat rickety undertaking became a more stringent course; I eventually taught full-time in that department and kept at it for thirty years, and over the first few of them I gradually became aware of all the other dance-related jobs *he* had taken on and would continue to take on.

He taught at New York's High School of Performing Arts. He choreographed numerous works for his own group, The Ballet Team, and for other companies. He served the field as "Dance Associate" on the New York State Council on the Arts and on the Dance Advisory Panel of the National Endowment for the Arts, both of which recommended grants to choreographers and companies. He directed The Kitchen Center and was instrumental in getting the organization out of debt. In 1988, he took part in the weeks-long American Dance Festival's Critics' Conference, during which he and his peers wrote about every performance they saw (I never asked him why). In 2009, he wrote *Graham Vs. Graham: The Struggle for an American Legacy,* an account of the trial over the rights to Martha's work (unpublished but in the New York Public Library for the Performing Arts). All these are just a few of his jobs and accomplishments, and all are in *Onstage with Martha Graham,* described with compassion, nononsense linguistic flair, and sly wit. That he remembers Martha's dances well and can describe how they have changed in recent decades gives any worthwhile dance historian much to think about.

And consider this. Through it all, he never stopped dancing. He is currently in his nineties and apparently hasn't considered retirement. I remember well seeing him with Alice Teirstein in their 1996 duet *I Thought You Were Dead.* How suavely and charmingly these greatly gifted senior citizens flirted and waltzed! In a 2007 iteration of Tina Croll and

Jamie Cunningham's semi-improvisational talking-dancing work, *From the Horse's Mouth*—this one devoted to Graham—he performed his "Martha's Rap," which ends: "Now every day on celestial grass/ Heaven is taking Martha's class." I can imagine that, down the line, he'd enjoy being part of that group.

A great deal that Stuart Hodes was stimulated to learn and to document in *Onstage with Martha Graham* can be traced back to the day some seventy years ago when he walked into her studio. That moment generated—indirectly of course—his ongoing voyage through an extraordinarily rich life in dance.

Deborah Jowitt

Preface

I've been warned that long conversations in memoirs generate doubts; who remembers exactly what was said many years ago? So let me state that all quotations in this memoir are to the best of my memory, from off-stage conversations to fights with Martha. All convey the truth of the moment: from surprising to inspiring to infuriating to funny. What is written in this memoir is what I remember and how I remember it.

Prologue

In the 1970s at Manhattan Community College, a late-blooming peacenik—long blonde hair, headband, ragged jeans—asked, "Did you really drop bombs on people in World War II?"

"Yes."

"What a bummer!"

I'd been a B-17 bomber pilot. On my seven missions before Victory in Europe Day, I'd had no qualms about dropping bombs on Nazis. And when I read the headline that an atom bomb had been dropped on Hiroshima, to me it bookended Pearl Harbor.

The army I served in for almost three years, was Jim Crow. The Tuskegee Airmen were black, pilots and officers, yet no less segregated.

After discharge I couldn't vote because I was under twenty-one.

On my first dance tour, when our train left Washington, D.C., a white conductor came through to see that blacks and whites were in separate Jim Crow cars.

On Broadway, chorus dancers were all white, except for the rare cast that was all black.

Violence against women went unmentioned. Clarence Thomas became a Supreme Court justice despite credible testimony by Anita Hill.

Fashion models all looked like they were starving. Black models never appeared in white publications.

Four-letter words were replaced with euphemisms. Norman Mailer, in *The Naked and the Dead,* ended a chapter with, *"Fug it."* In *West Side Story,* a song ended, "Officer Krupke, vrup you."

Today, racism, sexism, ageism, etc., are less apparent, but who dares say they no longer exist?

The latest attempts to root out bias are toward beautism, colorism, and "plus-size" people.

Read on.

Primary trainers in formation, class book, Claiborne Flight Academy. Courtesy of the U.S. Army.

I

·　·　·　·　·　·　·　·

Airborne

On my eighteenth birthday, I was drafted, became an Aviation Cadet, won my wings, flew a B-17 bomber across the Atlantic and seven combat missions before Victory in Europe Day. Seven missions weren't enough to earn quick return to the U.S.A., so I went into the Army of Occupation where an unofficial army newspaper, *The Foggia Occupator,* needed a pilot to fly reporters around. The editor, Sgt. Milton Hoffman, a journalist in civilian life, offered me a jeep, green "U.S. Army Correspondent" press patches for my shoulders, and a Speed Graphic camera. I flew to Rome, Naples, Pisa, jeeped around southern Italy, wrote a column, then news, features, and finally became managing editor.

Dancing had never entered my life. As a preteen in Sheepshead Bay, Brooklyn, I played stickball on East 27th Street, fished in the bay, swam at Brighton Beach, biked to Coney Island for a twenty-five-cent ride on the Cyclone, and to Floyd Bennett Field to watch airplanes. I took violin lessons, played in the Brooklyn Tech orchestra, and swam backstroke for the swimming team.

One Sunday afternoon while in Basic Flight Training at Minter Air Force Base in Bakersfield, California, I saw a Fred Astaire movie, *Holiday Inn.* Afterward I felt something different from the itchy disquiet of a kid far from home. Waiting for the military bus on the empty main street, I thought, "Astaire can dance, but I can fly" and wanted Sunday to be over so I could be back in the air, cutting arcs in the sky. Years later, when I told this to Martha Graham she said, "What you really wanted was to dance."

I'd just climbed the Leaning Tower. Photo by Eugene Cowen.

Home on leave after graduating in class 44F (June 1944) wearing my new pilot's wings, I visited my uncle, Navy Commander Ira Hodes, who'd won a battlefield commission in World War I, and when World War II began joined the Navy and was refitting destroyers in the Brooklyn Navy Yard. He took me below into his realm, a boiler factory from hell. But he was proud of it, and when he introduced me to his Navy friends I realized he was proud of me.

Five years later, after I'd danced all over the U.S.A. and Europe, he asked, "When are you going to stop this dancing and go to work?"

"Dancing is my work," I replied, wondering if I could ever earn a living at it. I was Martha Graham's third military pilot. David Zellmer had flown B-24 bombers in the Pacific, and Douglas Watson had flown F4U Corsair fighters in the Navy. Both had seen combat.

"I cannot know what it is to fly a combat mission," Martha said. "But every life has its mission, and some demand all that we can give."

The day I soloed I fell in love with flying. Three years later, September 16, 1946, war over, I took a dance lesson at the Martha Graham Studio and fell in love with dancing.

Above: Stearman PT-13 "Primary" trainer. Goggles on head (instead of around neck) mean I've soloed. U.S. Army photo.

Left: In a "basic" trainer, Vultee Valiant BT-13. U.S. Army photo.

Right: Cessna AT17 "advanced trainer." In my new pilot's wings. U.S. Army photo.

Below: B-17 Flying Fortress and crew. Me, top row (*2nd from left*). U.S. Army photo.

I'm asked, "How do you go from flying to dancing?" To me it seems natural; both need space and yield new concepts of it. Both demand skills and practice. And both can become pure action in which self-awareness vanishes, leaving unearthly joy.

A few weeks before my first performance—I'd been dancing less than half a year—I confessed to Martha that I worried about forgetting my moves onstage. She told me to lie on my back and proceed mentally through the entire dance. "Don't move a muscle. The body learns first, and although you may be able to do the dance on your feet, until you can do it in your *mind*, you don't really know it."

"That's how we practiced aerobatics!" And I told her about the cadet's handbook that instructed us to lie on our backs and imagine each kick on the rudder, press on the stick, and view of earth and sky.

A stage performance, like a combat mission, is complete in itself yet part of a far greater enterprise. After each performance, I'd replay it in my mind, after which it faded unless something unusual made it stick in memory, like my first performance when I got my foot entangled in the backdrop. Or when I danced with a broken toe in Bombay. Or the Broadway musical, *First Impressions,* where I forgot my lines and improvised, next day to have writer/director Abe Burrows say, "Those were some interesting lines I *didn't* write."

I'd also replay each flying mission, transferring to permanent memory only a few, like a training mission when I'd "buzzed" (flown) fifty feet above the rooftops of Rock Hill, South Carolina. Or when I flew a four-engine bomber across the Atlantic Ocean. Or my first sight of flak exploding. Or the bombing mission to Inn Rattenberg, a railroad bridge in the Austrian Alps hidden by clouds. No enemy fighters in sight so we were ordered to break formation and seek "targets of opportunity." I spotted another bridge and after "bombs away" tilted the plane and peered down. The valley was hidden by smoke. That night two pictures flickered through my mind: an Alpine village nestled in a green valley and a village aflame, shrouded in the smoke of my bombs.

Now, in my tenth decade, flying, which I did for less than three years, and dancing, which lasted more than sixty, tower over everything but love and family.

I began as Martha's student and (because few other men were available) soon became a dancer in her troupe. In a few more years, I was her partner. Yet almost from the start, we clashed. She was known for her fierce temper, but the first time she unleashed it at me it triggered my own. From then on, she sometimes seemed to provoke me deliberately, and because I always blew back it gave her a kind of power over me. Martha was driven to dominate people, and although I welcomed her as a teacher and creative polestar I could not allow myself to be dominated.

Nevertheless, from that day to this, when I encounter her detractors I leap to her defense. Many were fascinated by Martha, others stood in awe; she scared not a few, some resisted and some opposed. For those genuinely unmoved, I feel pity, as for someone tone-deaf or without rhythm.

I never did "figure out" Martha. She could be selfish and cruel but was most often giving and warm. Intellectually brilliant, she sometimes acted with no thought at all. Everything she did was without reservation. She was also a public genius and fair game for every kind of treatment, from Agnes de Mille's patronizing, error-riddled, soap opera biography to the thought-provoking "deconstructions" of Susan Leigh Foster.

Martha's vision, her dances, and her dancing were her everything. To become an object of her interest was intoxicating, and to dance with her was to be part of a soaring enterprise. It was a challenge I was powerless to resist. Yet it took me a while to realize that I was stuck with her and with dancing for the rest of my life.

In May 1978, Alan Tung calls from Kennedy Airport. He had danced in my young audience troupe, The Ballet Team, and is now director of the school of Maurice Béjart's Ballet of the 20th Century in Belgium. He wants to see dancing on his first night back in New York City. I get tickets to Martha Graham's *Clytemnestra* at the Met, Lincoln Center.

Clytemnestra had premiered in 1958, my final year with Graham, and although not in it, I'd returned to the troupe in order to dance my old roles. Now, twenty years later, Bertram Ross, the original Agamemnon, is even more arrogant and swaggering. When he takes his first fatal step toward the bath, the sudden entrance of Death literally raises the hairs on my neck. And when Clytemnestra strikes, I want to shout, "Take that, you smug bastard!"

The original Aegisthus, one of Martha's most sinister villains, had been danced by Paul Taylor. "He's kind of shifty, so I turned him in," Paul had said, reducing his eerie characterization to not turning out his legs. Alan and I saw the role danced by Mario Delamo who has a slithery sensuality that makes Clytemnestra's fall more of a seduction than the capitulation forced on her by Paul Taylor.

Gene McDonald played the dual role of Death and Paris, whose lust for Helen started the Trojan War. He is tall and cadaverous, and Martha further elongated him on twelve-inch-high platform shoes, giving him a heavy-footed lurch, like zombies in *Night of the Living Dead.*

The evening-length drama opened with the entrance of the Messenger of Death, originated by David Wood, bare-chested, a twisted skirt low on his hips, thumping a staff on each leaden step as if dragging the whole saga onto the stage while a baritone voice utters howls of despair.

Yuriko Kimura triumphed in Martha's role. I wondered if that pleased Martha or enraged her. Probably both. The great theater of the Met was fulfilled by *Clytemnestra,* a work of dance theater still masterful and magnificent after twenty years.

Afterward, Alan said, "To step off a plane from Europe and walk straight into *Clytemnestra. . . ."* I found myself wondering what could have made me give Martha up twenty years before.

"Can you teach two or three classes a week?" It's Diane Gray, director of the Martha Graham School. Running NYU's dance program had kept me away for four years.

"Put me down for two evening classes."

I arrive to see Martha at the front door waiting for her ride home. "Martha! It's so good to be teaching here again. It reminds me of so many things."

Her eyes meet mine. "What things?"

"Things that happened in the years I danced with you."

"Write it down."

This is unexpected. Ever intent upon her next creation, she had never showed any interest in looking back.

"I am writing things down but am never sure what comes after what."

"That doesn't matter. Write it down."

Her ride appears. She starts toward the limo, turns back. "Remember, Stuart, write it down."

Twelve years, 1947 to 1958, is my time in the Martha Graham Company. In 1971, LeRoy Leatherman, her general manager for twenty years, furious because she won't answer his calls, rages, "She thinks only about herself!

She's a complete egoist! She cares nothing about the school, the company, or history." He soon quits, or is fired.

Now Martha is asking me to write down my part of that history. Does she want the adventures, the glories, the triumphs? Or the battles, cruelties, defeats? I know, of course. She wants me to write *everything* down.

2

· · · · · · · ·

Moves

March 1942

After four years at all-boys Brooklyn Technical High School, I'd been gal-
vanized by coeds at Brooklyn College until the all-male U.S. Army yanked
me back into a barren one-sex world.

Basic training finished, I tried to check on my application to the aviation cadets. Learned only that it was "in the pipeline." Meanwhile, I was
sent to radio operator mechanic school in Sioux Falls, South Dakota.

To complicate matters, I was deeply in love with Selma, whom I'd spotted when registering for classes at Brooklyn College, got in line behind
her, and peeked over her shoulder. She signed up for English and Philoso-
phy, so I did too. When she joined the drama club, Masquers, so did I. I
only wanted to be around Selma, but Masquers was fun, and at its theater
party I saw my first Broadway play, Chekhov's *The Three Sisters,* a mighty
production with Judith Anderson, Katharine Cornell, Ruth Gordon, and
Edmund Gwenn.

I didn't dare tell Selma my real feelings (don't ask me why) so filled my
letters with lighthearted banter about army life, to which she replied with
breezy chit-chat about the home front. It was not what I wanted, yet I de-
voured every syllable.

College men were scarce in September 1942, so I landed a role in *First
Lady,* Senator Keene, who had to light an actress's cigarette. Book matches
were fussy so I put a couple of wooden matches in my pocket and as I

Selma in front of hydrangea bush.

took one out, scraped it on a piece of sandpaper I'd glued inside. Big laugh. It looked like I'd taken a lighted match out of my pocket.

Also in *First Lady* was another freshman, Fred Sadoff, and a sophomore, Jerry Solars, who played the lead. Jerry, with a profile like John Barrymore, also seemed interested in Selma.

The Masquers faculty advisor, Professor Patricia Casey, told me I was round-shouldered and should work on my posture. Three years later, she took Masquers to see Martha Graham, my first Broadway appearance. "And to think," she said, "that when you joined Masquers you had bad posture."

I went to a beach party with Selma, and on three dates. The first was a movie and I held her hand. A month before I was drafted, we had dinner at the Taft Hotel with a live orchestra. I asked her to dance. Once. A foxtrot. In the army I wrote, asking her to send me a picture and she did, standing in front of a hydrangea bush, ravishing in her T-shirt and slacks.

My last date with Selma was on leave after winning my wings. By sheer luck, Fred Sadoff was on leave from the Navy. We double-dated, me with Selma, Fred with a friend of hers. Both worked at radio station WNYC in the Municipal Building, where we went to pick them up. We arrived early and being exactly the same size, ducked into the men's room and traded uniforms. The girls spied us from the end of a long hall, waved gaily, then stopped, squinted, shrieked. We had dinner and listened to jazz in the west 50s.

I took Selma home in a taxi, slid an arm around her, and after a long goodbye on her front stoop, moved in for a kiss. But she seemed reluctant so I backed off. Alone on the subway ride home I regretted my lack of nerve and full of self-pity thought, "It'll serve her right if I'm killed in action."

Three years later, back in Brooklyn after discharge, I telephone Selma. Her mother answers.

"Is Selma there?"

"Who's this?"

"Stuart."

"Selma's out."

Half a dozen calls and Selma is still out. With Jerry, I'm sure.

Fred Sadoff is now an apprentice actor in Bennington, Vermont, so I call, mention I'd spent a year writing for an army newspaper. He tells me their publicity guy just quit, so I dash up to Vermont and get a job placing posters in store windows, writing program bios for actors and news releases for the *Bennington Banner*. Fred says he had danced with the Martha Graham troupe, so I put it into his bio, later to learn that he'd only taken her classes at the Neighborhood Playhouse. It is the first time I hear Martha Graham's name.

One afternoon I drop in to watch rehearsal of *Ladies in Retirement*, hoping to see a compelling young actress named Maureen Stapleton, but they are doing lighting. Fred has the boring chore of standing onstage for the lighting designer and passes time declaiming Shakespeare, singing show tunes, and dancing. One of his moves catches my eye.

"What's that?"

"Martha Graham. You can't do it."

"I could. And better than you."

"Anything I can do, you can do better," sings Fred, adapting lyrics from *Kiss Me Kate*, Broadway's recent smash, and does the eye-catching move in a circle until the lighting designer shoos him back into place.

Early September, after re-registering at Brooklyn College, I find myself in downtown Manhattan, look up Martha Graham in the telephone book, and go to her studio at 66 Fifth Avenue. The man at the desk, Donald

Duncan, says classes will start in a week but that visitors are not allowed. He introduces me to Robert Cohan, a vet like me. Cohan has been dancing six months.

"What's it like?"

He leads me into the studio, grabs a wooden rail fixed to the wall, drops into a split, bounces up, turns and splits to the other side. "I couldn't touch my toes when I started."

Another man, Tony Charmoli, says he'd been studying for the priesthood until he decided he wanted to dance. Ten years later, Charmoli's choreography is a regular feature on TV's *Your Hit Parade*. "I also take ballet," he says.

"What's the difference between modern dance and ballet?"

"Well," says Charmoli, "in ballet you do two or three turns. In modern dance you do only one turn."

To Donald Duncan: "Is it too late for me to start?"

"How old are you?"

"Almost twenty-one."

"Many beginners are older."

"Will everyone in my class be a beginner?"

"Yes."

"I'll try a month. After that, if I'm the best in the class, I'll try another. Then, I'll see."

I'm thinking that I have to make rapid progress if I intend to be a dancer. *Be a dancer?* Heaven knows how such a notion entered my brain twenty minutes after walking into the Martha Graham Studio.

My family thinks of dancing as a lark after the army. My mother confesses that when I was seven, she'd considered sending me to ballet school but, sure I'd refuse, opted for violin lessons. I wish she'd thought of tap dancing.

September 16, 1946

I arrive for my first class carrying bathing trunks and a T-shirt, change in a tiny alcove separated from the studio by a split bamboo partition. On the other side a pianist is pounding out dissonant rhythms. The air is humidified by sweat. Another man enters, Alvin Epstein. In a few years I'll see him on Broadway, opposite Bert Lahr as "Lucky" in *Waiting for Godot*.

I join other beginners watching intermediates hurtle across the studio,

Photograph of Woody and Marjorie Guthrie. © Woody Guthrie
Publications, Inc.

twenty-five or so women, most bare-legged in leotards, some with tiny
little skirts tied around their waists. And three men. After a cascade of
leaps the teacher says, "Thank you," the dancers applaud, and all leave. I
edge in with others to stand self-consciously along the back wall. A statuesque woman enters. "I'm Nancy Lang, your demonstrator." She shows us
how to sit on the floor, soles of the feet pressed together, hands on ankles,
knees flopped out to the sides. I feel foolish.

The teacher returns, droplets of water sparkling in her glossy black hair.
"My name is Marjorie Mazia." She radiates freshness.

Later, I dance with her and once meet her husband, folk singer Woody
Guthrie, who shows up at the studio, whispers to Marjorie, and leaves.

"Off on a singing tour," she says, "All he takes is his guitar. Not even a toothbrush."

"How long will he be gone?"

"Could be months. Even he doesn't know." She sees the question in my eyes. "Oh, he's impossible to live with but who can help loving him? I can be sitting on his lap kissing him while telling myself, I ought to leave this guy."

Marjorie demonstrates the first move, a pulsing torso stretch over folded legs. She calls it *bounces,* and chants out sixteen slow counts, one *bounce* to a count. She explains again and we do it again, then a third time, each set accompanied by piano chords.

Thinking: "I'm a grown man. I fought in a war. Why am I sitting on the floor in bathing trunks doing these weird moves?" But the moves feel good, and before the lesson is over I realize I am among people who want not just to dance but to change themselves. And after I join the Graham troupe I learn the ultimate goal: to change the world!

I start with the minimum, three classes a week, soon up it to five. When Marjorie enters, we pop to a sort of sitting attention. She looks us over, nods to the pianist, says, "A-a-n-d . . ." The word *and* marks the upbeat and begins every dance class, every exercise, every rehearsal, the dancer's equivalent of "Ready, set . . . ," followed by *one,* which is "go!"

Marjorie teaches *prances,* the move Fred Sadoff had done in Bennington, body hefted smoothly, leg to leg by calf muscles working the feet. Marjorie's soft voice would reassure nursery tots, and she does treat us a bit like babies. But she is marvelous Margie and can treat me any way she wants. After four weeks, Erick Hawkins strides into the studio, big as me and bristling with high seriousness. His strong sculptural moves fit my body better than Marjorie's deft maneuvers. Hawkins is ballet-trained and Martha uses his classical *double tours en l'air* in *Deaths and Entrances* and *pirouettes* in *Every Soul Is a Circus.* When Erick defects after the 1950 European tour, John Butler takes over his roles, but Butler cannot do ballet "tricks" so Martha changes the choreography. I resolve to master every move, and when I dance the Dark Beloved in *Deaths* I put the *double tours* back, also the *pirouettes* as Ring Master in *Circus.*

My schedule: 9:00 or 10:00 a.m., class at Brooklyn College, home by 1:00 or 2:00 p.m., lunch and half an hour nap, wake and study until 5:00 p.m., leave for dance class, 6:00–7:30 p.m. Home by 8:30, study until midnight. Muscles ache, but I'd never felt better. I'd always been a C student but that semester get Bs, plus A in Italian.

All Graham Studio classes except the 10:00 a.m. company/professional have a "demonstrator" who sits in front facing students. The demonstrator does every move in mirror image along with the students, plus extra times when the teacher asks. A demonstrator is like a live textbook and always dances "full out."

My first demonstrator is Nancy Lang, long-haired, long-legged, with the wiry body of a marathon runner. I see her dance in *Primitive Mysteries* where she doesn't stand out, but then no one is meant to. Ethel Winter, Helen McGehee, and Yuriko, on the school faculty, also demonstrate for Martha. After four years, I'm asked to demonstrate. Being a demonstrator is "boot camp" for Graham teachers. Army Air Corps basic training is not nearly as tough as being a Graham demonstrator.

Teachers often touch students to re-position an arm, loosen a tense hand, press down a raised shoulder, or run a finger upward along a spine, saying, "Lift." When I taught, I emulated Merce Cunningham, who always asked, "May I touch you?" And since most students are women, I make sure that my touch as a teacher is nothing like my touch as a man.

Martha's touch was mostly gentle except one day when she passed behind me and scratched her fingernails roughly upward on my spine, hissing, "Lift!" Another time, she faced me, and with both hands raked outward from my breastbone across pectoral muscles, fingernails stinging through my T-shirt. She glared at me. I glared back. She said, "You're a great big man. Dance like one."

She also worked on my "turnout," that 180-degree outward leg rotation perfectly achieved by very few and never by me. One day she stared dubiously at my turnout. "Turn out!" I responded with extra effort, but not much happened.

"Not from your feet, from your hips." And reached between my bare thighs and clawed outward with both hands. After class, I sat in the outer office and when she passed exhibited my bright scratches with a challenging smile. She returned an oblique glance. "Hope I don't get you in trouble with your girlfriend."

All touching ended in 1953, after Martha was sued by a forty-year-old Cornell dance teacher named May Atherton. It was said that Martha had merely run her finger along the woman's spine while making a comment.

Atherton claimed it had given her such a start that her back "went out," which, claimed her lawyer, ended a "brilliant performing career." After a jury awarded $40,000, it was announced that no teacher was permitted to touch a student.

When the Graham troupe toured, there were no company dance classes so dancers gave themselves individual warm-ups lasting an hour. A warm-up is not a class, but my technical progress continued because I was putting my rudimentary skills to work onstage. I'd also begun to realize that dancing and flying have curious parallels. First is the need for technical mastery.

A subtle yet major difference between dancing and flying is simply that the dance experience peaks before an audience whereas the peak of flying is alone in the sky.

In mid-December, Donald Duncan approached before class. "The company's going on tour in February and Martha wants to know if you'd like to come along."

"Doing what?"

"Dancing."

"In the company?"

"Yes."

"I'll quit college tomorrow."

"No, finish the semester. It's only a few weeks, isn't it?" He adds that I don't have to pay for any more lessons and to add intermediate classes but continue elementary, and to take as many as possible.

"Great. I'll clear up my bill for the past month."

"Forget it."

In *Letter to the World*, I replace Douglas Watson, who is pursuing an acting career. In the Christmas break, he teaches me the Party Dance which begins with the Party Step, not difficult except for quick front and back "cuts" on the balls of the feet. We work two hours, and that evening I rise and step on what feels like a stone. It's a collapsed left metatarsal arch. I press it back into place and tell Mark Ryder who says, "Get Dr. Scholl's metatarsal supports and put them in all your street shoes." He shows me how to strengthen my metatarsals by gripping my toes inside my shoes. I do it on the subway.

Once I know the steps, I do them with Ethel Winter, one of my teachers. Dancing with a group is like flying in formation but cozier. The Party Step is exhilarating in a group of eight.

On the day we're to show Martha, the women don long black skirts and Marjorie Mazia runs us through the moves. I do *pliés* at the *barre*, keeping an eye on the studio door. So far, all I've seen of Martha are fleeting glances of a small, dark-eyed woman who appears in the studio doorway to peer intently, but never for long. She arrives with pianist Helen Lanfer, speaks to Sasha, who picks up a white bench and places it against the mirror. Martha sits straight-backed upon it. We line up, Martha signals Lanfer, and we dance the Party Scene. Then we gather at her feet. She speaks softly, explaining that the Party Scene comes early to establish Emily Dickinson's male-dominated world. She demands that we muster a bearing more rigid, more arrogant than anything we imagine, describing the tightly fitted clothing and stiff collars of the era, which our costumes will evoke, adding, "But if your body does not bear its arrogance deep within, your costume will not give it to you."

I whisper to Sasha, "Poker-assed," not intending Martha to hear, but she catches something, and turns to me. "I was just saying, we know an army term."

"What is it?"

"Poker-assed."

"Precisely." No smile. She continues and I get the impression that *Letter to the World,* her future, life on Earth as we know it, hangs on how we perform the Party Scene. She concludes with a phrase I will hear again. "Success will be *your* success. Failure will be *my* failure."

Rehearsals are in full swing when my World War II buddy, Eugene Cowen, invites me to his wedding and assigns me a mission. Gene has relatives with primitive notions about wedding nights, and none he can trust with a secret, so asks me to book his hotel room and deliver the reservation at the wedding. The wedding is on a Sunday, a big rehearsal day. Martha does not consider it sufficient reason to miss rehearsal.

"He's my war buddy. We flew combat together. I have to go to his wedding."

"What time is the wedding?"

"Noon."

"You can be at rehearsal by two."

"The reception starts at two."

"No reception."

Doug Watson also teaches me his *Dark Meadow* role, one of They Who Dance Together. It includes a trio for the men called the Fetish Dance.

Noguchi *Dark Meadow* set piece with fetishes. Photo by Kevin Noble, Courtesy of Noguchi Museum.

Each fetish is a distinctive prop by Isamu Noguchi. We burst out of the wings doing double jumps followed by a violent shake of the fetish, thud across the stage to a slanted platform on which Martha had earlier reposed, to plunge the fetishes into fitted holes. Clumsy and pounding, it's the antithesis of what many consider "dancing." I like to dream up scenarios, including who we are and what we're doing. Some of my Fetish Dance answers: we are wild creatures leaving a spoor. We are vandals who desecrate a shrine; fanatics who ravage a gentle faith; puritans who destroy worshipers of love. Eventually the obvious; the fetishes are phalluses and we are plunging them into Martha.

Bob Cohan's fetish is a smoothly lacquered wooden stick with three white horsehair plumes. Mine is a crook-shaped flexible plastic rod with a black ball on one end. Sasha's resembles a metal tomahawk.

Bob flourishes his fetish. "It's elegant, I like it better than either of yours."

Me: "Mine looks like modern sculpture. I like it better than yours."

Neither of us like Sasha's tomahawk. He says, "Well, I like it. That's how it is with fetishes. You're only supposed to like your own."

Martha sends me to fetch a book from her flat on West 10th Street in Greenwich Village. I'm struck by its monkish spareness, bare, off-white walls, a single bed with a white coverlet and wooden headboard. On her night table is a crisp square of linen on which rests a book bound in black leather. Not what I was sent for. Beside it is a flower carved of sandalwood. I like the scent of sandalwood but do not take a sniff.

Her book is on a wooden chest at the foot of the bed next to a carved wooden *santo* from the American Southwest. In the studio a fierce *santo* frowns down from a perch atop the women's dressing room partition. But Martha's bedroom *santo* has a sweet, gentle face. I touch nothing, just get the book and leave.

Twenty years later, I go to a party in Martha's apartment on East 63rd Street, a short walk from her school. The entrance leads into a large living room, kitchen on the left, then a door to Martha's bedroom, where I add my coat to a pile on the queen-sized bed. Art covers the walls.

Her living room is dominated by a canopied Chinese bridal bed, gift of Bethsabée de Rothschild, who bought it for her in Malaysia on the Asian tour. Martha sits on it throughout the evening.

The walls are crowded with paintings, prints, icons. Tabletops and glass display cases hold carvings and bric-a-brac, including a tiny Buddha Yuriko had given her one Christmas, and an antique jade circlet which the company had chipped in and bought at Chait Galleries. (All have since disappeared into the possession of Martha's designated heir.) If this apartment is unlike her austere one on West 10th Street, it yields the same sense of a private place where a powerful presence reigns.

In January, I leave Brooklyn College. I'll want more education, but a degree can be safely delayed, dance cannot. My lack of technique hounds me. A role is more than the sum of its moves, yet with only three-and-a-half months of training, it's moves I need.

Two weeks before the tour, I ask Sasha about makeup. He writes a

Martha on Chinese bridal bed. Photo by Martha Swope. © The New York Public Library for the Performing Arts.

list: greasepaint, eyebrow pencil, rouge, sponge, cold cream, face powder, powder puff, facial tissues.

"Some people have tackle boxes full of makeup."

"Some people *like* makeup. They like costumes, applause, flowers, cast parties, and their name in the paper. *Dancing,* they're not too sure about."

"Tell me about the women in this company."

Straight to the point. "They don't want to be fucked, they want to be loved."

February 11–22, 1947, the Hurok Tour

We open at Hofstra College, Hempstead, Long Island, then Pittsburgh, Philadelphia, Baltimore, Washington, Norfolk, Lynchburg, Durham, and back to New York City with a week before eight performances at the Ziegfeld Theater. Martha calls the last her "season."

I am not in the program at Hofstra so plan to watch from out front. Small emergencies keep me running errands backstage, but I do see part of *Deaths and Entrances,* impressed by Erick Hawkins's entrance as the arrogant Dark Beloved, striding in backward as though, "Anyone in my way I'll run 'em down."

After *Deaths and Entrances* I slip backstage intending to go out front again for *Every Soul Is A Circus*. But I'm grabbed by Ethel Winter holding a coil of rope, one end looped around her waist. She asks me to hold the free end when she prances on as one of the Ponies in the equestrian dance. Formerly held by David Campbell or Douglas Watson, she'd forgotten that neither would be around.

"What do I do?"

"Stand in the downstage-left wing. When I hand you the end, hold it taut while I dance, then reel me in when I *chaîné* toward you on the exit."

"Can we try it?"

"There's no time but it's simple. Just don't drop the rope." From my spot in the wing, I watch Ethel prance in with three other women, each with a coil of rope. They prance center, prance to their corners where Ethel hands me the coil of cottony stage rope. I loop the end around my wrist thinking, *Don't drop it,* paying it out as Ethel prances to center. When she starts back, I hold it taut as she *chaînés* toward me, spooling the rope around her waist.

"Pull the goddam rope, you idiot!"

Jean Rosenthal, Martha's lighting designer, reaches from behind me and tries to grab the rope. I shoulder her aside. Ethel reaches me, slips out of her coil, and dashes off to her next entrance.

"Who the hell said you could handle a rope?"

"Ethel."

"You're supposed to pull it, not stand like a goddamned post."

"If you don't like the way I pull it, pull it yourself." I fling the rope at her feet.

After the dance, Ethel apologizes, saying she should never have asked me to do it without rehearsal. "It was an emergency. I'll explain to Jean."

"She's the one should apologize."

"She didn't mean anything," and explained that Rosenthal, the only female lighting designer on Broadway, works with men not used to taking orders from a woman. She dominates them with high expertise and a very rough tongue. Rosenthal was Martha's lighting designer as long as I was in the troupe. She never apologized, and I never spoke to her again.

The second night on tour, I'm invited to Marjorie Mazia's hotel room, where the dancers make a doll out of pillows, give it a red lipstick penis, dub it Erick, and stick pins into it. There's tension between Erick and the dancers, yet I admire his dancing, including the ballet skills that Martha puts to such good use.

February 12, 1947, Pittsburgh, Pennsylvania

As our train nears Pittsburgh, the sky turns silty gray and my eyes burn. Our theater, despite the name Syria Mosque, is just a theater, but the thought of dancing gives me stomach pangs, fast heartbeat, weakness in the knees. I tell myself: no matter how terrible I am onstage, I won't *die*. Doesn't help.

I wonder how I'll do in front of an audience. Everyone performs somewhere: sports, business or PTA meeting, classroom.

In the military, combat can expose the hollow insides of awesome training-camp warriors. In Italy, as the 772nd Bomb Squadron was climbing to altitude, a waist-gunner on his first mission sank to his knees, then to the floor, and curled into a ball. He couldn't be roused so the pilot was ordered to abort. As the bomber descended, the gunner uncurled, rose to his feet, and by the time they landed, was manning his gun and ready for action. A second chance, same thing. He went home with a Section 8, the "psycho" discharge. "Psycho like a fox," said some.

Martha and the dancers were in the theater when I arrived at 4:00 p.m. I gave myself a long warm-up, then danced through all of my moves, "spacing" the stage. Dripping sweat, I went to the dressing room for a shower, but the water was icy so I sponged off then found a place at the makeup table between Sasha and Bob, copying Sasha as he applied greasepaint, eyeliner, powder, eyebrow pencil, lip rouge, final dusting of powder. Bob, on my right, is using mascara. I ask him if he feels stage fright.

"Mmm-hmm."

"Is it anything like what you felt in the Battle of the Bulge?"

Bob turned to look at me. "Why do you ask me that?"

"Because I feel like on a bomb run with flak exploding." A corner of Bob's mouth curled.

Actually, I felt worse. I tell myself that fear of death is reasonable but not fear of dancing. What is the *worst* that can happen? I forget my moves, trip on my feet, drop my partner, slam into Martha, knock her down, get fired, never dance again.

Better than dead.

Does failure as a dancer mean failure as a man? A few years later Erick Hawkins and Martha are having tea in the top floor lounge of the Neighborhood Playhouse. Both are facing windows overlooking 54th Street. A body hurtles past. They rush to the window, look down at a crumpled figure on the sidewalk. With a cry, Erick dashes to the stairwell, trips, tumbles down the flight, and ends on the landing unable to move. Martha telephones for an ambulance, takes the elevator down, drapes her coat over the body, and after the ambulance arrives, goes back and ministers to Erick. Years later in Tel Aviv, an Israeli pays Martha a serious compliment: "I'd go to war with that woman."

I must be the only one ever to dance in Martha's company without having seen her dance. She is fifty-two years old. Ballet stars stop much younger. If she no longer does the spectacular split leaps Sasha described, she can still jump cleanly, fall to the floor, and rise in one continuous arc, or hoist a leg over her head and hold it there, rock steady on the other. Yet Sasha says this pales beside her sheer magic. By 7:30 p.m., an hour before curtain, I'm made up and in costume. I find a spot in the downstage-right wing with a view of the whole stage. I'm in *Letter to the World,* second on a program that opens with *Appalachian Spring.*

Appalachian Spring opens quietly. The Pioneering Woman enters, followed by the Preacher, the Husbandman, the Bride, the Flock. Martha wears a beige taffeta dress with a flounce, fancy for a farmer's wife yet not for a bridal gown, and although *Spring* does not depict a wedding, its joyousness pervades the dance. The Bride enters, hands modestly clasped, gaze humbly down, nears her husband, raises her face to his, stops before they touch, slowly part, the Bride to her place by the house, the Husbandman to the fence.

The dance has barely begun yet I've felt Martha's magic, sheer charisma intensely focused and writ large. One sees it in great leaders, teachers, charlatans. Rhapsodic prose and lyrical poetry try to capture it in words but Martha onstage must be experienced. I'm also impressed by Erick as the sturdy Husbandman, May O'Donnell as the Pioneering Woman, Mark Ryder as the Revivalist, and the Flock: Yuriko, Pearl Lang, Helen McGehee, and Ethel Winter. Also by conductor Charles Muench, a rare chance to see his face, blissful in lyrical passages, frowning when the music swells, contorted during climactic heights. But afterward, the women complain about his tempos. Before long, I too am critical of conductors. When I buy Serge Koussevitzky's recording of *Appalachian Spring,* his exaggerated *ritardandos* and frantic *accelerandos* sound schmaltzy and worse, undanceable. I complain to Erick who says, "But at least Koussevitzky plays contemporary music."

After *Appalachian Spring,* stagehands haul off the set and replace it with *Letter to the World.* I'd rehearsed with the set for weeks but onstage it seems different. I pace through my sequences until the stage manager calls "Places!" then slip into the upstage-left wing with Ethel Winter. Three couples behind us. *Letter* begins with a stately pavane between Martha, One Who Dances, and Angela Kennedy, One Who Speaks. Ethel and I stand between the upstage wing and a shimmering billow of filmy white voile that hangs in front of the black backdrop. My costume is brand-new and on my feet are new Capezio ballet slippers of nappy gray suede. Ethel hooks her hand in the crook of my left elbow. I tell her I feel stage fright.

"Everybody feels it. Some people never get over it."

Our music cue. I step out on my left foot, sweep my right in a wide arc. It brushes the voile—and sticks. The gauzy fabric clings to the shoe's rough nap. I yank. It tightens. Ethel can't move without me, and the other couples stack up behind us. I lurch like a bear in a net, rattling the chain weights that keep the voile anchored. A desperate lunge, the voile rips, I hurtle forward yanking Ethel with me.

Afterward, no one says a word. "That voile really had me," I say, hoping Ethel will say it wasn't too horrible.

"Thought you never would get loose," she mutters.

In *Deaths and Entrances,* Bob Cohan and I each partner an older sister. Mine is Pearl Lang, a fierce beauty, beside whom I am utterly outmatched. Bob has May O'Donnell, a powerful earth-mother. *Deaths and Entrances* evokes the antagonisms between women and men, and dancing with Pearl feels as much like wrestling as dancing. We exit locked hand-to-hand, arms stretched high, as do Bob and May. One day Bob says that May is stretching his arm so high he feels a pull on his ribs under his war wound from the Battle of the Bulge. A square of skin from Cohan's thigh covers a scar on his chest where flesh is still fused to his rib. It limits torso movement, a real disability for a dancer. The army sends Bob a monthly disability check.

"Tell May." He won't.

A week later: "You know that high reach? May stretched my arm so high, something tore. I could feel it."

"Does it hurt?"

"Not exactly."

After the tour, Bob goes to the Veterans' Administration doctor, who checks the wound, discovers that the flesh over his rib cage is completely free. Now 100 percent fit, the VA stops his disability check.

Our next performance is in Philadelphia. I'm in *Dark Meadow.* Throughout Martha and Erick's ecstatic duet, the men stand on one foot, hands clasped prayerfully. I'd rehearsed it countless times, but, afraid I'll lose my balance and imagining two rock-steady guardians and one tottering boob, I play it safe and keep a toe on the floor. Afterward, pitying snickers from Sasha and Bob are worse than razzing. I resolve to take my chances next time.

During the Funeral scene in *Letter to the World,* the men are pallbearers in black coats. We march toward Martha who waits in a posture of aching grief. As we lift her to our shoulders, her body arches, becoming a corpse in its casket. With slow funereal steps, we bear her upstage, then lower her, as if into a grave.

In the wing, Graham Black whispers, "Martha yanked my coattail."

"When?" asks Sasha.

"While we were carrying her. Two hard yanks."

"Maybe there's something wrong with your coat." Sasha looks him over and finds it, a white cleaner's tag the size of a postage stamp stapled to the inside of the slit in his coattail.

My sister, Malvine, lives in Washington, D.C., where her husband, Gordon Cole, is a reporter on the *Washington Post.* Gordon tells his editor that four war vets are dancing with Martha Graham and a reporter/photographer pair show up at rehearsal.

Next day, a two-column spread: "Veterans Turn From Battlefield to Modern Ballet."

Photo of Mark Ryder, Graham Black, Bob Cohan, and me. And under the photo: "Barefoot Men Give Preview of Dance Act."

I proudly show this to Martha who regards it coldly. Later, Malvine says that if she'd known Dorothea Douglas was the daughter of Senator Paul Douglas of Illinois, she could have gotten us on page one. I've learned enough to be thankful she hadn't.

Our last booking is in Durham, North Carolina, Duke University's Paige Auditorium whose generous stage has a rich black velour backdrop.

All our theaters had been similarly adorned so I remark to Sasha how lucky that all have such nice black drapes. He stares at me in disbelief.

"Those are not the theater's drapes, they are *ours*. And *our* lights. They travel with us. Our stagehands are in the theater hanging them before you've had your breakfast and are taking them down and packing them away after you've had your dinner and are back in your hotel room sound asleep."

May 1947, New York, New York. Back in New York City, we start rehearsals for the Ziegfeld Theater. Martha's season includes a solo by Erick, *Stephen Acrobat,* with lines spoken by an actor. I learn that after the Ziegfeld, Martha will start a new dance to be premiered at Harvard. *Dark Meadow* will open the program, so I'll get to go.

Martha designs, fits, cuts, and pins costumes, assisted by a professional designer, Edythe Gilfond, who gets program credit. Final sewing is by Mrs. Hatfield, an elderly black woman whom Martha considers a colleague.

Martha will give me a swatch of fabric. "Try to match this. You won't find the exact thing, so bring back samples." I return with swatches pinned to a sheet of paper with the shop, price, and yardage on the bolt. Martha and Erick mark what they want, and I go back often to buy the whole bolt.

Our first New York rehearsal is interrupted by a man from AGMA, the American Guild of Musical Artists. He reads us union rules, hours we can rehearse, rest periods every two hours, twelve hours between calls, etc. Our elected representative is Pearl Lang, to whom we are told to report violations. Pearl Lang? It's a farce. We've been rehearsing without pay for months, and the union guy knows it. We know he knows, and he knows we know he knows. But if AGMA came clean it would have to expel Martha from the union, and of course there is no changing rules written with the premise that choreographers and dancers are adversaries, like General Motors and assembly-line workers. We have our adversarial moments, but Martha is our teacher, mentor, and creative polestar.

In 1952, I join Chorus Equity to dance in *Paint Your Wagon,* then Actors' Equity for *Peer Gynt.* For The Latin Quarter, a nightclub, I join the American Guild of Variety Artists, and when television gets going, TVA, the Television Authority. When TV and radio unions merge, it becomes AFTRA, the American Federation of Television and Radio Artists. I pay initiation fees and dues to all these unions to do one thing, dance, and envy musicians who have one powerful union whatever instrument they play and wherever they play it. No surprise, they are much better paid than dancers.

I get to know some very decent stagehands, but brushes with their union are toxic. In the rehearsal studio of the Ziegfeld Theater, Sasha and Pearl are preparing to rehearse a duet from *Every Soul Is a Circus*. It is performed on a prop drum. Sasha drags it from the corner but before they start, a stagehand appears saying that if they so much as put a foot on it, the Graham Company will have to pay four stagehands for four hours of work. Sasha draws a chalk circle on the floor and they rehearse on that.

The set for *Every Soul Is a Circus* includes a richly upholstered black satin divan, our most fragile and expensive piece, never touched except for performance. Stored in a remote corner of the Ziegfeld stage, it is discovered by a bulky stagehand who takes possession for a snooze, booted feet splayed on the delicate silk. I shoot Erick an indignant glance. He puts a finger to his lips: *"Let sleeping stagehands lie."*

Getting the Ziegfeld had been a coup. No theater owner books a single week that might block a musical that could run for years, so Martha had to find one between productions. The Ziegfeld fills the bill, but owner Billy Rose doesn't want to bother. Martha calls Katharine Cornell whose husband, producer, Guthrie McClintic, calls Billy Rose urging him to book Martha, saying, "She will *hallow* your theater." Martha relates this with glee.

Professor Patricia Casey and the Brooklyn College Masquers choose Graham for their theater party, come backstage, and I introduce them to Martha.

After the final curtain call, bouquets clutched, visitors gone, I step onto the elevator with Martha and Dorothea Douglas. It had been a long haul, and thinking of that, or perhaps because she only wanted to break the silence, Dorothea says, "Well, I'm glad that's over."

Martha glares at her coldly. "I'm not!"

Night Journey

Season over, Martha begins a dance based on the Oedipus tale. Erick plays Oedipus, Martha is Jocasta, Mark Ryder (Sasha) is Tiresias, the blind seer, and the women are chorus, termed Daughters of the Night. It premieres at Harvard on May 3 in a program opened by *Dark Meadow*.

Night Journey is the first dance I watch Martha make. Her reading list is on the school bulletin board:

Prolegomena to the Study of the Greek Religion, by Jane Harrison
Ancient Art and Ritual, by Jane Harrison
The White Goddess, by Robert Graves
Gods, Graves, and Scholars, by C. W. Ceram
The Hero with a Thousand Faces, by Joseph Campbell
The King Must Die, by Mary Renault

Once Martha has the story and characters, she plans the dance, then goes into the studio to carve it out of space, time, and bodies. She demonstrates moves on her feet and draws others out of the dancers. If someone makes a move she likes, she may ask everyone to learn it. Dancers work off to one side knowing Martha will sometimes say, "Ethel (or whomever), can I see that?" Never does anyone say, "Martha, how about this?"

Only the cast is called, but I'm allowed to watch. One day things are moving slowly so I pick up a book. Erick whispers that reading in rehearsal is *not done* and suggests I read in the office. If reading in rehearsal is taboo, walking out to read will not be appreciated. I put the book away.

Martha attacks her toughest projects, solos and duets with Erick, early in the day, stopping for morning class at 10:30 a.m. Class ends at noon, lunch in Harlow's Drugstore across Fifth Avenue. Martha often has a can of boned chicken and drinks honeyed tea. Or she might send for a sandwich on white toast and a "Martha Graham flip," which the Harlow fountain man makes of orange juice, ice cream, and a raw egg whipped in a mixer. All are back by 1:00 p.m., to work on Daughters of the Night until advanced class at 4:30 p.m. After the 6:00 class ends at 7:30 p.m., she rehearses *Dark Meadow* until 10:00, then spreads her notebook on the floor and makes out the next day's schedule. Not knowing schedules until the night before makes personal life impossible, yet does not seem unreasonable. Creativity doesn't run on schedules.

One afternoon, Martha has Sasha show us his new Seer's solo, the dire revelation in which Tiresias reveals that Oedipus had murdered his father and married his mother. The entrance, traveling flex-footed jumps across the front of the stage, is one of the most arresting ever choreographed. The dancer gains elevation by pounding a stout Isamu Noguchi staff into the floor, making a terrific racket. We are dazzled and Martha is pleased. Critics witlessly liken those jumps to a man with a pogo stick. But pogo stick

Noguchi bed from *Night Journey*. Photo by Kevin Noble, Courtesy of Noguchi Museum.

and rider go up and down together, while Seer and staff go in opposite directions. And a pogo stick is hoppity and cute, while the Seer is jolting, disruptive, demented. The Noguchi set arrives. Upstage center is a surrealistic "bed," two vaguely human forms, male, female. A series of stepped pieces constitutes a stairway for Oedipus. Downstage left is a stool backed by a twisted shroud of white fabric, Jocasta's intimate space, into which she invites Oedipus. A couple of weeks before we leave for Boston, *Night Journey* is finished, except for the end, where Oedipus blinds himself leaving Jocasta to commit suicide.

In addition to the set, Noguchi had sent a prop, a surprisingly realistic painted plywood "eye," clear and blue on one side, red and blood-veined on the other. Erick's opening solo as the arrogant Oedipus, is danced holding the clear blue side toward the audience. After the deadly revelation and blinding, he's supposed to hold the bloodshot side front.

That eye is trouble. About two feet wide and eighteen inches high, its clear side remains glassily aloof. The bloodshot side looks like something from *Mad Magazine*. It is also hard to keep the proper side facing the audience. And being only one eye, it is *Cyclopean*—wrong myth. Yet how Martha strives to make the wretched thing work, right through the Cambridge premiere. After that she gets rid of it and finds powerful movement for Oedipus's self-mutilation and blinding. The groping, stiff-legged exit seen today was devised with Erick but gained potency when Bertram Ross took over the role. And with the invention of Velcro, Bertram suggested that Oedipus tear off the barbaric Noguchi jewel Jocasta wore on her breast and gouge his eyes out with that.

Martha explains: "Tiresias is Oedipus after his crime, condemned to wander the earth. He is blind but at last can see the inner truth."

Opening dances, "curtain-raisers," are traditionally lighthearted or flashy. *Dark Meadow* is neither. Our brainy cosponsors, Harvard and MIT, are in for a double whammy.

Martha, Erick, and Helen Lanfer rehearse in the morning and break at noon, whereupon Yuriko or Pearl rehearse *Dark Meadow*. After dinner *Night Journey* again. On the second day, I notice shards of wood on the floor near the piano and pick one up. One surface has a shiny shellac finish. I show it to Sasha.

"That is a piece of Helen Lanfer's metronome. I figure Helen Lanfer referred to it once too often."

When Martha says a tempo is wrong, Helen often sets the metronome clacking: "Tell it to the composer."

I'm taken aback. "You think Martha deliberately smashed the metronome?"

"No," says Sasha impishly. "I'd say she smashed it accidentally when she threw it at Helen." Adding, "She once threw her dachshund at Louis Horst."

"I don't believe it!"

"She was so upset she gave it to Katharine Cornell. Now she misses it and says it's her punishment."

Martha's travails also turned on William Schuman's score. I hear: "I'm so tired of scratchy music!" But Daughters of the Night is brilliant. Not the first time she'd used a Greek chorus, or the last—the *Night Journey* Furies are the most powerful.

Costumes are ready but not hairdos. A day before the premiere, Helen

McGehee and Pearl Lang shop for materials and after dinner invite us to their residence, the female-only Brattle Inn. Yuriko has the largest room and suggests we work there. We pass through a lobby crowded with Victoriana, pass the front desk to the foot of a carpeted stairway. Yuriko appears on the landing. "Come on up." But the little desk clerk scoots out and plants herself at the foot of the stairs.

"You can't go up there."

Yuriko comes down. "We just want to work on costumes."

The clerk gives Bob, Sasha, and me a dubious glance. "We never allow young gentlemen in the young ladies' rooms."

So the headdresses were created in the Victorian lobby, and I believe that their bizarre shapes owe something to that desk clerk's lascivious interdiction.

May 3, 1947

The three-day Symposium on Music Criticism includes music by Aaron Copland, Paul Hindemith, Arnold Schoenberg, and others, presentations of scholarly papers, and finally dance, with music by William Schuman for *Night Journey* and Carlos Chávez for *Dark Meadow*. The performance is followed by a buffet supper. We are driven by a graduate student. I sit in front and ask, "How come MIT and Harvard cosponsored us?"

He explains that he is studying cybernetics, a field created by his professor, Norbert Wiener. "It deals with thought-like processes in machines."

"How does dance fit in?"

"We believe that art is the link between science and metaphysics."

Martha was right to hit them with two intellectual blockbusters.

In eight months, I'd taken some 300 dance classes, learned two small roles, performed on tour, at the Ziegfeld Theater, and at Harvard. Little air-conditioning then, Broadway takes a summer hiatus, the Graham Studio closes. Martha leaves for Santa Fe. Sasha is hired by Tamiment, a Catskills resort. They need one more man, says I should audition. Of a dozen, all are eliminated except for me and a man named Victor Duntiere, whose skills clearly exceed mine. The choreographer is Rod Alexander, but the final choice is up to producer, Max Liebman, who picks Duntiere.

I find a job as counselor at a family camp about thirty-five miles north of New York City. My nine- and ten-year-olds live with parents in cottages and spend days with their counselors. Among them is a sullen, pudgy ten-year-old I instantly dislike. It's so unfair I feel guilty and give her extra attention. She responds by never leaving my side. In a week, I'm so fond of her, I have to hide it or the other kids will be jealous. By then I know that in September when the Martha Graham Studio reopens, I'll be there.

3

· · · · · · · · ·

Dance Lessons

When I tell Martha I intend to give dance a try, she understands that, for me, dance is on trial. "I have a lot of catching up to do. Where should I study ballet?" It never occurred to me not to ask, although other Graham dancers are surprised I had, and by Martha's answer.

"Go to Muriel Stuart at the American School."

The School of American Ballet, SAB, is in the shabby, time-stained Tuxedo Building on Madison Avenue at East 59th Street. The registrar, Madame Eugenie Ouroussow, is a genteel White Russian with an elegant accent. I tell her I've had a year of modern dance, so she puts me in a baby class where I tower over nine-year-old girls. Afterward, the teacher, Elise Riman, asks, "How long have you studied ballet?"

"This is my first lesson. But I've had a year of modern dance." She returns a glassy stare and goes to a parent. The parent leaves, she looks in my direction. I approach.

"How long have you studied ballet?"

She didn't believe me! Only classical ballet is dance to her.

"I have never had a ballet lesson but my classes at the Graham Studio include *pliés, relevés,* and things like that." Madame Ouroussow tells me that I'm admitted.

A month later, Martha asks how my ballet classes are going.

"Fine, but I don't like ballet hands."

"What don't you like?"

I raise my right arm and let it fall, articulating my wrist so that the hand floats. "I do this," dropping arm and hand together, as in our modern classes.

"No," says Martha firmly. "Don't confuse the two styles. When you're taking ballet, be the most classical dancer in the room."

It makes an immediate change in my progress. The only way to study any kind of dance is without reservation. If you can't accept everything your teacher says, find another. After a month, I'm promoted to "A" level, taught by the first team—Anatol Oboukoff, Lew Christensen, Pierre Vladimiroff, Felia Doubrovska, and Muriel Stuart. It's a relief to be with grown-ups, although all are better than I. And I am light years from "D" level, often taught by "Mr. B," George Balanchine.

Saturday is children's day at the Graham Studio so I spend the day at SAB, first taking character dance taught by Yurek Lazovsky, which begins with a foot-stomping *barre,* then showy mazurkas and polkas. After that, supported adagio, or "partnering." Women always outnumber men so I get two or three to haul around. And finally, a modern dance class taught by Merce Cunningham, whose superb feet and perfect arabesque are the envy of every dancer, and whose cerebral choreography doesn't alarm Lincoln Kirstein, SAB's brilliant but anxious angel.

My view of dance is expanding. I'm captivated by Antony Tudor's stark dramas, the slick romps by Jerome Robbins, the coruscating designs of George Balanchine. But the classical warhorses leave me cold. Ballet females have a sort of Barbie Doll cuteness, but the males look like pompous twits. I scorn their starchy walks, weight in heels, legs poking out like nervous antennae.

Some ballet moves are tough to master, and when I achieve *double tour en l'air* and four clean *pirouettes* I possess something tangible if uncommon (like knowing how to fly an airplane). Following Martha's advice to "be the most classical dancer in the room," I indulge the fluttery hands and swooping *port de bras,* especially as taught by the fiercely elegant Anatol Oboukoff. I enjoy fast footwork, rare in Graham Technique, and the curious contradiction between trying to make moves look easy while making sure the audience knows they are hard.

I relish ballet lifts. Some demand strength, like straight-arming a woman overhead in a *bird.* Others require close coordination, like the *fish,* in which the woman perches on the man's thigh, legs swirled around his torso and rising behind his back, arms free. Catches require precise timing, and "supported" moves demand sensitivity of each partner to the other.

But one ballet move, *entrechat*, seems pointless. Dictionary definition: "A step of beating in which the dancer jumps into the air and rapidly crosses the legs before and behind." In many warhorse ballets, there comes a moment when one of the male principals jumps up and down doing *entrechats*, the expression on his face like trying to smile while drowning. Finally the audience obliges with half-hearted applause. I see no point except its difficulty and a pathetic plea for applause.

But I like the way ballet steps fit together. After *barre* and center work, comes "the combination." I relish those by Muriel Stuart, who, according to gossip, had frequently been mistaken for Pavlova when she danced with her famed troupe. One day, her combination is so exciting I catch her at the end of class.

"That was wonderful. You should choreograph a ballet."

"A ballet?"

"Yes!"

"No," she says a bit wistfully. "I just make up nice little things."

There's a big difference between nice little things and a ballet, yet many a choreographer would cherish Muriel Stuart's ability to whip up graceful combinations, and I still believe she could have made them into a lovely ballet if only she'd dared.

Ballet class over, I'm about to leave when James Waring, to whom I'd never spoken, says, "Would you mind going to the *barre?*" I comply, whereupon he tells me to do a *grand plié* and proceeds to make corrections of my placement, alignment, arms, hands, épaulement, the way I hold my head, etc. I had not been impressed by his dancing, and it was years before he achieved acclaim as an experimental choreographer. A few weeks later, we are watching an adult beginner's class, our eyes drawn to a man with superb feet. "I wish I'd started with feet like that."

Jimmy: "You should wish to end with feet like that."

I often see a lean, smallish man with a lofty, disdainful air who keeps his shock of black hair in place with a kerchief. One day he says, "I should imagine you have good elevation."

"Oh?"

"Well, do you?"

James Waring, 1962, wearing costume he designed for *Two More Moon Dances*.
Photo by Dan Entin. © The New York Public Library for the Performing Arts.

"About average, I guess."

"It should be better than average with your massive thighs."

Massive thighs (also called "thunder thighs") are not admired, so I wonder if he's trying to insult me. After that he initiates other exchanges, all subtly malign. One day, "Do you think dancers should suffer for their art?"

"Not if they don't have to."

"You think art can come easy?"

"No."

"Do you want to be a dancer?"

"I am a dancer." I expect a challenge since some at SAB deny that modern dance is dance.

"Are you suffering now?"

"No. Are you?"

"Of course."

After that, I'll say, "How was the suffering today?" to elicit a distant smile.

Another exchange followed a performance by Teresa and Luisilio. I like Spanish dance but this pair reveal new dramatic potential in that highly theatrical form. He dismisses them, mostly it seems, because he doesn't like Luisilio's profile.

Publicity photo of Luisilio and Teresa. Photographer unknown

"But he's changing Spanish dance."

"For which he should be banned from the stage."

"Do you expect art to stand still?"

"Spanish dance is a classic form."

"So is ballet and it's changing."

"So much the worse for ballet. But Spanish dance will not change because it has 300 years of Spanish culture behind it, and it certainly won't be changed by twits like Luisilio."

"If he's a twit, so is Balanchine."

"*Touché!* Your problem is that you don't comprehend art because you refuse to suffer. Millions of people had to suffer so that Spanish dance could flower. All the tortures of the Inquisition were worth it because it gave the world Spanish dance."

"Are you saying that if you could eliminate the suffering of millions by sacrificing Spanish dance, you'd keep Spanish dance and let them suffer?"

"Gladly."

Suddenly I'm angry. "Let me tell you about the Inquisition. They had this little wooden box about six inches square with a hole in the top, into which they stuffed your balls. Then they twisted the handle and the sides came together. Think of your balls in there! I'm twisting the handle! Waves of agony are passing through your body. You're sweating, shitting, vomiting, screaming your brains out!"

He draws back.

"Don't you *adore* Spanish dance? You're pissing blood! How about a little zapateado?" He backs away. I follow. "Your balls are crushed and bloody. Isn't it great to suffer for your art?"

"You're out of your mind." He stalks away and doesn't speak to me again.

I ask Jimmy Waring, "What's that one's problem?"

"Him? Oh nothing much. Just hoping to impress you enough to get a piece of your ass."

On reflection, that also explains Jimmy's far subtler approach.

As a member of the Graham troupe I take company class even though I'm not technically ready. I consider any correction to anyone a correction for me. One day, Martha asks how my ballet classes are going.

"Wonderful! I've been promoted to 'A' class."

"How many classes do you take there?"

"Eight, counting character and adagio."

I'm expecting a pat on the head but Martha's expression is stony.

"You don't take that many classes in *this* school."

I'd never encountered Martha's wrath but sense trouble. "Each day I take one class here and one there. On Saturday you have children's classes, so I take three there."

"If you want to join that company, join it!"

"But Martha . . ."

"You don't have to take *any* classes here." Her private cubicle is behind the front desk five steps away, but she manages to storm into it.

I stand dumbfounded, feel my face grow hot. "All right I won't!" and stomp into the men's dressing room, throw on my clothes, slam shut my suitcase, and stomp out. Martha is waiting between stairs and elevator.

"Stuart," she whispers. "You have the power to make me angry. You have that power because I care about you." I return a glare. "I care about you, very much."

Stiffly: "I intend to become a good dancer."

"That is all I want for you. But sometimes I am . . . possessive. I don't want to lose you."

My anger ebbs. "You will never lose me, Martha."

"You have a temper."

"You'll never lose me to ballet. If I leave, it will be to leave dance altogether."

"No. You will not leave dance. Your gift will not permit it."

My anger evaporates. "If you want me to stop taking ballet classes, I will."

"No, take ballet. But you must realize you are more of a dancer than that."

"How could you think I would want to dance *there?*"

"Ballet is a very old and very seductive art."

"All I want is to be a better *Graham* dancer."

She takes my arm and draws me back into the studio.

Dorothea Douglas had watched enthralled and tells me that Martha had twisted me around her little finger.

"Yep, I was putty in her hands."

She asked what I'd had in mind when stomping out of the studio.

"To leave and never come back."

"Really?"

"And to quit dancing."

"You mean, quit dancing altogether?"

"Yes."

She seems puzzled. "But you could dance with someone else."

"If Martha fires me, I'll quit dancing."

"Did you tell her that?"

"I'm not sure."

"I'm sure she'd like to know."

I'm aware that Dorothea is having problems with Martha. As for me, leaving dance is always in my mind and part of me would welcome an excuse. But that Martha so easily talked me back was not only her power of persuasion. Whatever my doubts about a career, dancing is terrific fun and I want to study every kind I can. But the only place I can imagine performing is in the Martha Graham Company.

The mirror is a dancer's tool, yet Sasha (Mark Ryder) always positions himself at a gap where a column sticks out of the wall. "I don't like to stare at myself."

"Because you're afraid you'll fall in love with yourself," I taunt.

"Maybe I am," he answers coolly.

As for me, my flawed reflection generates only an urgent hope that with hard work I can make it better.

Merce Cunningham, on the other hand, has an ideal body for Western dance: slender, strong, arrow feet, long legs, short waist (some Eastern forms favor a long waist), long neck, sloping shoulders, flexible spine. And he can jump higher than any dancer I've ever seen. Yet he is reluctant to exhibit his virtuosity. Sasha claims it is ego turned inside out. After reading Carolyn Brown's lucid *Chance and Circumstance: Twenty Years with Cage and Cunningham,* I think of Merce Cunningham as even more of a mystery.

Virtuosity is everywhere sought: musicians, athletes, gymnasts, kids with skateboards. Onstage it can reveal the demonic or the divine, which is where Martha's interest lies. In a dozen years, dancers doing "jazz" will say, "If you got it, flaunt it."

Martha's Class, 1947

The advanced class meets at 4:30 p.m. By 4:15, choice spots in the center of the studio floor and in front of the mirrors are taken, and latecomers pick their way to places near the back or at the sides. I sit with the soles of my feet together, letting the weight of my torso gently stretch the muscles of my lower back. The maple floor, clean as a cutting board, feels good beneath my bare thighs.

Ethel Winter, Martha's demonstrator, faces the class. A minute before 4:30, Ralph Gilbert enters, sits at the piano, and arranges his newspaper. Martha enters, looks the class over, glances toward Gilbert, who meets her eye.

"And..."

Gilbert's compressed chords mark each pulse as torsos drop into opening bounces: sixteen with soles of the feet together, sixteen with legs outspread, sixteen extended to the front. The Breathings follow, an expansion that fills the torso and lifts the gaze.

Then Contractions, Martha's signature torso modulations. From deep in my pelvis I draw my body into a concave arc from hips to head, relishing the feel of deep muscles working. A surge of energy seems to gather and shoot out of my flexed hands and feet. "Release" straightens me, like an uncoiling spring. As each Contraction begins, my face lifts, lengthening my throat. "Open your eyes," Martha commands. She hates seeing them closed, deeming it self-indulgent.

"Present your gaze."

I present mine to the vaulted ceiling, through the ceiling to the sky, to space, beyond space. My gaze feels weighted. I pan it like a searchlight, chop it down like a cleaver, as my body gathers into an accelerating sweep that articulates my spine and flows through my torso into my mouth, where it bursts into a second Contraction that begins the entire sequence again.

"Sit to the side, fourth position."

I am not comfortable in the "sitting fourth" and study Ethel Winter, trying to fathom her comfort and ease in this curious body posture. My tendons seem long enough, but I am not quite relaxed and believe it to be a conceptual flaw, some muscle group that hasn't learned not to resist. We change sides, each move marked by a percussive piano chord. Gilbert's improvised music follows familiar patterns yet is always fresh.

My left hip lifts, to insinuate a rotating wave through my stomach, chest, and head. My left arm engages, then my right, then both. Head and gaze sweep through an arc, and the room spins past my eyes. Within, I feel stillness. My torso arches up, back, and around until my weight hangs over my right forearm, where I pause in suspension until a Contraction sucks me in and draws me into a ball where the Release fills me once more. The move ends delicately, like silk settling. In the stillness that follows effort, I relish my quickened heartbeat and present my gaze to the mirror, where thirty others present their gazes to me.

Martha moves about giving corrections. She stops over me. "Go to the count of five." I spiral back, placing weight on my right forearm. She pokes me lightly under the ribs. "Lift, *there.*" I strive into my rib cage. "At least you're wet."

The floor is wet, too, as sweat runs off my thighs and drips from my arms. Heavy sweating feels cleansing, a shower taken inside out. The room is hot, comforting my muscles, the humid air as nourishing as broth.

"Over on your face." I stretch out, face down with my body parallel to the front wall. "Back on your knees. Exercise-on-six." Martha's most dramatic floor sequence is named simply by the number of its counts.

I take the starting position, weight on my knees and insteps, torso horizontal, body shaped like a Z. Martha looks us over. "Lengthen your torso. Keep your back parallel to the floor like a table." She presses gently on the hips of a dancer, lowering her torso, lifts another's shoulders, traces her finger along the spine of one who isn't in a full Release, presses down a pair of tensely lifted heels. She takes her time. Simply holding the position demands strength. I am uncomfortable with weight on my knees, actually on the tops of my tibias just below the kneecaps. I feel my jaw tighten and try to relax all muscles not engaged in holding the position.

"One." A powerful Contraction lifts the center of my back, as head and shoulders scoop toward the floor, coil, then uncoil into a steep backward tilt from knees to head.

"Two" catches the tilt and it holds there, thighs lengthened from within.

Years later a student from Japan, Akiko Kanda, transforms herself in the exercise-on-six. She'd arrived with muscle-heavy thighs, giving her slender torso a grounded look. She takes three classes a day and does the exercise-on-six relentlessly.

"She is *Samurai*," Martha says approvingly. In a year, Akiko's thighs are slender as reeds. When she became a leading dancer in the Graham Company, no one believed she'd ever been anything but the steely sylph who appears onstage. When she returned to Japan, she became a celebrated dancer, teacher, and "National Treasure."

"Three." From full body Contraction into Release, the body arches, knees to head.

"Four." The Release sucks back into a second Contraction and steeper tilt, buttocks inches from heels, the limit of my strength, held half a count.

"And, sit." Buttocks drop onto heels, head flung back, gaze straight up, spine striving for length as the torso folds forward toward the floor into an exaggerated "hyper-release."

"Five." The Release reverses, becoming Contraction. "And, six." We return to the cantilevered horizontal thrust of the opening. Immediately we do it again. Exercise-on-six is always done twice.

"Sit to the side." I settle gratefully off my knees. Martha nods to Ethel. Ethel had done every movement along with the class, now demonstrates the exercise-on-six, slowly, as Martha explains the impulse beneath each move. It looks effortless, her control rock-steady in positions that make my thigh muscles shudder. Then our turn again, four more times. It yields, at last, exultation.

A dozen years later when I am teaching regularly, musician Reed Hensen, accompanying the class, is inspired to play the dramatic opening of Richard Strauss's *Also Sprach Zarathustra*, surrounding the exercise-on-six with a shimmering musical aura. From then on I call it "The Zarathustra," but it doesn't catch on.

"Rise from the floor." We stretch out full-length, face down, then push back onto hands and knees.

"One." The left leg reaches back.

"Two." Step through onto the left leg, straighten the right, make one line through heel, hip, and head.

"Three." Rise onto the left leg as the body quarter-turns toward the mirror and the right scissors in, to meet the left in first position.

Mini-break, fifteen seconds. Men tuck T-shirts into trunks and subtly adjust dance belts. Women pull leotard bottoms over exposed buttocks.

"Brushes." We begin with the legs parallel, weight on one, the other beating like a bird's wing.

"Make arrows," says Martha. I am not happy with my feet and point hard on each brush. The brushes break free of the floor then rise parallel to the floor at a tempo faster than the natural pendulum rhythm, so the body must absorb the effort, or in weakness, reveal it.

Martha, in my ear: "You're gripping with your arms. Let go. Let light pass through your body." I respond with a shake of my torso as I try to disconnect my arms from the force energizing my leg. I want to feel transparent, to float above the commotion of my legs. I imagine the pumping leg is not part of me and encourage it in a friendly, yet impersonal, way.

We do deep *plié* (termed *grand plié* in ballet), done by every dancer who ever lived. My body nears the floor, knee angle acute as the bones lose mechanical advantage, spilling weight into thigh muscles that must support me with sheer strength.

"Lift, Lift!" exhorts Martha, and I try to imagine gravity flowing upward through my body, opposite to jumps where the thrust is down. Resolution is sought in opposites, and continue to imagine that with enough concentration effort will vanish.

"Slow sits-to-the-floor."

We begin in a wide second position, spill weight onto the left leg, body curved like a filled sail, right foot passing behind and to the left of the left, sickling at the ankle, an unmitigated sin in classic ballet.

In Bombay, 1956, a master demonstrated moves with a sickled foot—turned in, giving it an ugly "clubbed" look. I ask if the sickled foot has a special meaning, like so many Indian moves. He says, "No. We do it because it is *beautiful*." And then in the next instant it was beautiful to me too.

My instep caresses the floor and accepts my weight as I drop my right buttock all the way to the floor, settling into the *sit*. Thirty dancers hold it there, curving coils of muscle from shoulder to knee. Ralph stamps the piano's pedal down, letting the chord ring (as he turns the page of his newspaper), and Martha counts, "6, 7, 8." Then he slams his thick fingers down, hitting more than ten keys at once. Thirty backs snap straight, flinging weight through thighs and sickled feet into skin-polished floor. Thirty torsos cut upward, suspend, then settle carefully, like mountain birds landing. The music drains away.

Martha has Ethel demonstrate prances and then challenges us with a look: Why don't you dance like that? The first time I saw Ethel dance, it was in *Letter To The World* where she is chaste as Diana. Next, she's doing jazz improvisations at a company party, and after that steamy routines in Broadway's *Ankles Aweigh*.

Daydreaming, I miss an explanation, feel woozy, bend over to send blood into my brain. Then, *prances.* I do them as a rest step, letting the spring in my calves and feet carry me through the first set. We repeat, knees rising high, then with jumps in the middle, ending on a double up-beat. Martha works them into a turning jump combination with tricky syncopation, and I attack with gusto, no longer feeling tired.

A second mini-break while the class shuffles to the corner and lines up in pairs for the diagonal across-the-floor. Men dance last. We are only four: Sasha and Bob Cohan, both in the Graham Company, and a smallish wiry newcomer in a white leotard whose horn-rimmed glasses are tied on with elastic. Cohan and the newcomer hang back, wanting to go last, so I pair up with Sasha.

We begin with low walks, slow at first, then faster, keeping the body's weight centered between footfalls. After several crosses, Martha gives a ludicrous illustration, chest caved in, belly thrust out, chin poked forward. "This is how little babies walk. Selfish little babies."

Her smile fools nobody. She hates what we are doing. We start again. "No!" She stops us. "Watch Ethel."

Ethel moves in a seamless flow, knees flexing smoothly, toes touching the floor with the sensitivity of fingers, the heel following soundlessly to take the body's weight.

"*Do it.*"

We do it again, and again, then faster, the low walks becoming low runs that swallow the studio's sixty-five-foot diagonal in four seconds.

"Triplets." One low step, two high. Martha adds a wide turn, a traveling skip, and works it into a dancey combination that reverses and cuts back in a semicircle to end with leaps the length of the studio. Ralph hammers out the triplets on low notes, then switches to a four-beat for the leap—*one*-two-three, *one*-two-three, one-*two*-three-four—with a slashing chord on "two" instead of the down beat, giving us a musical lift at the crest.

"Stop!" Martha claps her hands together, halting music and dancers. "You're missing it," she says angrily. "Push off on one, stay in the *air* on two. Listen to Ralph. He's trying his best to help you. Sasha and Stuart, will you please demonstrate?"

A bouquet! We leap across trying to out-jump each other, followed by the eyes of the intermediates who crowd the doorway waiting for the class to end. Then everyone leaps continuously, a sustained crescendo until the clock says two minutes after 6:00.

"We've run over. That's all. Thank you."

We applaud as intermediates dash in to grab choice spots in front of the mirror.

A year after Merce Cunningham had left Graham, Sasha and I join four other dancers in a shabby rented studio where he's teaching, accompanying himself on a flat Wigman drum. He gives tough Graham floor moves, fast tricky standing work, and when we start across the floor, demonstrates traveling jumps on one leg. Sasha and I drop quickly to the floor to see how high.

"As high on one leg as we jump on two," says Sasha.

It is still pretty much Graham Technique yet on the brink of his own which dispenses with floor work. He curves his torso as in Contractions, yet purges it of emotion. His clean geometric moves spool out like line from a fishing reel. A dance writer (can't recall which) intriguingly termed it "movement by the yard."

Martha's dances, shaped like life, have cycles of birth, growth, climax, decline, and death, with stark openings and powerful endings. Cunningham renounces this, along with striving and heroics. His dances open quietly, develop serenely, and stop without really ending, a glimpse into a world that always was and always will be.

Whenever I watch his sublime dancers enact their mysterious rituals, moves that seem to follow rules that I will never comprehend, with only casual reference to one another and virtually none to the audience, I feel I am observing superior beings from some higher plane. (Natanya Neumann, dancing with Cunningham, said that just before a performance he said, "There is no one out front. This is just another rehearsal.") That is not Martha's way. Powerful she may be, yet always at the mercy of mightier powers. Martha's genius lies in being able to reveal the glory and catastrophe of being human.

In 1974, while I was running the dance department at NYU School of the Arts, my students complained because the English teacher supplied by the university said, "Forget rules of grammar and write what you *feel.*" This approach may produce original writing but dismays my students who *want* to learn the rules. Dance, not English, is their creative medium.

I'm wondering what to do about the teacher when he abruptly leaves "to follow my guru."

Gurus had begun appearing in the 1960s. Soon they're an invasive species. Below 14th Street, gurus and their followers wear untucked off-white shirts of ramie or pineapple fiber, bow their heads humbly, and press their palms together prayerfully. They accompany a zeitgeist, which includes Rollerina, a 6-footer who glides around East Village on roller skates wearing a Christmas-tree-shaped ball gown. There is also a bald-headed, white-eyebrowed Mr. Kleen, troops of chanting Hare Krishnas in airports, and the Jules Feiffer character who wails, "I want to be different like all those others!"

Dancers pick up moves from yoga, karate, tai chi, etc. Few submit to the rigors of these disciplines, limiting themselves to a few moves added into whatever they know, offering the undigested aggregate to audiences and students. Martha never allows raw exotica to creep into her technique. When a student learning Contractions whistles her breath in and out, yoga-style, Martha stops the class.

"These movements are not mystical, they are technical. In performance, you may have to do them while fighting for breath, so you must breathe as your body demands," adding that she respects yoga too much to do it superficially.

In the 1960s, Yvonne Rainer, in her ruthless *No Manifesto*, tosses out everything deemed dance to embark on a rigorous search for what remains.

No to spectacle.
No to virtuosity.
No to transformations and magic and make-believe.
No to the glamour and transcendency of the star image.
No to the heroic.
No to the anti-heroic.
No to trash imagery.
No to involvement of performer or spectator.
No to style.
No to camp.
No to seduction of spectator by the wiles of the performer.
No to eccentricity.
No to moving or being moved.

It strikes me as outrageous and brave. Presently there emerges "post-modern" dance, which some take as license to dance any which way, or not in any noticeable way. At NYU, a student shows a study in which she lies on her back, head pillowed on her hands, one knee raised. After a minute, the knee flops to one side. End. Her composition teacher, the ruggedly avant-garde choreographer William Dunas, doesn't scoff but asks, "Does that seem like a dance to you?" Years later, after I'd returned from Russia, I called Yvonne and told her that Russians in Voronezh had asked me to teach "post-modern" technique.

"What did you teach them, walking?"

I meet Ruth Mitchell in ballet class. Sleek, long-legged, fashion-model beautiful, very southern. One day she meets me at the Graham Studio, and, since Martha is sitting at the desk, I introduce them. Next day Martha asks, "How was your date with Ruth?"

"Very nice." She's waiting for more so I add, "She's in *Annie Get Your Gun*. When it closes she's going back to Atlanta to open a dancing school. When she leaves New York, maybe I'll date a modern dancer."

As Martha looks away I hear her muttered, "irrepressible drive toward women."

Martha urges us to see Swiss modern dancer Harald Kreutzberg. The audience under the marquee of the Ziegfeld Theater is older. A grizzled man in sandals and a toga-like garment of monk's cloth is Raymond Duncan, Isadora's brother.

Kreutzberg is in his fifties, compact and strong, no show-off, yet able and willing to produce soaring jumps. Every costume has a hat, so I assume he is bald. His dances, all solos, are finely wrought and performed to perfection. Some are little anecdotes, some are lively portraits, yet the one that sticks with me, *Seliger Walzer,* is pure joyous dancing. I sit high in the balcony, but his powerful presence penetrates every inch of the Ziegfeld Theater.

New York City attracts troupes from all over the world, including Trudi Schoop (Switzerland), Lotte Goslar (Germany), Kurt Jooss (Germany) with his famed *The Green Table,* The Royal Ballet (England), also Spanish, Balinese, and Indian troupes. Martha talks feelingly about Mary Wigman in East Germany who no longer dances. It is painful to think what European modern dance might have become if not destroyed by Hitler and his thugs.

Harald Kreutzberg. Photo by Siegfried Enkelmann. Courtesy of the Ann Barzel Dance Research Collection, The Newberry Library, Chicago.

Before SAB's elementary "A" class, comes the professional "D" class, taken by City Center Ballet company dancers and watched by all who can cram into the tiny landing above the steps down into the studio. When taught by George Balanchine, there are always two remarkable women, Maria Tallchief, his wife, and Tanaquil LeClercq, who, whisper students, will be his *next* wife.

Tallchief always leads across the floor, rising with majestic power into *grand jeté*, legs in a breathtaking mid-air split, to land smoothly, swallowing the sixty-foot diagonal in four leaps. LeClercq, as if to forestall comparison, crosses near the end. Lean and bony, she is preternaturally strong, appearing magically at the leap's apex, to float with gravity-defying *ballon,* a magical suspension some dancers have, some don't, her sharp-featured face serene while she utters the most demanding technical feats as naturally as a tree utters green leaves.

The class includes *corps de ballet* dancers in pink tights and pierced ears, all having danced since childhood, hoping to join a troupe even before graduating high school. They watch each other with predacious eyes, gobble like geese about their teachers and who "Mr. B" is noticing. Ballet males occupy a lower rung, even soloists like Nicholas Magallanes and Francisco Moncion, rock-solid partners, seldom given a chance to show their own virtuosity. Other ballet males are subdued and self-absorbed, in black tights and white T-shirts, called "boys," never men. Males are more highly regarded in modern dance, but with its minuscule audience it is hardly a promising field for a man hoping to build a career.

When the City Center Ballet begins its month-long season, I join SAB students sneaking in, led by Brendon O'Flanagan, a student who knows an unguarded rear door leading to a narrow stairway to the second balcony. We enter before the first dance and when the lights dim, descend to the first balcony, thence to the orchestra. Once I know the ropes, I sneak in on my own, seeing Spanish troupes, dancers of Bali, and Uday Shankar, rationalizing this larceny as essential to my education, and buoyed by a rumor that Merce Cunningham steals books that are essential to his work, which will one day repay society. Whether or not the rumor is true, Cunningham bountifully enriched society.

The City Center ushers are onto us and at occasional sold-out performances, after fleeing from section to section, we can be asked to leave with a courtesy that says they know we will likely perform on that stage one day. I'm grateful and believe that bona fide dance students should be issued permits to attend all the dance performances they can tolerate.

One day I mention to Muriel Stuart that Martha Graham had told me to study with her. Her patrician brow rises.

"You are in Martha's company?"

"Yes."

She puts her face an inch from mine. "I never miss her season."

One day, dancers are talking about a new teacher in town, Benjamin Harkarvy. Melissa Hayden, a Ballet Theatre star, takes his class. I show up, surprised to see a portly, balding, very young man. But less than halfway through the class I know he's a genius. Harkarvy's classes are quiet

Benjamin Harkarvy teaching at Jacob's Pillow, 1987. Photo by Timothy Cahill. Courtesy of Jacob's Pillow Archives.

yet intense. He never uses ridicule, common among the Russians. I never found out who his teachers were but soon I'm taking take all my ballet classes with "Ben."

I run into Muriel Stuart on 57th Street. "I'm sorry I haven't been in your class lately, but I am going to ballet class."

"As long as you are taking class, and as long as it's not with that twenty-one-year-old fat man." My expression gives me away. "Oh, Stuart. Not you, too!"

"He's a good teacher," I say lamely.

Many modern dancers take Ben's class, and one day Ben gives Contractions. I am there to gain ballet skills and resent being taught Contractions by a ballet teacher. Deeming it a sop to the modern dancers in his class, I go back to my traditional ballet teachers. Eventually I meet a ballet dancer, Elizabeth Wullen (today, Elizabeth Hodes), who tells me she'd never heard of Contractions until Ben gave them, and that they gave her new freedom in her upper body. Ben was teaching Contractions for classical dancers. That had escaped me completely.

Downtown at the Henry Street Settlement, Alwin Nikolais has a dance center complete with small theater. He creates stunning dances out of bodies, costumes, props, sets, music, and lighting. (I could never detect a story.) Himself the author of every element, his dances look like no one else's. He has no imitators because, I decide, his dances are impossible to imitate. The dancers, however, are swallowed by external elements and seem interchangeable. Martha's vivid individuality suits me perfectly.

One day, Mark Ryder and I are jump-kicking by the studio wall, each trying to leave a smudge higher than the other. Martha and the women enter, watch, and in a voice meant for us to hear, Martha says, "When I was in Yellowstone Park, a ranger pointed out scratches high on a tree trunk. He explained that bears put them there. A bear comes along and puts his scratch as high as he can to show how big he is. Then another bear comes along and puts his scratch even higher. That's what men are, bears."

During an intermission at the 92nd Street Y, a stranger approaches. "Are you Stuart . . . uh . . ."

"Stuart *Gescheidt,*" using my born surname.

"Yeah," he replies, unwilling to try saying it. "You dance with Martha Graham?"

"Yes."

"I tried to get in touch with you. I need dancers for a show at the Astor Hotel."

"You still need them?"

"Yes. One day's work, pays $100." (Useful money in 1947.)

I become one of four bearing a fifteen-foot-long, feather-covered train for Gypsy Rose Lee, who, before we start down a flight of steps, turns and says, "Anyone drops this goddam thing, I'll brain 'em."

The name of an author, painter, or photographer stays on the work of art. A performer's name on a program gets one glance. I ask Sasha Liebich where he'd gotten Mark Ryder.

"Out of the air."

I decide to stick with Stuart, and since "Gescheidt" means *smart* in German, try Stuart Smart, Stuart Bright, Stuart Keen, Stuart Sharp, Stuart Brilliant. Another list keeps my initials: Stuart Gillette, Stuart Geste, Stuart Glide, Stuart Gordon, Stuart Gorth. For a time I favor Gorth; Heaven knows why. I mention the problem to Uncle Ira, who says, "You have a perfectly good name. Hodes. Why not use it?"

Uncle Ira's son is named Stuart. "There already is a Stuart Hodes."

"Why can't there be two?"

I have it legalized eight years later, before my daughter Catherine is born. Cousin Stuart, I note, sometimes calls himself "the real Stuart Hodes."

Jean Erdman, one of Martha's most elegant and lyrical dancers, is from Hawaii. Her forbears were missionaries whose descendants, as James Michener tells in *Hawaii,* ended up owning much of it. As a child, she'd learned the Hula, a sacred dance of native Hawaiians.

I'd seen her powerful solo, *Transformations of a Medusa,* so when she asked me to be in a new trio, I expected something weighty. It turned out a romp—*Sea Deep: A Dreamy Drama.* Bob Cohan and I play shipwrecked sailors who sink to the bottom, there to encounter a mischievous mermaid played by Jean.

Choreographers in movies like *The Red Shoes, The Turning Point, Smile,* etc., are depicted as posturing twits who stop rehearsals screaming, "No! No! No!" Rehearsals are stop-and-go, of course, but Jean, prepared and thoughtful, has the dance on its feet in two weeks and invites her husband, Joseph Campbell, to a run-through.

Dr. Joseph Campbell, author of *A Skeleton Key to Finnigans Wake* and *The Hero with a Thousand Faces,* had met Erdman at Sarah Lawrence College, where she was a student and he a professor. She introduces him, we dance, are dismissed. At the next rehearsal, Jean reworks the whole dance from notes. Campbell shows up several more times, each time going head-to-head with Jean, followed by more reworking. The final version seems decent enough, although to me, no better than what Jean had done the first time.

I meet Campbell again at a concert by ex-Graham dancer Marie Marchowsky. In the intermission he asks how I like Marchowsky.

"I don't."

"Why not?"

"Every dance is the same, and all her movement looks like something Martha threw out."

"You have no right to such an opinion."

"No right?"

"You have neither the background nor the experience to make such a judgement."

"But I still have the right to an opinion."

"No, you don't."

I know I am tilting against a mighty intellect, yet the exchange with Campbell reinforces my impression that where Jean Erdman is concerned, he's an arid intellectual parasitizing a creative artist. Campbell goes on to become America's reverently embraced all-purpose guru, whose musings on the meaning of life are seen during PBS fund-raising drives, along with Deepak Chopra on health, Jonathan Pond on money, and Dr. Phil on whatever. And after a few years, I completely reverse my opinion of Marie Marchowsky. But since when do ignorance and lack of comprehension deny one the *right* to an opinion?

Linda Margolies, who'd started with Graham at age nine, asks me to be in a duet. I'd seen her biting solo, *Small Fiasco,* evoking an embarrassing moment and am eager to dance with her. She's only seventeen yet has already danced in a Broadway musical, *Make Mine Manhattan.* She's not in the Graham Company because Martha considers her too young. Her duet is based on the barn scene in Steinbeck's *Of Mice and Men,* where big Lenny accidentally strangles the flirtatious wife of ranch boss Curley.

First rehearsal. Linda turns in (sickles) her right foot against her left ankle, leans sideways until about to topple, then stumbles to catch her weight. *More clumsy experimenting.* I resolve not to say yes again without knowing what I'm getting into. Thus began *Curley's Wife,* which was immediately called by reviewers "a miniature masterpiece," and, repeatedly, "the best dance on the program."

It fell into place with a piano piece by Marc Blitzstein. *Variation II, from Show.*

We give a private showing at the Weidman Studio Theater. Louis Horst comes with Valerie Bettis, and we're gratified by his gruff "Mmph, good dance" and by Bettis's generous praise. But before dancing at the 92nd Street Y, we need permission to use the score from composer Marc Blitzstein. I go to his apartment on University Place and describe how Lenny strangles Curley's wife. He's taken aback. "It's a classical *pas de deux.* I don't see how you can use it for such a dance." But he attends the concert and comes backstage to congratulate Linda. Never mentions money.

In September 1947, when Martha returned from Santa Fe, she started technique class in a new way. Instead of bounces followed by sitting Contractions, she began with *breathings.* In sitting position, a wave rises from the "sitting bones," up though the spine. A second *breathing* lifts the face

Stuart and Linda doing lift from *Curley's Wife* in Logan, Utah. Photo, Gertrude Shurr.

to the sky. After the breathings, then the older contractions, both moves from the breath, which goes in and out.

John Butler returned to dance with Martha in 1948, and after his first technique class, said, "If you leave for a year, you come back and feel like a beginner."

Soon after the Breathings, Martha added Spirals, which today illuminate virtually all her moves. Martha urges us to see a French film, *Farrebique ou Les quatre saisons* (1947), a documentary of a French family farm. She'd been transfixed by stop-motion sequences of plants growing. "They spiral upward toward the sun. Life flows along a spiral path."

In 1953, scientists Crick and Watson announced that the DNA molecule is a spiral helix. Martha's intuition about life flowing along a spiral path was scientifically confirmed.

Gertrude Shurr told me how the Graham Technique really began. I met Shurr at New York City's High School of Performing Arts. She is Martha's size, and like her, said Ruth St. Denis, has "a fascinating homely face." Unlike Martha, Shurr is not mysterious, but spunky and peppy, like a bright little bird. She told me exactly when Martha started teaching her own technique.

Ted Shawn, who never missed a chance to earn a buck, began his classes with a warm-up, after which he made up a long combination while a member of his staff watched and made notes. During the last half hour, while the students practiced, the notes were typed out and mimeographed, copies placed on the desk, and sold for two dollars. Since many of Shawn's students were dance teachers who needed material for their own classes, Shawn earned good money that way.[1]

Shawn also licensed the term "Denishawn Technique." (His wife was dancer Ruth St. Denis). He wouldn't license anyone to use it whose studio was near enough to compete for students, but others could pay $500 a year (multiply by 12 in today's dollars) for the right. When Martha started teaching in Rochester, Shawn sent her a bill. Martha replied that she was not teaching Denishawn Technique, but her own. "And that," said Gertrude Shurr, "was when Graham Technique really began."

Shawn's licensing policy suffered the "law of unintended consequences." Dance technique, like riding a bicycle, is not forgotten, even after muscles no longer respond, allowing aged dancers to continue as teachers. Most Denishawn alums could not create their own techniques, so if they wanted to teach Denishawn without paying, they called it something else. As a result, Denishawn Technique, whatever it may have been, disappeared from the earth. Martha, creating something entirely new, codifying every move, equipped her students to teach Graham Technique and seemed unconcerned when they did. So it spread into studios, academies, and colleges all over the world.

After Martha's death there arose a copyright claim on Graham Technique, whose moves are now deeply embedded in world dance. If the claim had been upheld, it would simply have stripped Graham's name from what is universally taught. Eventually people would be dancing Graham's moves without knowing they were Graham, soon forgetting that they ever were. And that would have been a shame.

Martha "codified" her technique, specifying body shapes, counts, which muscles do what, how weight is transferred, where to exert strength, and other specifics. Isadora Duncan made a powerful impression but codified nothing. Nevertheless, today there is something called "Duncan Dancing," with notable practitioners like Lori Belilove. If Belilove codified enough Duncan moves to comprise a teachable technique, it's a plus, although it might legitimately be termed "Belilove Technique." Yet there is no official Duncan Technique or Ted Shawn Technique because neither codified the vocabulary. Graham Technique, like classical ballet, is taught all over the world. But because she never stopped adding moves, it was never "closed." A creative teacher or choreographer can add moves and it will still be Graham Technique. Thus, every strong teacher has a personal stamp. Recently a French dancer said she was studying in Paris with a teacher who taught "authentic" Graham Technique. Such a teacher will presumably claim that this move is authentic, that one is not. I give such teachers a wide berth.

Martha was content to see her teachers further codify, within limits. One day, in the studio lounge, Bob Cohan and I argued the counts and moves of a class exercise: where the upbeat came, exact flow of the body's arch, swing to center, precise "and-a," until Martha, sipping honeyed tea, said mildly, "You're codifying it to death."

December 31, 1951

At a New Year's Eve party I am sitting on the floor, back propped against a pair of female shins. After my fourth drink, a complete dance idea pops into my head, including music of descending scales. The idea is still there the next day, so I get Linda Margolies and John Smolko, a dancer from *Paint Your Wagon,* to be in it for my 92nd Street Y concert.

I have a title from a poem, *No Heaven in Earth.* The woman echoes my moves, then leaves. The man and I fight. Eugene Lester writes a score based on descending scales. We perform it at the 92nd Street Y. Louis Horst, in *Dance Observer,* says it seems to be about a man trying to decide if he is straight or gay. I resolve to ignore the next dance idea that comes in a half-drunken stupor.

"Floor for Rent," in a loft window on East 21st Street. Too narrow to dance in, no heat on weekends, illegal to live in (it is years before Artist-in-Residence—AIR—lofts), although everyone above the street floor does. The rent is thirty-six dollars a month. I grab it. Even thirty-six dollars a month is steep when your income is zero, so I ask Eugene Lester, playing piano for classes and rehearsals at the Graham Studio, to share. He also takes over my musical education.

I'd studied violin, played easier pieces by Vivaldi, Telemann, Mozart, and Bach. Eugene had studied with Paul Hindemith at Yale, has me listen to Gustav Mahler and Anton Bruckner. We teach ourselves to play recorder (*blockflöte*), a cross between a flute and a pennywhistle. Dancers James Waring and Job Sanders play recorders too, so we have musicales joined by Helen Lanfer playing *continuo* on piano. I write a recorder piece for Linda's solo, *World On a String:* a child with a balloon whose world ends with a pop. I play it live for her concert at the 92nd Street Y.

On the floor below lives a German refugee family, Paul and Ilse Mattick and Bubi (Paul Jr.), their toddler son. Paul, a master machinist, anti-Nazi, and social theorist, had been lucky to escape Germany. One day, on our mutual front steps after small talk, I say, "Well, I'm off to work."

"You don't work. You dance."

"Dancing is work."

"It's effort, not work."

"Why isn't it work?"

"Work is effort that leads to a product. You produce nothing."

"I produce dancing."

He thrust out both hands. "Can you put it there?"

"There are many important things you can't hold in your hand."

"Such as?"

"Love."

Paul frowns. "Well, I don't *need* dancing."

That changes Paul's definition of work to effort that leads to a product he personally needs. But he does not acknowledge the flaw in his reasoning or accept the idea that dancing is work. I'm not entirely sure either, yet whatever dance is, I need it.

December 1947

Rehearsals get under way for the season at Maxine Elliott's Theater. Graham Black is gone, opting for a career in radio. A dancer arrives—John Butler, six foot three and silky smooth—to dance in roles originated by Merce Cunningham. I get Graham Black's role as a Cavalier in *Deaths and Entrances*, also the Highwayman in *Punch and the Judy*, once danced by Douglas Watson. I learn from a 16-millimeter silent film, fitting the moves to music assisted by pianist Helen Lanfer, whose scores are marked with entrances, exits, and distinctive moves.

There is also a new man, Dale Sehnert, lean, wiry, an inch taller than me. Martha adds him to *Dark Meadow* and he goes into the Fetish Dance. Up to now there have been three fetishes and three holes in the bias-sliced cylinder fashioned by Isamu Noguchi. Our production manager calmly drills a fourth hole into Noguchi's sculpture (!) and gives Dale a wooden dowel for rehearsal. A week before opening, Dale still doesn't have a fetish. Martha is consumed by details, and Erick says that Noguchi is not in New York. I volunteer to make something to see us through the season, cut a saucer-sized disk out of plywood, bend a wire bottle brush around its edge, fasten it to Dale's dowel, and spray-paint it black. *Dark Meadow* goes on.

Fifty-seven years later, December 4, 2004, I am at the Noguchi Museum, Long Island City, in a panel discussion about the Isamu Noguchi/ Martha Graham collaboration. Around us are sets, and sticking out of the original *Dark Meadow* piece are three original Noguchi fetishes and a fourth—mine! Elizabeth Auclair, a principal in the Graham troupe, says that the dancers refer to my fetish as "the toilet brush." I reveal this to the panel, the audience, and Ms. Shirley Taylor, director of the Noguchi Museum.

Martha doesn't play favorites, although the women say she favors the men. And she will hear nothing—*nothing*—critical of Erick. But exultation in the studio and on the stage make such matters fade. Exultation is not a daily experience, but its recurring gleam glorifies life as a Graham dancer.

One day Martha takes me aside and says that Erick is forming a troupe of his own, wants me in it for a bus tour to begin the day after we close at the Maxine Elliott. She will schedule rehearsals so I can do both, saying it is a fine opportunity. It is also an order.

I learn I'll be the Interlocutor in *John Brown*, read poetry in *Salem Shore*, a solo of Martha's danced by Ethel Winter, and speak as Stephen Trainer in *Stephen Acrobat*. When I express doubts about my speaking voice, he sends me to voice coach Constance Welch and pays the bill.

Stephen Acrobat had premiered at the Ziegfeld but I hadn't seen it. Reviews ranged from dismal to vicious. Walter Terry in the *New York Herald Tribune*:

> New York: February 2, 1947—"'Stephen Acrobat,' a new dance work by Erick Hawkins, last evening was given the first of what one hopes will be but few performances.

Erick's tour will also include Martha's *El Penitente*, in which I'll dance the Christ Figure, originated by Merce Cunningham. John Butler had danced it at the Maxine Elliott, and if he's not there both Sasha and Bob are ahead of me. So Erick's tour is my chance.

Erick is enthusiastic about plans to revise *Stephen Acrobat* with a new set by Isamu Noguchi. But his enthusiasm is not catching. He rambles on in a breathy monologue that never calls for a response, and although he doesn't mention his dreadful reviews, his tone is full of reproach.

Erick has his own studio on Fifth Avenue, five blocks north of Martha's, a narrow loft with a linoleum floor. On the upright piano is a large kachina doll. Erick speaks worshipfully of Hopi and Navaho cultures: "Everything they made was a work of art, every pot, every blanket, every article of clothing."

In a small room off the studio, he has a cot covered by a Navaho blanket. A bookcase of polished maple holds a dozen books, a smaller kachina, and bone china cups and saucers. Erick's coffee maker is a Chemex shaped like an hourglass, with a wooden collar around its middle tied on with a leather thong. He holds it up. "Glass, wood, leather. Why can't more manufacturers make things like this?"

Despite the voice coach, I continue to dislike the sound of my voice. I do come to like *John Brown*, a stalwart dance I think would be well received if it could be revived today.

I learn the Christ Figure from a 16-millimeter film of Merce Cunningham. John Butler had changed some moves, but I restore them and Martha approves.

The Noguchi *Stephen Acrobat* set arrives. The backdrop has an iconic tree with a bright red apple dangling from a branch. But the major object is a twelve-feet-high, three-sided tower of steel tubing, three-and-a-half feet on a side. It stands mid-stage left, and Erick wants me to clamber through it while speaking lines. Not fastened to the floor, it can easily topple over with me inside. I start gingerly, but, after a week, have enough confidence to "walk" it across the studio by rocking gently from side to side. One day, rocking toward Erick like a twelve-feet-tall mechanical zombie, I suggest he use this in the dance. He rejects it with a shudder.

Erick takes a full hour to warm up, urges me to do the same, and although my roles do not require it, I do. Erick tries scores of moves while I hang in the Noguchi tower repeating a line. Deadly boring, yet I grow to like Erick. He's helplessly sincere and honest to the point of innocence. On a break, he makes coffee in his Chemex and when the liquid has filtered through, holds it to the light, giving me a look at its clear umber depths before pouring into bone china cups and saucers. He tries numberless endings, none right until he begins to climb into the Noguchi tower. It suggests a union of Stephen Acrobat and his Trainer. Curtain.

An item appears in the *New York Herald Tribune:*

> New York. July 14, 1947. Erick Hawkins, principal male dancer in the Martha Graham Company, has announced the formation of a touring unit to be called "Erick Hawkins in Theatre Dance Pieces." A group of six dancers headed by Ethel Winter and Stuart Gescheidt will accompany Mr. Hawkins on a spring tour of the Middle West. The repertory will feature "El Penitente," "Salem Shore," "Stephen Acrobat," and "John Brown," all of them created either by Martha Graham or Mr. Hawkins for Miss Graham's repertory."

Erick Hawkins (jumping) and Stuart Hodes (hanging) in *Stephen Acrobat* set.
Photo by Philippe Halsman, copyright Halsmann Archive. Used with permission.

Not six dancers, three: Erick, Ethel Winter, and me. Plus pianist Hazel Johnson, stage manager Stuart Talcroft, and technical director Pamela Stiles. In the weeks before Martha's season at Maxine Elliott's Theater, I take two daily technique classes, dash from rehearsal with Martha to rehearsal with Erick, eat on the run, leave my bed unmade, laundry piled up; barely enough sleep, no social life. If this is a dancer's life, it suits me.

February 17, 1948

Maxine Elliott's Theater. I don't dance opening night, so Donald Duncan passes me into the audience and in the first intermission introduces me to Jerome Robbins whose *Fancy Free* and *Interplay* are wowing ballet audiences. Robbins asks if I've seen rehearsals of *Night Journey*.

"Yes."

"Has Martha invented lots of new movement?"

"Lots."

"Good. I'm working on a new ballet and need ideas."

I relay this to the Graham dancers, who seem surprised. Everyone is copying Martha, yet few come right out and say so. I see Robbins's next ballet, *Afternoon of a Faun,* and many others. Not a single Graham move that I can see.

But in 1952, I see a solo at the 92nd Street Y, titled *At the Recital.* The program is by Ronne Aul. He wore black tights, a long-sleeved white shirt, bow tie, black vest, and a derby. He carried an umbrella and worked with a chair. Section titles were "The Grand Entrance," "He Came By Mistake," "The Sponsor," "The Critic," and "The Artist."

Four years later, 1956, Jerome Robbins premiered *The Concert,* which is set at a piano recital. The costumes are identical to Aul's, except that the tights are white. They carry umbrellas and folding chairs. Jerome Robbins's program note:

> One of the pleasures of attending a concert is the freedom to lose oneself listening to the music. Quite often, unconsciously, mental pictures and images form, and the patterns and paths of these reveries are influenced by the pure music itself or its program notes, or by the personal dreams, problems, and fancies of the listener.

Three Robbins biographies (by Greg Lawrence, Deborah Jowitt, and Amanda Vaill) reveal him as a brilliant but desperate soul, often doubting his own genius, terrified of being exposed as a homosexual, a punishable crime then. And in the House Un-American Activities Committee, corrupt pols like Joseph McCarthy and Richard Nixon flaunt bogus patriotism by bullying, threatening, and destroying the careers of theater artists. Robbins acknowledged that he was influenced by Martha Graham, yet there was nothing about other influences. I wrote Deborah Jowitt. Her reply:

I found no reference to Ronne Aul among Robbins's papers, but, then, I didn't peruse every scrap of paper in the zillions of boxes. There was a box of programs I had hoped to go through, but time ran out, and I imagine the Library scattered them.

As I noted in the book, Jerry did map out a ballet about a woman having fantasies while listening to music. That was in 1953, but still after the date you mention [1952].

You say that Aul's dance, unlike "The Concert," was a solo? Of course Robbins could have seen it. And maybe been influenced. Who knows? I suppose umbrellas are a natural response to the "Raindrop" prelude.

Ronne Aul at Jacob's Pillow, 1951. Photo by John Lindquist. © Houghton Library, Harvard University.

I wrote back that using the "Raindrop" prelude could have been Robbins's response to Aul's umbrellas.

Deborah Jowitt seems to doubt that Robbins copied Aul. A note to Amanda Vaill elicited the news that on the date of Aul's Y concert, Robbins was out of the country. But the Y was not a premiere. In 1951 Aul did his dance at Jacob's Pillow and who knows where else?

Ronne Aul was the most brilliant male dancer of my generation. I first saw him in Sophie Maslow's *The Village I Knew* and wondered why he never took a class at the Graham school where Martha would have grabbed him. But not every male dancer wanted to dance with Martha. After two years in Italy, Aul emigrated to Martinique, where he became a major figure in the development of dance there. The U.S.A.'s loss.

Robbins's *The Concert* is a great comedic ballet. But can you believe he independently came up with Ronne Aul's entire idea, virtually identical costumes, and also props? I cannot.

After the last performance at Maxine Elliott's Theater, February 29, 1948, I stay up late packing for Erick's tour. We leave in the morning. Erick's program:

1—JOHN BROWN, A Passion Play,
Dance by Erick Hawkins, Text by Robert Richman,
Music by Charles Mills,
Set by Isamu Noguchi
The Interlocutor. . . . . Stuart Hodes
Captain John Brown. . . . . Erick Hawkins

A few months after the hanging of John Brown, James Redpath published a biography of him with this dedication: "To Wendell Phillips, Emerson, and Thoreau, Who, when the mob cried 'Madman' said 'Saint.'"

2—EL PENITENTE
Choreography, Martha Graham, Music, Louis Horst,
Decor, Isamu Noguchi, Costumes, Edythe Gilfond
Penitent. Erick Hawkins
Christ Figure. . . . . Stuart Hodes
Mary Figure. . . . . Ethel Winter

3—YANKEE BLUE BRITCHES, A Green Mountain Dance
Dance by Erick Hawkins, Music by Hunter Johnson, Set and
Costumes by Charlotte Trowbridge

The ghost of Yankee Doodle rises from the valleys, crosses mountain ranges at a single step, and encompasses the earth which loves him. But whenever he is surprised by enemies and is downed, he comes to life again, as a hero has always done, dances a jig out of joy and gladness, and calls out to let the nations know "I wasn't brought up in the woods to be scared by owls."

4—SALEM SHORE
Choreography by Martha Graham, Music by Paul Nordhoff
Set by Arch Lauterer, Costume by Edythe Gilfond
Reader: Stuart Hodes
A ballad of a woman's longing for her beloved's return from the sea.
Danced by Ethel Winter

5—STEPHEN ACROBAT
Dance by Erick Hawkins, Poetry by Robert Richman
Music by Robert Evett, Set by Isamu Noguchi,
Costumes by Kenn Barr
Stephen Trainer . . . . Stuart Hodes
Stephen Acrobat . . . . Erick Hawkins

March 1, 1948

On arrival at Skidmore College, Ethel discovers that her *Salem Shore* costume had been left in New York City. When Erick chides her, she points out that packing is the stage manager's job and that neither he nor I had checked our costumes. The costume is sent for and arrives in time—by taxi.

After the show, snowflakes drifting down, students walk us to a cozy common room, fire burning in a great hearth, table deliciously loaded, and we dine surrounded by delectable young women in plaid skirts, angora sweaters, and saddle shoes, who tell us that they loved our dancing.

Next day at Bard College, two-thirds of the way back to New York City, Erick is doing warm-up bounces when Stuart Talcroft steps up and blurts,

"The *El Penitente* props aren't here. They were left at Skidmore." (Couldn't make himself say, "*I* left them at Skidmore.")

Erick stops mid-bounce. In the strained silence, he does a half bounce, then a full bounce, and like the Little Engine That Could, picks up speed and is bouncing full-speed again. Talcroft slinks away.

The Flagellation rope and Penitent's cloth mask are easily found but not Isamu Noguchi's artful Cross and distinctive Death Cart. Erick finishes his floor warm-up and starts on *pliés* while staring at the smoothly crafted fence of the *John Brown* set, also by Noguchi. He stops, takes the fence apart, separates two sections, and lo! one is a lopsided square, which, draped with black cloth, makes a serviceable Death Cart. The other is a kind of *art moderne* cross. The Bard kitchen supplies a Red Delicious apple, and *Penitente* goes on without a hitch. Erick Hawkins, I decide, is a real pro.

In Baltimore, the tiny stage has no backstage crossover. With no way to go unseen from one side to the other, Erick makes some changes in choreography. Pianist Hazel Johnson is squeezed into a sliver off-stage right. Playing Erick's *Penitente* solo, she snakes out a hand to turn the page, to have the entire accordion-folded score spill onto the floor. With her left hand plonking any old keys, she gropes down with her right, but each time she catches hold of a page and sets it on the piano, the other pages pull the whole thing back down like a Slinky toy.

Stuart Talcroft is in the opposite wing with no crossover. I am twelve feet from Hazel but cannot leave the stage. She keeps groping while making tuneless plonks, to which Erick does his entire solo. Then comes Ethel's Magdalen dance. It ends when she offers Erick the Temptation Apple. Now it is my turn as the Christ Figure. To a scatter of tuneless, rhythmless plonks, I stalk to Erick and gently slap each cheek, whereupon he throws his arms around my waist. When I back up he is supposed to let go, but he hangs on so I drag him upstage.

This audience is seeing something rare: Martha Graham dancers *improvising* choreography. Finally Hazel stops plonking, reaches down with both hands, grabs the score, sets it on the piano, and plays to the end.

A looming disaster I never let happen is to topple over *inside* the Noguchi tower. But one night during bows, the curtain, a "traveler" that closes from the sides, catches one of the tower's projections. Erick yells for Talcroft to stop pulling the curtain rope, but the tower crashes, and

Erick shrieks as pieces snap off and fly into the audience. No one is hurt, and the tower is repairable, but Erick deplores this as unprofessional.

On our way upstate, the temperature plunges. After a show at a woodsy college miles from any town, we plan to drive straight to the next town and sleep late. But the bus won't start. At two in the morning, a rattle-trap replacement arrives. It has no heat. Bundled in sweaters and coats, we hunker down.

I am roused by a gleam of light inches from my face. I'd been breathing on a wheel well, and it is sun reflected off ice that had condensed from my breath. I sit up to see Ethel, Hazel, and Erick staring numbly at the snowy landscape. They turn bleary eyes to me, I hold up an index finger—wait!—reach down and tug at the ice. It comes off in my hands, a clear curved slab a foot across and an inch thick, and I hold it overhead like a tennis trophy. Ethel starts to laugh, then everyone does, helplessly, until we arrive at the hotel and stumble to our rooms for a few hours of rest. The remainder of Erick's tour was without incident, but Ethel was left with a chill. Back in New York, she stayed bedridden for a week.

One day, company class seemed charged. Afterward, Martha said, "You're all so beautiful I'm going to make a dance just for you." *Diversion of Angels* had been conceived. Rehearsals began in silence, but soon Norman Dello Joio was composing a score and sending it over page by page. Helen Lanfer would play the new passage and Martha immediately flung out moves. She didn't usually work that way, but then, she had no usual way. *Primitive Mysteries* had been choreographed to counts and Louis Horst composed music to the counts. Aaron Copland and Martha are said to have had a rapturous correspondence leading to *Appalachian Spring*. William Schuman gave her a score for *Night Journey* that began with a prelude meant to be played before the curtain rose. Martha let about twelve seconds play, the curtain rose, the dance began. Schuman composed Martha's next score for *Judith* but left the prelude out of the piano reduction. She rehearsed for months and only heard the prelude at an orchestra rehearsal a week before opening night. On opening night she danced to it.

Mark Ryder told me that Martha approached Paul Hindemith with an idea but that he rejected it and returned a score based on an idea of his own. I knew no more until I read David Zellmer's book.[2] Zellmer had left Martha to become a World War II B-24 pilot; he flew in the Pacific, and they corresponded. One of Martha's letters to him said that Carlos Chávez had failed to deliver a score based on Shakespeare's *King Lear,* so she offered the idea to Paul Hindemith who rejected it but sent a score based on a Stéphane Mallarmé poem, suggesting that Martha's dance be based on that. Martha accepted, and the result was *Hérodiade,* a masterpiece. Some choreographers are so unsure of their talent that any suggestion is taken for criticism. Martha is so sure of hers that she can make any idea her own.

Dello Joio kept the music coming: one, two, three pages a day. Helen Lanfer played the pages, Martha made moves. Soon she'd thrown away enough for several dances. If the dance had a form, I couldn't tell. Dance composition teachers are mad about form. Someone read Martha a review in which a critic described *Deaths and Entrances* as a perfect study in form. She said, "I never think about form." Yet she was sensitive to it. One afternoon rehearsing the new dance, after a romantic duet she said, "Now I must sweep the stage," and she gave the women a tilting crossover that swept it clean.

Everything about the new dance has baited-breath excitement. Helen McGehee and I are thrown together and immediately torn apart: "Adolescent Love." Pearl Lang and Bob Cohan circle and cling to one another: "Romantic Love." Natanya Neumann and Mark Ryder are serene in "Mature Love." On early programs, the couples are not identified. "Duets for Adolescent Love" (later, "Yellow") and "Romantic Love" (later, "Red") are soon completed, but not "Mature Love" (first "Blue," finally "White"). Until one day at the start of rehearsal, Martha had us sit and watch Natanya and Sasha. Serenely paced, no flashy moves, "Mature Love" is breathtaking. At its climax, both dancers pitch forward, the man falling across the woman, as if sheltering her body with his own. Sasha, strong and gentle, is a superb partner. He has a striking girlfriend and, while not boastful, makes no secret of the fact that he considers himself an ardent and skillful lover.

"Don't lose the embrace," says Martha sharply as Sasha falls athwart Natanya. Martha is too small to demonstrate so Sasha tries again, pitching his body over Natanya, taking weight on his hands, one on either side of her shoulders.

"No, Sasha. Hold the embrace."

"I am holding it."

"You're not," she says, "Hold it—there." She guides Sasha's knee to a place above Natanya's hips.

"Oh. You meant with the leg."

"Haven't you discovered that a lover's embrace is with the legs as well as the arms?"

The great lover draws himself up haughtily but does not reply.

The non-dancing staff is in a continual state of flux. Pianist Ralph Gilbert, who has the ungainly good looks of Ernest Borgnine crossed with Burt Lancaster, leaves to work full-time with his wife, the stunning dancer Iris Mabry. Succeeding pianists include Ada Reif, Betty Walberg, and Eugene Lester. When manager Donald Duncan leaves for a post at *Dance Magazine*, Martha engages a bright lad named Doug Hudelson who soon defects to manage folk singer Susan Reed (for which Martha devises a stinging rebuke). Eventually she finds Craig Barton in Texas, and, with LeRoy Leatherman, they manage the Graham Company for the next thirty years.

Spring 1948

Martha announces that the company will spend the summer in residence at the Connecticut College American Dance Festival. One hundred dollars for six weeks, plus room, meals, transportation, rehearsals, and all the dance classes we can squeeze in.

With an open ticket on the New Haven and Hartford line, I decide to go Sunday, a day early. Martha is on the train but there are no other dancers, so she invites me to join her for lunch with company manager Doug Hudelson. We're in the dining car at a cloth-covered table with china dishes, glass tumblers, heavy silverware, and silent waiters, waiting for cooked-to-order food. Martha is by the window facing front, Doug beside her, me opposite, gliding by green, sun-drenched New England.

Hudelson, young, smart, and ambitious, had declined Martha's offer to be her general manager. After introducing us, she turns to me and says pleasantly, "Doug is going to be Susan Reed's new manager," and shoots him a teasing glance. "He could have been ours, but his vision doesn't reach that far." Doug's smile grows strained. She pats his wrist. "But he did agree to see us through the summer."

She and Doug talk about theater, art, ambition, relationships, love. I'm silent yet feel included by Martha's glances and smiles. Hudelson, stimulated by Martha's interest, grows effusive. Suddenly she leans toward him and whispers in his ear. All I hear: "But Doug, what about......?"

His face falls. "Oh, Martha. It didn't work out." He stares down at his plate.

Martha puts a sympathetic hand on his sleeve. "But Doug, what will you do?"

"There's nothing I can do. It's a disaster."

Martha's head pops up. She cocks a glance at me, back to Doug, smiles perkily. "A disaster? How perfect! Makes me feel so good, I think I'll put on another pound." Snatches up a soda cracker and bites off half.

Hudelson sits like a stone, reddens, struggles against tears. After a long moment, Martha touches his cheek. "Oh don't mind me, Doug. You know I just like to get a rise out of you," and turns her prattling attention to me while Hudelson collects himself.

The New London station is deserted. She sends Hudelson to look for an open drugstore. When he's out of sight she smiles coyly. "I was naughty, wasn't I?"

"Yes, Martha."

"I hope I didn't disillusion you."

Disillusion *me?* I want to convey that I am too sophisticated, and anyway, if she'd disemboweled Hudelson with her steak knife, I'd still be her faithful minion. "You didn't disillusion me at all." A shadow crosses her face. Too late I recognize the nasty implication.

"You'd better get Doug," she says. "I don't think he'll be able to find that drugstore." She wants to be rid of me. I am glad to escape.

Someone that summer is teaching Wigman Technique. After watching a class, Martha says, "The movement has mechanical power." She lifts and drops a shoulder, whiplashes her head, slices an arm through the air. "You can see why it appealed to them." Is "them" Germans in general or the Nazis, who banned modern dance, allowing only "rhythmic gymnastics," which had originated in the eighteenth century, blossomed in Sweden, and become an Olympic event?

That summer Martha completes a strong draft of the new dance: *Wilderness Stair*, later titled *Diversion of Angels*. Helen McGehee, my partner, is five feet tall, 100 pounds, steely slim, with patrician features, blue/green eyes, Virginia accent, and barbed wit. But no matter how many times I fatuously call her hometown Lynchville or Lynchtown, she patiently says, "Lynchburg."

Helen and her husband, Umaña, invite me to dinner in the loft where they live with his paintings and two Siamese cats. The bouillabaisse is so spicy my eyes water. Everyone is eating it, so I do, too, following each burning spoonful with a gulp of ice water. Next day, Helen mentions that when shaking in dried chili pepper, the top of the jar had come off, emptying the entire shaker into the bubbling pot.

"But why did you serve it?"

"I wasn't going to throw it out."

"You seemed to enjoy it."

"I thought I was going to die!"

Our duet is shattering first love, not cute, not puppy-love. The moves are breathless, eager, halting. I think of Selma, my lost (my eternal!) love. Helen is light, strong, fearless. She takes chances, trusting me to catch her however she flies at me. When a good move emerges, Martha weaves it into the dance and we are glorified. Today, when I watch *Diversion of Angels* and see those very moves, I'm glorified again.

Martha's *Notebooks* reveal the complexities of her thoughts when making other dances, but nothing about *Wilderness Stair*. I suspect there wasn't much cogitating. Moves seemed snatched out of the instant. One day, Sasha and I are sitting on the studio floor watching Martha in mid-stride, feet parallel, torso spiraled, gaze turned and raised, as though listening, left arm at shoulder level and folded at the elbow, fingers brushing her cheek. "That's for Pearl," Sasha whispers, and as if on cue, Martha says, "Pearl?"

Thirty years later, I see a Graham performance in which the Red duet originated by Pearl and Bob in the program is called "Erotic" love. Martha's erotic duets—Jocasta and Oedipus, Eve and the Stranger, Phaedra and Hippolytus, to mention three—have a turbulent physicality unseen in *Angels,* which is extravagantly romantic. But that was not the only coarsening of Martha's language. I had often heard her say that all movement begins in the body's "core," sometimes its "generative core." Decades later she's "quoted" as saying, "Movement begins in the vagina."

Martha was proud of her Victorian heritage and neither reticent nor blatant about sex. But when I was taking her classes, late '40s through early '70s, she would no more have said "movement begins in the vagina" than Jack Cole's "fuck the moon." In *Dancing with Cuba,* Alma Guillermoprieto's luminous memoir, she quotes Martha as saying, "From the vagina, girls. Movement is born in the gut."[3] All I can say is that Guillermoprieto's class surely had no men in it. If it had, Martha would not have left them so pointedly out, although she might well have added "testicles" to her taunt.

All of which has little to do with changing "romantic" to "erotic," which I attribute to Martha's waning energy in the 1980s, when program material, once carefully wrought, was being debased by parasitic minions.

Martha invented and tossed out many openings for *Wilderness Stair*. Once, the whole company was onstage; another time, three couples; still another, the men and one woman. One day, waiting to begin, we were all lounging against the *barre* at the back wall. Martha entered, said, "Take hands," and had every other dancer pitch deeply forward while the others pulled back to hold their weight. Alternating pitches and pulls, the line traveled downstage, where it split, dancers exiting left and right except for Natanya and Sasha. It was stunning but lasted only a week.

She got close to what became the opening when she had the four men gather about Natanya, who tilted against each in turn, to stay against Sasha as the others exited. But she changed it completely for the 1950 Paris premiere. The curtain rose on the entire group facing upstage. On the opening chords, slow back falls in unison, then all rose and broke for the wings leaving Natanya and Sasha onstage.

Doris Humphrey was also in residence at Connecticut College, and the two troupes became instant colleagues. José Limón, Humphrey's star, taught technique at eight in the morning. I roused myself at an unholy 6:30 a.m. to take his class.

If modern dance had a *danseur noble*, José Limón was it. All knew that Martha had asked him to dance with her. As a peasant in *Day on Earth*, he glowed with the nobility Doris Humphrey revealed in that humble life. Person to person, Limón maintains a friendly distance. Meeting me on campus he'd say, "Ahh, Stuart. Good morning, Stuart. How is Stuart today?"

Properly awed, I'd reply, "I'm fine, Mr. Limón. How are you?"

But not Al Shulman. Al Shulman is dancing like some men join the Navy, a bit of adventure before settling into life. He has torrents of energy, will dance with anyone who asks. When José Limón says, "Ahh, Al. Good morning, Al. How is Al today?" Al replies, "Al's fine, José. How's José?" After dancing a few years, Al Shulman becomes a veterinarian.

At the dance festival is a sixteen-year-old named Claude Rapkine who claimed to be French, although her perfect English (with a faint New York City accent) makes me wonder.

"Can you speak French?"

"I *am* French."

She also claimed to be in a movie called *The Illegals,* about Jews running the British blockade to get into Israel. "I give birth on the deck of a ship." (Sure you do.)

Back in Brooklyn, I pass a theater where *The Illegals* is playing, walk in to see Claude's face filling the screen, a hand with a cloth gently wiping beads of sweat from her brow as she gives birth. I dig out her Paris address, write with chastened respect, and two years later she greets the Martha Graham Company when it arrives in Paris where she is a working actress: her professional name, Louise Vincent.

Doris Humphrey is making a new dance, too, titled *Corybantic.* I read up on the Corybantes, orgiastic dancers who accompany the Earth goddess, Cybele. Yet the dancing seems more ceremonial than orgiastic. I am eager to watch her rehearsals but assume that, like Martha's, they are closed to outsiders. Her pianist, Simon Sadoff, says I should ask permission, but sure I'll be refused, I suggest a ruse. Her music is Béla Bartók's dazzling Concerto for Two Pianos and Percussion, which Sadoff had reduced for one piano and a clanging metal ashtray. Fearsomely difficult, he needs a page turner and I ask him to let me be his. Pretending to have my eyes glued to the score, I watch rehearsals every day for a week. One day, Sadoff says Humphrey had asked about me. Told I was in Martha's troupe, she said, "I don't understand that one. He comes to rehearsal every day but never watches the dancing."

Norman Lloyd, like Louis Horst, is a musician who teaches dance composition and also, like Horst, bases it on musical principles. Horst is crusty but you *know* he likes you. Maybe Lloyd does too but you'd never guess from his mocking style. I hear him describe "monkey mother" choreography:

> The monkey mother sits in a tree eating a banana. She scratches her armpit, hikes her baby onto her back, tears off and nibbles a leaf, hoots at another monkey, leaps to another branch.

Uneasy laughter as Lloyd makes the point that non sequiturs produce chaotic dances. But something tells me that if monkeys behave that way, it does not have to be chaotic because monkeys are unified by their monkeyness, as dances can be unified by elements other than movement alone. And ever since, if I bog down, I summon the monkey mother, who often comes up with a refreshing non sequitur.

William Bales also teaches composition. One day he assigns a study based on water. Students dance water running, flowing, raining, bubbling, babbling, boiling—all pretty much alike. Then a student approaches the water, touches it with a toe, wades to his knees, hips, neck, over his head—and *drowns*. It is the first dance I see by Donald McKayle.

Erick Hawkins is at work on a solo titled *The Strangler*, which, with Martha's new dance will be premiered at the end of the summer. He asks me to be in it, yet another speaking role. My heart sinks, but how can I refuse?

It is based on the Oedipus myth—Erick tells me to pronounce it *Oy-de-poosse*. His script is dense with Freudian folderol. Working on this piece I come to recognize what I must describe as Erick's curious gift; he does not sense when he's become ridiculous. This may be true of many avant-garde artists, but I am not convinced Erick is one. He begins on his back, arms and legs paddling the air—an infant, he explains, and while I chant the riddle of the Sphinx (*"Four legs, then two, then three. Four legs, then two, then three."*), he slowly reaches toward his crotch and covers it with both hands.

Grabbing one's crotch is cool in the 1960s, but in 1948, Erick, supine on his back, legs in the air, hands covering his genitals, is not. I long to escape his endless rehearsals. About two weeks before the premiere, Erick, ill at ease, tells me he's decided to replace me with actor Joseph Wiseman. I hide my relief, especially when both he and Martha *apologize*. At the premiere, Erick's hands move toward his crotch and from the audience comes a raucous, "Grab it!"

Erick presents *The Strangler* in New York City in January 1950 at the Forty-Sixth Street Theater. John Martin of the *New York Times* calls it "a thoroughly embarrassing piece of ineptitude that should have been quietly interred back in 1948."

Several years after that, when Erick is well along toward creating his own distinctive style, he evokes an angry reaction from the mostly dance audience at Hunter College Playhouse. I was in the mezzanine, a couple of rows behind Anna Sokolow, and in the middle of one of Erick's dances she uttered a loud "Boo," setting off a chain reaction of boos and opposing applause. I join the applause and, although not yet one of Erick's admirers, consider it wrong for one dancer to boo another in this modern dance sanctuary. Helen McGehee was there, too, and wrote about it.

> I was sitting with Bertram Ross. We were in the mezzanine behind Anna Sokolow, Muriel Stuart, and Betty Walberg, and Anna yelled "Booo." Bert spoke loudly to Anna criticizing her behavior and identified himself saying, "My name is Bertram Ross." It was a lovely and stimulating gesture on Bert's part. I was grateful to him especially since I felt so implicated in Erick's performance. One of his dances, "Chimeara," called for hooves, and Umaña [Helen's husband] had made him two pairs. He rehearsed in one pair and saved the other for performances, but decided to use the rehearsal pair for the performance. The elastic broke and Erick calmly said, "I have another pair," left the stage, and returned with the new pair and finished the performance. For me, that performance really opened up Erick's art in a way that was new. A while after that, the word came around that Bertram Ross and Anna had had a public spat.[4]

At Connecticut College's Palmer Auditorium, the Martha Graham and Doris Humphrey companies share a dressing room. I notice that Limón's costumes are painted and mention it to Helen McGehee.

"Spray-painted. Martha would never do that."

"Why not?"

"Spray-painting makes cheap fabrics look rich onstage. Martha uses rich fabrics."

Wilderness Stair got its title from a poem by Ben Belitt, professor and resident poet, who watched rehearsals. The whole poem became our program note:

> *It is the place of the Rock and the Ladder, the raven, the blessing, the tempter, the rose. It is the wish of the single-hearted, the undivided; play after spirit's labor; games, flights, fancies, configuration of the lover's intention: the believed possibility, at once strenuous and tender, humors of innocence, garlands, evangels, Joy on the wilderness stair: diversion of angels.*

Martha designs and makes the women's costumes. The color of their dresses identifies their roles: yellow for "Adolescent Love," red for

"Romantic Love," blue for "Mature Love," shades of beige for the others. Blue later becomes white, and today the couples are "Yellow," "Red," and "White." The men wear earth-colored tights, chests bare. Martha demands that all exposed skin be covered with body makeup, so the men sponge on "liquid pancake" that dries to a powder. But when we sweat it goes liquid again. Martha respects sweat as a sign of work, but New London is so hot and humid we sweat after a few *pliés*. After pre-performance warm-ups, we shower, sponge on body makeup, pull on tights, but in the few moves before curtain we get so sweated up that our torsos gleam and pancake comes off leaving broad swathes on the women's costumes, which must be sent out and dry-cleaned after each performance. This annoys Martha.

"There's a limit to how much you need to sweat, and you are sweating more than is necessary." She dismisses our protests. "There is something in a man that drives him to leave *his mark* on a woman."

If *Corybantic* was less than a triumph, Doris Humphrey's *Day on Earth* and *The Shakers* are masterpieces, and I envy the dancers in them. I know enough not to reveal this to Martha and not for an instant do I think of leaving her. But I develop deep admiration for Doris Humphrey, as an artist and a person. She has a second superb man, Lucas Hoving. Tall and lean but neither the airy spirit of Merce Cunningham nor sleek and polished like John Butler, Hoving projects iron intensity, a perfect foil for Limón's rich earthiness—Lucifer to Limón's Everyman. In a few years, Hoving will create the role of Iago in Limón's *The Moor's Pavane*. I never hear Martha speak badly about Doris Humphrey. Their almost polar difference is illustrated by the significance each gives to the *left* side. Both deem it the "dark side," except that to Martha it is her own left—stage left, while to Doris Humphrey it is the audience's left—stage right. Thus, Humphrey makes dances imagining how the audience will experience them, while Martha seeks to draw the audience into her own experience.

That summer I took classes in Humphrey-Weidman Technique as taught by José Limón. The central theme is said to be Fall and Recovery, which some compare to Martha's Contraction and Release. But I think Doris Humphrey sought to capture nothing less than mortality itself. "Fall and Recovery" seems like the purest metaphor for the biblical fall and the human potential for rebirth. Her dances could be dramatic, like *Lament for Ignacio Sánchez Mejías;* dark and brooding, like *Ruins and Visions;* exalted, like *The Shakers;* or serene and joyous, like *Day on Earth.* She finds moves from the "ritualization of gesture," and actions like walking, running, leaping, falling, rising, etc., enriched by dancers like Charles Weidman with his comic genius and José Limón, whose name her technique now bears. Graham too used such moves and invented others, but behind all lurks the mysterious Contraction, drawn from breath, which is close to life itself.

In my first performance of *Wilderness Stair,* stage fright transmutes into boundless energy and mental alertness. Maybe it was the role, the first Martha made specifically for me. I began to imagine dancing bigger roles.

New York Times critic John Martin was kind to Doris Humphrey. "*Corybantic,* like most works of substance, no doubt, requires further seeing before it yields its full impact." He dismissed *Wilderness Stair,* saying, "The group of six girls and four men danced superbly, and if the work itself can scarcely be considered one of its creator's happier or more important achievements, it at least provides material for a stunning performance."[5]

In another column, he ignored Martha completely:

LIMÓN UNIT SCORES
HIT AT DANCE FETE
New London Audience Cheers
Company—Martha Graham
and Troupe in Program.

Martha never comments on criticism, saying she does not read reviews. (Sasha says she lets Louis Horst read them to her, but I'll bet he didn't read her that one.) But Martha is far from finished with *Wilderness Stair* and works on it for the next *five years:* tried new openings and endings, re-costumed the men, and gave it a new title, *Diversion of Angels.* I was sorry to lose the euphonious *Wilderness Stair* yet understood why it had to go. It isn't much of a leap from *Wilderness Stair* to *Jacob's Ladder,* and that is no leap at all from Jacob's Pillow, where Ted Shawn is still reigning lord. By changing titles, Martha put more distance between herself and Denishawn.

Martha's early concerts had been in recital halls, the dance equivalent of off-Broadway, ignored by major critics. John Martin of the *New York Times,* dean of dance critics, never went to the 92nd Street Y, scene of many historic performances, nor would he go to Brooklyn, even when Rudolf Nureyev played the Brooklyn Academy of Music. Yet any attraction in a Broadway house drew critics from the *Times, Herald Tribune,*

Daily News, Daily Mirror, Post, Sun, World-Telegram, Journal-American, PM, and *Brooklyn Daily Eagle.* In 1947, Martha wanted such coverage.

Most newspapers had no dance critic so assigned a drama critic to Martha. But John Martin and Walter Terry (of the *Tribune*) were full-time dance critics: Martin, the lofty pundit, and Terry, didactic and chatty. The importance Martha gave this pair was seen one evening when she turned rehearsals over to Yuriko.

"I'm having dinner with Walter tonight," Martha says with a roll of her eyes.

"Who's Walter?" I ask Sasha.

"Walter Terry, the *Herald Tribune* critic. She'll have dinner with John Martin tomorrow."

"What happens at dinner?"

"She explains the dances to them so they can look good in print." Sasha grinned. "Doesn't hurt her reviews either."

"Who pays for dinner?"

"I don't know."

I never did find out.

A drama critic writing about the Broadway musical *Texas, L'il Darlin',* which had tap and hoofing, overheard from the audience, "I like this kind of dancing better than choreography."

The first person I heard use the phrase "make a dance" was Merce Cunningham, classing dances with other things one can make, like a picture frame or dinner. Soon I was using the term. Now it seems natural, although I wonder how it sounds to you.

September 1948

Martha tells me to take Louis Horst's dance composition course, Pre-Classic Forms. I'd watched dance composition classes at Connecticut College, but I never tried to make up a dance or even thought about how it was done, accepting Martha's moves as handed down like the Ten Commandments.

Louis explained that each pre-classic form was once a living dance. Some, like the *minuet,* done by the upper classes, others, like the *galliard,* by peasants. Music is preserved in music notation, but all we know of the dances are verbal descriptions and drawings. In his class, Louis described a dance's historic and cultural roots, meter and tempo, and played ten or so musical examples, each one to three minutes long. He counted out the number of measures. A student picked one musical example and made a study outside of class. Not having a studio was no excuse. "Work between the bed and the bureau," said Louis.

We did not try to re-create a historical *minuet,* say, but to capture its spirit in an original way. Each choice had to be titled, encouraging us to make it "about" something. At the succeeding lesson, all were shown while Louis played. Then came his critique, which, I was warned, could be pitiless. In a way it was because it was rational, impersonal, and clear. But he never made anyone feel small and welcomed disagreement, saying, "You don't have to listen to me. I'm just an old man." Nothing pleased him more than a good study.

Our first subject was the *pavane,* Spanish for "peacock." Louis explained it as a dance of sixteenth-century Spanish nobility, all steely arrogance and lofty display. He played a dozen or so *pavanes,* and each student picked one, wrote down its counts, and made up the dance outside of class. I cannot recall one scrap of mine, but the idea of using movement to explore ideas is intriguing. The course included *minuet, allemande, galliard, gigue, gavotte, courante, sarabande, bourrée, rigaudon, passepied,* and *chaconne.* Each piece had "structure," theme, variation, recapitulation—A-B-A—or a variant, so we were learning about form itself. For years I assumed form originated in music, although Louis never said so. Eventually I learned it had originated in "rhetoric," the classic Greek art of discourse. The course climaxed with a showing for invited guests, each student presenting one or two examples. My mother came.

I showed three studies, "Knight Errant," about a knight who has trouble mounting his horse, "Pre-Paternal Anxieties," depicting a man awaiting the birth of his baby, to collapse with joy when it arrives, and "Interrupted Jaunt," of which I recall nothing but the name. While performing, I heard Martha's chirping laugh. Martha told my mother, "Stuart has *something.* . . ." That night, Mom said she understood why I worked with Martha.

A year later, I took Louis's other course, Modern Dance Forms, which drew from the visual arts. One student, Shirley Clarke, later a filmmaker, made a study in which her hand and two fingers became a tiny person who ran up her torso, down her leg, and around her feet. When it slipped under her heel, she squashed it flat. This was about thirty years before *Saturday Night Live* and its Mr. Bill, a clay lad who is regularly squashed and chopped.

Louis composed scores for Martha's *El Penitente* and *Primitive Mysteries.* About *Mysteries,* he said, "Martha handed me a sheaf of paper with all the counts written out and said, 'Put notes to these counts.'" She performed it without changing a move or a note. Louis and Martha had met in Denishawn where he was pianist, conductor, and occasional composer. They are said to have been lovers, but by the time I knew them, that fire had banked, leaving a deep bond. She didn't always take his advice but needed his support.

The best personal description of Louis is Agnes de Mille's in her biography, *Martha.*[6] She dotes on his adorable side. Louis was always surrounded by dewy young things. One, Nina Fonaroff, remained for decades and cared for him in his final illness.

In the 1960s and 1970s, postmodernists tried to dismiss Louis's courses as doctrinaire and old-fashioned. One dance writer said Pre-Classic Forms had outlived its usefulness. Deborah Jowitt, a *Village Voice* critic and one of the few dance critics who is also a dancer and choreographer, had taken Louis's Modern Forms course. In 1996 she made a dance titled *The Body (in print),* an exploration of her odyssey from dancer to dance writer. It also revealed an enduring warmth for Louis, whose composition courses were also primers on music, art, and an introduction to Louis himself, one of the great mentors of modern dance. After taking both of Louis's courses, I tell him I want to take them again. He returns a curmudgeonly scowl.

"No. Make dances."

April 1949, New York, New York

Every dancer in the Graham troupe is either making dances or dancing with someone who is, so I'm pleased when Miriam Pandor, a Doris Humphrey dancer I'd met at Connecticut College, asks me to be in a trio with Betty Jones and Bob Cohan.

Pandor is lean and sleek, speaks with a soft German accent, has been in movies and Broadway musicals. Yet her work is not remotely "commercial," or anything like Humphrey's or Martha's. Everything seems to be raw experiment. She usually begins by tying the three of us into a knot:

Stuart, stand behind Betty, bend your torso to the left, reach your right arm around her legs in front, then wrap it around her right ankle and grab her left foot from behind. Bob, kneel on your left knee in front of Betty. Take her waist with your right arm. Betty, put your right hand on Bob's left shoulder, no, in front of his face. Hang on to the ankle, Stuart. Bob, reach up with your right arm and grab the belt of Stuart's pants. Now move forward together without losing your connections.

If it works, it goes into the dance, if not, Pandor tries something else. After a while, she stops calling rehearsals. But I file away her approach for when I start to make my own dances.

I see a studio concert by Normand Maxon, who takes Graham's classes. His cast includes a very young Donald McKayle. Maxon puts moves together well, devises nice lifts, and the finished dance flows smoothly, like water in a pipe, but to little effect. Maxon soon gives up choreography to become a successful costume designer.

In 1950, after Martha's troupe had danced in Santa Barbara, California, Mills College offered me a job, with the amazing prospect that resident composer Darius Milhaud would write scores for my dances. I'm astonished yet not tempted. Dancing with Martha hardly pays but I cannot give her up. The other dancers are my colleagues and several become lifelong friends. The men are also my rivals, and when the day comes that I feel I am not getting roles I deserve, I fight for them. Martha observes a seniority that puts me behind Robert Cohan and ahead of Bertram Ross. Yet when Bertram takes over Erick's role as Oedipus in *Night Journey,* and when she chooses him to create St. Francis in *Seraphic Dialogue,* it is for what he alone can bring to the role. Bertram dances elsewhere, including in a Broadway musical, *Bless You All.* He makes his own quirky dances and lavishes love on his cocker spaniel, Cedric. But Martha comes first, and he'd abandon all but Cedric were she to ask. At a party I hear a professor type expand on his thesis that George Balanchine suffers "a dichotomy of the emotions," claiming that the great choreographer, who married five ballerinas, really prefers boys and doesn't know it. It is the professor's way of impressing a callipygian female modern dancer who is hanging on his words. I leave him to his quest, convinced he knows little about ballet women in their look of lacquered innocence, and nothing about George Balanchine.

At SAB, an expressionless blonde with the picture-perfect features of a Walt Disney princess asks me to explain modern dance. I do my best and offer to take her to a modern dance concert, but she walks away. Donald Driver says, "She'll never go out with you. She only goes out with gay men."

A couple of years later, in *Paint Your Wagon,* a woman dancer says, "Of course we go out with them: they're gentlemen and wonderful dates. They treat you like a lady, hold doors and chairs. They're elegant, know how to dress, how to order food and wine. And they can talk about any subject."

"You mean girl talk."

"No. They're more cultivated than you, and they've got more than one thing on their minds."

"You mean, there's one thing they *don't* have on their minds."

"Right."

"Is that what you really want?"

"Why not? It's a relief to be with somebody who's not undressing you with his eyes or cruising every other woman in the room."

"They're cruising the men."

"Not on a date. They know how to behave in public."

"What about in private?"

"If you must know, they're better in the sack, too."

"They don't do it with women."

Hoots of laughter. "When a gal wants a simple roll in the hay, a gay man is better every time." I'm shocked. "Poor baby, doesn't know the facts of life. Time he learned. Did we upset him? Is 'ums jealous?"

One day at SAB, a notice appears on the bulletin board.

Why Do You Dance?
Dr. George Amberg invites all dancers
to an open discussion: "Why I Dance."

Below is a list of Amberg's books. It's at the Museum of Modern Art. I decide to go. In the first row is Tanaquil LeClercq. Dr. Amberg, tweed jacket, is on a dais scanning the alert faces, stops on LeClercq and offers a serious smile.

"Thank you all for coming," and waits for silence. "Dance is universal human behavior. Every race, nationality, and tribe has its own dances. And you," with a sweeping gesture, "are the highest expression of dance in the Western world." He seems to have a trace of foreign accent. I dislike him immediately.

"Psychologists, anthropologists, and dance historians have theories on why human beings dance. It has occurred to me, that one way to approach this question is to ask you, who give your lives to this art. So I ask, Why do you dance? What is your reason?" He spots a hand shyly raised. "Yes?"

A thin female voice. "Does there have to be a reason?"

"Do you think you are dancing for no reason?"

"No. I mean . . . I guess there is a reason, but I never thought about it."

The smile grows kindly. "Exactly. So I ask you to think about it now. Why do you dance? What makes you work so hard to join a professional elite that, for most, promises little in terms of material reward, and," with a glance at LeClercq, "even for those with great gifts, offers the prospect of a woefully short professional career?"

A hand rises. Amberg nods.

"Um . . . I have wanted to dance since . . ."

He interrupts. "If you will stand, we will all hear you better."

"Um, my parents always had music playing. I began to dance when I was three. They bought me a tiny tutu, and I would put it on and dance. When I was six they sent me to ballet school. Now I just dance."

"I see," said Amberg, "Thank you." Points to the back.

Another rail-thin girl. "My nanny taught me to waltz when I was four. I was a holy terror, so my mom figured dancing would sop up some of my energy."

"And does it?" asked Amberg.

"I guess so."

"Is that why you dance now?"

"Oh no. I dance now because I love it."

"Can you explain why?"

A small frown riffled the smooth face. "I just love it."

Amberg turns to LeClercq in the first row. "Miss LeClercq, why do you dance?"

She didn't rise. "Me? I was sent to ballet classes to keep me out of trouble."

"And did it?"

"Some people might not think so."

A hand poked up behind LeClercq, and a young woman rose. A full figure and flowing hair set her apart from the toothpick bodies and bun heads of the ballet girls. "I dance because I believe that human beings are meant to dance. It is an expression of nature. When people dance they express their inner selves and are allowing nature to fulfil them."

"May I ask where you dance?"

"With Anna Sokolow."

"You maintain that human beings dance for the same reason that peacocks dance?"

"Peacocks?"

"Or pigeons? On any ledge in New York City you can see pigeons dancing to attract mates." With an impish smile. "Many species dance to attract mates."

The standing woman flushed. "That is not why I dance."

"Forgive me. I thought you said it is an expression of nature."

"It is, but . . ."

"Do you think there is anything wrong with dancing to attract a mate?"

"What I said. Uh, no. There is nothing wrong with that. But it's not the only reason." She sits down. I find myself resenting Amberg's blatant manipulations.

"Let me pose something. When you dance, you enter a fairy-tale world of princes and princesses. Are you happier in this make-believe world? Have you ever thought that dancing might be a way to escape quotidian realities, that is, the real world?"

So *that* is his theory, and he needs dancers to support it.

He goes on. "Is it not true that you prefer your fantasy world to the ordinary everyday world? Tell me, why is this make-believe world better? Can anyone explain?"

I rise. "You've got it wrong, Dr. Amberg. You call everyday life the real world? To me it's meaningless junk forced on us, like the army marched us through mud, then made us clean and shine our boots like mirrors. We called it chicken shit; excuse me, ladies. If that's what you mean by the real world, you can have it. When I dance, I enter a world of meaning and purpose. Dancing *is* the real world to me." The room explodes with applause. Amberg spends the next few minutes chatting up LeClercq, but the meeting soon ends.

January 1949

We rehearse at night so are not aware of a big network radio contest to identify "Miss Hush," part of radio's last-ditch effort to fend off television.[7] One afternoon, Sasha answers the pay telephone.

"What?" Shoots me a glance. "I don't know a thing about it." Then, "I'll ask, but I seriously doubt it." Hangs up. "Is Martha 'Miss Hush?'"

Donald Duncan, our manager, says that such calls are to be ignored, confirming that Martha is involved. Clues appear in newspapers. A recent wrong answer is "Mary Garden." During the next broadcast there is no rehearsal so I tune in to hear a woman say "Martha Graham" and win the prize.

In her biography, *Martha*, Agnes de Mille wrote, "This was fun for Martha" (p. 290). It wasn't. Martha hated it. She alluded to pressure from people who had insisted the publicity would attract audiences. "They are not *my* audience," she said. "I haven't worked all these years to become famous as Miss Hush."

4

· · · · · · · · ·

The Green Tours

September 1949

Twisting his *art moderne* wedding ring, Sasha introduces his bride, Emily Frankel, who had danced with Charles Weidman. Martha invites her to take classes. Lithe and quick, she breezes through everything. Emily is so strong and self-confident I am not surprised that when Martha offers her a place in the company, she turns it down. She and Sasha start their own troupe, The Dance Drama Company. They make dances, commission others, including Todd Bolender who creates *At the Still Point,* and book their own nationwide tours.

In 1944, Martha had wanted to make a dance based on Shakespeare's *King Lear* as seen through Cordelia's eyes. She commissioned a score from Mexican composer Carlos Chávez, but he failed to deliver. In 1948 she returned to *King Lear* to make a dance for Erick Hawkins. Pearl Lang is the virtuous Cordelia, Helen McGehee and Yuriko the wicked sisters, Goneril and Regan, Sasha is Edmund the Bastard, Bob Cohan, the Fool, and I am Mad Tom.

A huge tree stump is dollied into the studio and Erick sits upon it—Mad King Lear upon his throne. Virtuous Cordelia stands aside as fawning Goneril and Regan slither over their father, all three inside a huge fabric cylinder that reveals every twist and pull as the scheming sisters

Patricia Birch on *Lear* stump. Photo by Stuart Hodes.

lavish false love upon the doddering king. Vincent Persichetti's score is clamorous and percussive, the choreography moves quickly, Cordelia is banished, Lear thrust into the storm, accompanied by the Fool and Mad Tom. I'm excited when Martha schedules a rehearsal for me alone.

Shakespeare's line: "Mad Tom's a-cold."

"Mad Tom is naked in the storm," says Martha, "so you will be wearing very little."

I fold my arms in front of my chest, hunch my back, tread as if barefoot in the spiky grasses of a wild moor. Martha asks for a hesitating step-jump. I do a sort of skip-hop, like a child playing jacks.

"Do that again, and vibrate your legs." I do *something. "Yes!"*

It is my first Bicycle.[1]

The choreography is roaring along until one day Martha starts throwing out sections. The dance bogs down. Sasha has a theory: "The problem is Erick. She's trying to create a role that fits him, so she's having him play a madman. But Erick is already mad and a madman can't play a mad character. What comes across is Erick's madness, not Lear's."

Martha soldiers on, completes the dance, first titles it *Lear,* then *The Eye of Anguish.* Louis Horst dubs it *The Angst of Eyewash.* Martha changes the title back to *Lear.* It premiers on the first of the three national tours booked by Charles E. Green, the "Green Tours."

According to Sasha, Sol Hurok deems Martha a prestige-maker but not a moneymaker, so keeps her tours short. They're also posh; we travel by train, play downtown theaters, three or four shows a week. Martha, wanting to perform more, switches to Consolidated Concerts whose Charles E. Green books eight shows a week, six nights plus Wednesday and Saturday matinees, a different city every day. And we travel by bus.

January 31, 1949

Green One starts with a day trip to Upper Montclair, New Jersey, then six-and-a-half weeks on the Eastern seaboard. After that, a six-month hiatus before Green Two, another six weeks, followed by five weeks of rehearsal in New York City for a one-week "season" at the 46th Street Theater. Then Green Three, eight-and-a-half weeks ending April 1950.

Each tour carries one program. Green One is *Diversion of Angels, Cave of the Heart, Lear,* and *Every Soul Is a Circus.* Three are masterpieces, and although *Lear* is not Martha at her best, it's action-packed and audiences can follow the story. I'm in *Angels* and *Lear,* delirious at the prospect of dancing every day. Helen McGehee, dedicated to Martha, is also a devoted wife and homebody and not happy about a long tour. At lunch in Harlow's she pulls out a newspaper article about spring floods.

"We really shouldn't be going on this tour. By March every state we're supposed to dance in will be under water."

"Don't worry Helen. I'm a certified Red Cross lifeguard."

"That won't do us any good if we're trapped on flooded roads between washed-out bridges."

"What should Martha do? Cancel the tour?"

Thoughtfully, "That wouldn't be a bad idea."

"Because of a little rain?"

"You fool! Don't you realize that we're all going to die?"

Four marrieds: Marjorie Mazia, May O'Donnell, Ethel Winter, and Yuriko, who has a newborn, decline Green One. Helen McGehee, pressured by Martha, goes. Pearl Lang says yes, but just before we leave, cancels for knee surgery. Natanya Neumann and Dorothy Berea split her roles. The other women are Dorothea Douglas and Joan Skinner. The men are Mark Ryder (Sasha), Bob Cohan, and me, ten dancers including Martha and Erick. Our orchestra is four winds, percussion, and Eugene Lester conducting from piano. Stage crew of three, one doubling as tour manager, plus a sleepy old man who sells souvenir booklets in the lobby. Twenty people with baggage, costumes, sets, and lights.

The souvenir-book man is also responsible for theater programs, but neither he nor Charles Green inform sponsors of cast changes so there are no program inserts, not even an announcement. One morning, a local paper has a glowing review of Pearl Lang as Cordelia, useless to Natanya, who had danced the role. She shows it to Martha, saying she'd been asking for the change for weeks. Martha explodes. "You should be grateful for a chance to dance!" Natanya, weeping, retreats to the rear of the bus. I am in no position to interfere, but had it been me, I'd be gone.

February 4, 1949, Altoona, Pennsylvania

After our performance, station wagons take us to a large homey house for a hot buffet of ham, turkey, roast beef, fresh vegetables, salad, cheeses, fruit, pastries, punch, and coffee. The hostess, a sparkling woman in her forties, gushes. "I loved your dancing. Tell me, do you make up the steps as you go along or do you practice them first?"

I'm staggered, but Dorothea Douglas says calmly, "Oh, we practice them first."

February 5, Harrisburg, Pennsylvania

Adjacent to the stage is a large dance studio. Martha is at the *barre,* no one else there. I find a spot across the room but she catches my eye, a quiet invitation. I approach. "Martha, I've realized something."

"What is that?"

"You are not a saint."

"Congratulations."

February 17, Louisville, Kentucky

We are *ordered* to attend an after-show party and to wear our best. We pay for taxis to an address out of town, where people in evening gowns and dinner jackets are holding drinks. Bourbon neat, bourbon and soda, bourbon on the rocks. No food, not even peanuts. An hour later, famished and reeling, we pay our way back to the hotel where the dining room is closed. Sneering at the myth of southern hospitality, we dine on potato chips and Baby Ruth bars from a vending machine. The next day, Martha commiserates but says our presence had been important because the hosts, trustees of the Louisville Symphony, are considering a commission. They come through with two, *Judith* and *The Triumph of St. Joan.*

February 18, Nashville, Tennessee

I glance out of the bus window to see that the road we are on is named Deaderick Street. (Dead-Erick, get it?) I whisper it around and soon everyone is chortling. Erick, in the front next to Martha, turns back with a grin wanting in on the joke, but no one dares.

February 19, Chattanooga, Tennessee

Saturday matinee. Bob calls Sasha and me to the dressing room window. In the rear alley, a black family—mother, father, and two preteen girls in starched dresses—pick their way past garbage and trash. They find the rear door, knock, and wait to be admitted.

"I don't want to dance here," says Bob.

"Me neither," I say.

"We have to dance for *them,*" says Sasha.

Next day we tell Martha. "The South has endured great pain," she says. "And there is more in its future."

After Mary Hinkson and Matt Turney join, Martha is invited to tour the South again, assured that her black dancers will receive every courtesy. She refuses, saying she will not dance where all members of her troupe are not welcome on their own. This echoes her refusal to perform in Germany at the 1936 Olympics, despite assurances that her Jewish dancers would receive every courtesy. After the Green Tours, the company does not dance in the South until segregation ends.

Tower Theater, Atlanta, after sign had been changed. Photo by Stuart Hodes.

February 20, Atlanta, Georgia

Heading to the hotel on Peachtree Street, we pass the Tower Theater. Big letters on the marquee: "In Person, MISS HUSH." Our stage manager says we are not to go to the theater until notified. Two hours later, on the marquee: "In Person, MARTHA GRAHAM."

Diversion of Angels gets applause all the way through. *Lear* is watched with baited breath. In *Cave of the Heart,* Martha's snake-eating solo gets applause. Wrong to applaud there, but so what? The audience loves us! *Every Soul Is A Circus* is last, and I decide to watch from out front. In the first minute comes a comic gesture. Half the audience laughs out loud, the other half goes "Shhhh." Abashed, no one utters a giggle for the rest of one of the funniest dances ever made.

February 21, Travel Day

Two weeks in, four weeks to go, we're exhausted. After Sunday matinee in Atlanta, Monday morning 8:00 a.m., we climb into the bus for an eleven-hour ride to Baton Rouge. This constitutes our day off. Four hours into the trip, seven hours to go, we're passing a huge cemetery. Helen McGehee says, "Look at all those lucky people . . . resting."

February 22, Baton Rouge, Louisiana State University

When the stage manager calls "Places," we take our opening poses for *Diversion of Angels,* listen for the hush that means the houselights have dimmed. No hush. The rising curtain catches us by surprise. The audience is chattering. The music begins. It keeps chattering. Martha, furious, will not allow a curtain call.

"They haven't figured out it's not a basketball game," says Sasha.

They quiet down for *Cave of the Heart,* so Martha allows one bow, and after enthusiastic applause for *Lear,* relents and gives normal calls. *Every Soul Is a Circus* gets peals of laughter.

Crossing campus to a reception, we pass magnolia trees laden with fragrant blooms. One of the women picks a magnolia and pins it into her hair, then the others, and all arrive magnolia-adorned. This bothers me, so I ask a student, "Was it okay for our girls to pick magnolia blossoms?"

"Sure, they're not students."

"What about students?"

"Twenty-five dollar fine." (About $300 in 2020 money.)

This, everyone agrees, is southern hospitality.

February 26, Tallahassee, Florida

Bill, our bus driver, is a sullen almost wordless slob. When forced to speak he squeezes out words like constipated little turds. This makes it imperative to Martha that she conquer him, so she favors him with small confidences and regularly invites him to dine with her and Erick. But Bill is not conquered. He chooses the most run-down rest stops with the filthiest latrines. One had an outdoor privy reached by a path twenty yards through a swamp. Natanya Neumann stepped in a scum-covered mud hole and returned with one leg soaked past the knee.

Erick carries a list of good restaurants and any time we're near one, directs Bill to it. I hear Bill mutter, "It's twenny miles extra at fitty cents a mile." Erick does not back down.

But this tale begins on February 1st in Poughkeepsie, New York, the third date of our tour, at a snowy campus where our hotel and the theater are a few miles apart. The sponsor provides Martha and Erick with a car and driver so Erick orders Bill to take us from hotel to auditorium, wait during rehearsal, return us to the hotel, and then take us back to the auditorium for the show. Bill usually has this time off.

He drops us at the stage door, but after rehearsal isn't there. Eugene Lester and I spot the bus on an empty campus road a quarter of a mile away. We cut across a field of grassy stubble covered by crusty snow. The bus is by a parking meter. At our knock, instead of swinging the door open, Bill cracks it an inch. As I take hold of the edge I notice a dent, slowly swing it wide seeing that the dent meets the top of the parking meter. When he'd parked, Bill had opened the door into it. I peer at the dent, frown, peer at the parking meter, shake my head, peer at Bill, *"Tsk, tsk,"* back to the dent, again at Bill. *"Tsk, Tsk."*

"Whatcha tryin' a do, put a dent inna door? It's Erick hasta pay fer it."

"Nothing out of my pocket."

As we take our seats, Eugene Lester says, "He's trying to blame you for the dent." I deem this preposterous.

[Fade out, Poughkeepsie, New York, fade in Tallahassee, Florida.]

After the show at Florida State University, only one nearby restaurant is open. We slide into booths, except for Erick, Martha, and Bill, who sit at the only table. The vegetables are canned, mashed potatoes runny, chicken-fried steak is gristle, barbecued pork mostly fat and sickly sweet. Erick calls the tired middle-aged waitress and asks for the manager. She is the manager. He rises to his feet, proclaims, "We have been traveling through fourteen states and this is the worst food we have eaten on the entire trip!" And marches out.

Next morning, a chill in the air, I don my fleece-lined bomber jacket, pick up my suitcase, and take it to the bus. It's a solemn duty to load one's own bag into the luggage rack but all the bags are on the sidewalk, Erick in their midst. I start to put mine aboard but Erick stops me.

"Leave it on the sidewalk. I'm working out a better way to pack."

"Do you want some help?"

"No, no." Gene and I drop our bags on the sidewalk. Clearly, Erick is skipping breakfast because the ill-starred restaurant of the night before is the only one open.

The air is brisk and fragrant. I pick up a fallen branch and bear it like a staff.

Southern breakfasts are a happy exception to the fare at other meals and the restaurant is aromatic with bacon and sausage. Dancers and musicians occupy the booths. Martha sits at the table with Bill.

I lean my staff against the edge of the booth, have fresh orange juice, eggs-over-light, sausages, grits with melted butter, corn bread, and three cups of coffee. Pleased with life, I rise, don my bomber jacket, pick up my staff, and head for the door.

"Stuart!"

I stop, turn, approach Martha at her table. "Did you put your bag in the bus?"

"Yes."

Then, again. "Did you put your bag *in* the bus?"

I remember. "Oh, Erick told me to leave it on the sidewalk."

"You oaf! How dare you come in here and stuff yourself while Erick loads *your* bag on the bus?" The restaurant falls silent. I am too dumbfounded to reply.

"And I *know* what you said about not caring if Erick has to pay for damage *you* did to the bus. Don't think I don't know about that."

Bill sits, liverish face blank, one fat finger hooked through the handle of his coffee cup. It hits me. Voice soft: "You listen to *liars*." On 'liars,' I pound my staff into the floor, snapping off a piece that flies across the room. Voice rising: "You listen to people who care *nothing* about you, and believe any lie they *tell* you. You believe the *worst* about those who love you and give their lives to you. You don't *deserve* people who love you and give their lives to you. You don't deserve their *devotion*. You are *unworthy* of them. You are unworthy of *me*."

With that I turn, stride out, slam the glass-paneled door behind me, and stand on the sidewalk, regretting my outburst.

Eugene Lester emerges. "She deserved that."

I mutter, "No one should talk to Martha Graham like that." Still furious, I start toward the bus thinking I'll grab my bag, hike to the nearest Greyhound station, leave Martha, the tour, and dance. Forever.

"Erick, was I supposed to help you re-pack the bags?"

"No? No?" voice rising on each word. "You were not."

"Can I help you now?"

"No. I'm finished."

I wait by the bus door as dancers and musicians straggle back, ignoring their "thumbs-up" glances. As Martha nears me, I say, "I'm very sorry for the things I said."

"You should be."

"Well, I am. No one should speak to Martha Graham like that."

"But you did, didn't you?"

"Yes. And I'm sorry. No one should speak to *Martha Graham* like that."

I've twice referred to her in the third person, to Martha Graham, the great artist, to whom no one should speak as I had spoken. As for pettish, irrational Martha, she damn well deserved it. Martha knows what I mean. Her eyes find mine. "The day you get a starring role, the world will fall!" And climbs aboard. I follow.

Why I didn't grab my bag, hike to the nearest Greyhound bus station, leaving Martha and dance forever, I can't explain.

As we get under way, I ponder her remark. Did she mean that a starring role will so inflate me that metaphorically, the world will fall? Or that the world must literally fall before she, Martha Graham, gives me a starring role. I decide it is the second, and that I will not wait that long.

February 28, Auburn, Alabama

A shy young man is assigned as a backstage "helper." During *Diversion of Angels,* he asks if any of the women are married. I point out Helen McGehee, Natanya Neumann, and Dorothea Douglas. He asks what state each of the others is from, if they live with their parents, how we travel, where we stay on tour, what we do when not touring.

"Doesn't seem like much of a life for a girl."

"They're dancers, and this is their chance to dance."

"It looks very strenuous."

"They're in excellent physical condition." He studies their physical condition. "Are they virgins?"

I shoot him a suspicious glance, but he's just trying to understand this odd variety of female.

"Absolutely. They're all virgins."

March 5, 1949, Natchitoches, Louisiana

My salary is $72 a week. Sasha earns a little more, and we both want to save. I set a goal of $200 for the whole tour. A decent hotel is $5 tops, most of ours less, and $4 a day is enough for food. No one "ghosts," that is, one person checks in and others sneak in, because Martha would be furious. When a musician is discovered to be stealing towels, he's fired.

Our manager calls every hotel, and if a towel is missing, sends reimbursement.

Sasha and I sometimes stay at a local YMCA, where a room can be as little as fifty cents. A hotel chain, The Milner, charges $1.00 and $1.50, not as nice as the Y, but the sheets are clean. We eat breakfast and dinner in restaurants, for lunch buy cold cuts and fruit. One week I send home $30.

Sasha jokingly suggests we sleep in the bus. I jokingly agree. Bob Cohan, who spends every penny of his salary, tells Martha, who summons me and Sasha. "There will be no sleeping in the bus. Your responsibility is to your dancing and to me. If you haven't any self-respect, at least respect your need for a decent night's rest."

Sasha tries to explain that it was a joke, but Martha does not smile.

After dancing we're ravenous, so on arrival ask the hotel where to eat after the show. If there's no restaurant, we buy sandwiches. One hotel offers to keep the dining room open and after the show we get tender steaks with baked potato, southern greens, salad, and corn bread. Helen McGehee, under 100 pounds, says, "That was so good, I think I'll have another" and does, with all the trimmings.

Martha and Erick always sit in the first two seats on the right side of the bus, Martha by the window, Erick on the aisle. Dancers, musicians, and crew switch around. Occasionally I sit with Joan Skinner, a strong disciplined dancer who had danced with Merce Cunningham. She is not talkative and often seems occupied by her thoughts.

In the mid-1960s, some fifteen years after the Green Tours, I begin hearing about "Skinner Releasing Technique."[2] I never see any physical moves so have no idea what it looks like. By the 1980s, it is simply called "Releasing Technique." It clearly has staying power, but I still have no idea what it is, so I class it with Feldenkrais Method, Alexander Technique, yoga, tai chi, and other regimens of which I am respectfully ignorant. In 2001, Lone Larsen, who teaches Graham Technique in Denmark, comes to New York to teach for the Graham Summer Intensive. She mentions that Danish dancers are wild about Releasing Technique.

"You mean Skinner Releasing Technique?"

The name Skinner draws a blank. "Exactly what is it?" I ask.

"One of those ways to dance *without* technique."

I Google Joan Skinner to find an impressive website titled "Joan Skinner Releasing Technique." Among the essays is "Imagery and its Application to Movement Training." From that essay:

In the Skinner Releasing Technique the image serves as the carrier of a patterned whole of information—a metaphor for kinesthetic knowledge—which "formulates a new conception for our direct imaginative grasp," and this metaphor is apprehended intuitively rather than analytically.

Another is titled "The Pedagogy of Imagery."

In Professor Skinner's application, she discovered that excess tension is the most common cause of inability to realize the Releasing principles. The twentieth-century person exhibits a variety of tension patterns: hands are gripped, breathing is held, jaws are clenched, shoulders are hunched. The list of tension patterns and tension diseases is long.

I recognize this nonsense as scribblings by dance-blind eggheads, like Mortimer J. Adler and Judith Butler. If you can stand one more: "As Professor Skinner says, 'One releases immediate fixed states of being to become available to the aligning process. In turn, the aligning process releases psycho physical energy.'"

In March 2004, I'm teaching Intermediate Graham Technique at the Martha Graham School, trying to get students to loosen up. "Just throw it away," I say, using a show-biz term for a relaxed enactment that is more than "marking," which reduces moves to gestures. When you "throw away" a move you dance loosely. I demonstrate.

"Oh," says Cara Gardella. "You mean Downtown Style."

"What's Downtown Style?"

"Like Releasing Technique," and she does the move with an exaggerated looseness which is close to what I want.

"You mean *Skinner* Releasing Technique?" "Skinner" elicits no recognition, so I explain. "Releasing Technique was invented by Joan Skinner. She used to be in the Martha Graham Company."

Cara had never heard of Joan Skinner but is delighted to hear that, like Cunningham and Hawkins techniques, Downtown Style *qua* Releasing Technique was invented by someone who'd begun with Martha Graham.

But Skinner Releasing Technique has taken on a life of its own and is, moreover, trademarked. The Skinner website lists "authorized" teachers all over the U.S.A., in Australia, Canada, England, Germany, Hungary, New Zealand, and the Netherlands. Yet most dancers know it as Releasing

Technique minus Skinner's name. And now, a variant called Downtown Style.

What Cara showed me (moves with the loose, dangling, Ray Bolger-as-Scarecrow-in-the-Wizard-of-Oz-look) is the only sample I see of Downtown Style-cum-Releasing Technique-cum-Skinner Releasing Technique. A few months later, another dancer shows me actual bits of something being taught as "Downtown." Joan Skinner is left out because of her trademark, as Steve Paxton is left out of Contact Improvisation, to-day just called "Contact."

If you're talented, original, and industrious enough to devise a physical regimen deserving of your name, be proud and happy. But try to own it and all you end up owning is the name.

Lately I've noticed that Skinner Releasing Technique has acquired a new attribute. It is accompanied by mystical hand passes. One person stands on both legs. Another stands behind, tracing the body's outline with open hands. This is so ineluctably mystical, so impossible to nail down, we'll never be rid of it. I hope Joan Skinner makes a few bucks from her brainchild.

Occasionally we play old vaudeville houses with ancient splintery floors. The crew lays out a huge bale of canvas, dancers bunch up in the center, fan out kicking it taut, and the crew tacks down the edges. The canvas causes floor burns but saves us from splinters. One day we arrive at an old theater to find the decayed pine floor covered with four-foot squares of tempered Prestwood, silky smooth yet not slippery, and perfect for bare-foot dancing. It turns out to be Paul Draper's tap dance floor. Knowing Martha was to follow, Draper had left it in place. We think warm thoughts of this great and generous artist.

Dorothea Douglas is the daughter of Senator Paul Douglas of Illinois, but no big deal. She's "Duggie," Bennington grad, serious and thoughtful, long dark hair, long face, firm chin, unplucked eyebrows, large deep-set eyes. Duggie is a clean mover, strong, athletic, and jumps with the men. I often watch her to see how a move should be done.

Duggie and I enjoy a palsy rapport and have conversations, discussing, for instance, Albert Schweitzer's "Reverence for Life," or who is the greater composer, Igor Stravinsky or Cole Porter. One day I am sitting behind Duggie who is kneeling on her seat facing the rear of the bus. We are discussing who are better dancers: "the girls or the boys." We actually say, "girls" and "boys." All ballet males except stars are "boys." On Broadway it is "dancing boys" and "singing men," "dancing girls" and "singing women."

Duggie: "Girls are better coordinated."

Stuart: "Boys are stronger."

Duggie: "Girls learn faster."

Stuart: "Boys remember better.

Duggie: "No, they don't. Anyway, girls dance longer."

Stuart: "Boys jump higher."

Duggie: "Girls are better than boys because they live longer and so get to be better."

Stuart: "Boys are better because they don't live as long, which means their dancing life is compressed and if you multiply how good they are by the compression, they are better than girls."

Duggie: "Girls are better because they have to be lifted, and knowing how to be lifted is much harder than just lifting someone else."

Stuart: "Boys are better because when they lift girls they are responsible for their lives which is much, much better than just knowing how to be lifted by someone else."

WHAP! Duggie slaps me full across the face.

I'm astonished. Slapping is *not* part of the game. And by the look on Duggie's face, she is more astonished than I am.

"You . . . slapped me."

Shakily: "That's right."

Uncertainly: "I ought to slap you back."

"Go ahead." She tenses up.

If I'd reacted instantly I could have slapped her, but there is no way I can slap Duggie in cold blood. "Well, you sure proved who's better."

She's wavering toward an apology.

"Don't bother to apologize," I say, hoping she will. But she doesn't.

Sitting beside me at the window is Natanya Neumann, whom I deeply admire. I turn to her for sympathy. But she is choking with laughter. "Too late to apologize," she gasps.

Suddenly I'm furious, lapse into a stony sulk, and don't speak to either for two days. On the third morning, Duggie, at breakfast: "Isn't it time we ended this?"

"Do you apologize for slapping me?"

"I apologize. Abjectly." Big hug and we sit together in the bus.

Sasha comes over and asks what the fight had been about. I tell him we'd been discussing who are better dancers, boys or girls.

"That sounds silly."

"Of course it's silly. Boys are so much better there's no argument."

WHAP! A hard slap, and instantly—*WHAP!*—I return it full across Duggie's cheek. She bursts into tears.

"Duggie, I'm sorry." I really am. "But why did you have to slap me *again?*"

"I don't know," she sobs.

"It's obvious," says Sasha. "She wanted to give you another chance to slap her back."

Duggie and I are friends again, but I stay mad at Natanya, an innocent bystander, for two more days. Somehow I'd expected her, *needed* her to take my side. When we do speak again, she says she had assumed that I just wasn't interested in talking to her anymore, or ever had been. This is devastating because I am hopelessly in love with Natanya, like a peasant in love with a princess.

March 8, 1949, Denton, Texas

Around three in the afternoon, after lunch in a cute little Tex-Mex res- taurant near the college campus, I go to the cashier, a bulky middle-aged woman whose dyed black hair is knotted into a tight Katzenjammer bun, and put a dollar bill on the counter: "May I please have change to tip the waiter?"

She sweeps the bill up with a fat hand, slams four quarters on the coun- ter. "He's a perfectly nice boy."

"What?"

"You heard me." She leaves the cash register. Back at my table, I recount the curious exchange.

"Maybe she misunderstood you," said our clarinetist.

"I asked for change. What could she have misunderstood?"

The woman is back at the register, fleshy face tilted up, eyes rolled down so that the whites fill most of her eye sockets.

"That woman hears voices," says Bob Cohan.

"I'm going to speak to her." Back at the register, a little man comes out of the kitchen and stands near. I say, "Excuse me, ma'am, but I asked for change to tip the waiter. If it sounded like anything else, I apologize for not speaking clearly."

"See, he apologized," whined the little man.

"I heard him perfectly clear." She starts toward the kitchen. "He can apologize to the police."

Back at my table. "I think she called the police."

"Maybe you should get out of here."

"I will not."

Three minutes later two bulky town cops come to my table. "C'mon."

From the back of the cruiser: "What is happening, would you mind telling me?"

"We don't 'low cussin' in public," said the one not driving.

"Cussing? I don't cuss." No answer. "What was I supposed to have said?"

"Y'said y'wanted change t'tip th' son-of-a-bitch waituh."

"I don't talk like that." Silence. "I never use profanity What kind of a place is this to arrest a visitor having dinner?" My temper is rising. "I am a member of the Martha Graham Dance Company. We are here at the invitation of the president of the university. Is this southern hospitality? Or isn't Texas the South? Or the United States of America?"

Somehow, I arrive at the police station neither bloody nor bruised. Soon Erick Hawkins and our tour manager arrive. After consultation with the desk officer, Erick says, "They've agreed you can go if you apologize."

Loudly. "Apologize? That would be *admitting* I used profanity. Have you ever heard me swear? *Ever?* No. I do not swear. I did not swear. I spent three years in the army without swearing, and I don't swear in restaurants in Denton, Texas, if that's where we are. I will not apologize for what I did not do."

The tour manager whispers, "Look. This constable can lock you up overnight. If you apologize, we can get out of here."

Very loudly. "Overnight? Lock me up overnight because a deranged woman hears voices in her head? Fine. Next week she'll hear the president of the university swear and they can lock him up."

"Stuart," pleads Erick, "We've got to dance tonight."

I am beyond reason. "Call the president of the university. Let him dance."

Another conference. The constable peers at me in disgust. "Ya claim ya didn't use perfanity. Awright. But don't go inta that rest'rant agin."

"You'd have to hogtie me and drag me to get me in that place again."

The silly part of this is that until that day I never did use profanity. I was a verbal prude. Almost still. Almost.

March 10, 1949, Dallas, Texas

The troupe is invited to an after-performance party in the home of Craig Barton, whom Martha described as "a six-foot Texan." Waiting taxis take us to a house that, in the light of the moon, looks conventional but has a living room dominated by two large looms, each holding a half-completed rug. The rooms are filled with objets d'art, chrysolite, jade, turquoise, small tapestries, a Navaho kachina, a Mexican *santo*, tin masks, antique brass candlesticks, a teak Buddha. When we ask about the looms, Barton obligingly sends the shuttle back and forth a few times. Martha watches with a beneficent smile.

Craig Barton is six feet tall and lives in Texas, but he does not evoke "six-foot Texan." He moves skittishly, speaks rapidly, and, despite a square-ish handsome face, has a puppy dog demeanor. He settles Martha in a chair and fetches a plate of the bland food she favors.

Agnes de Mille had this to say about Craig Barton: "Like all young men, he fell in love with her," and goes on to imply that he and Martha have a torrid physical affair. Claptrap. Barton is as capable of having sex with Martha as climbing Mount Everest on stilts. As for Martha, she's a goddess—Terpsichore, Athena, Hera—but not Aphrodite. De Mille frequently injects herself into Martha's life, but the only mention I ever heard Martha make of de Mille was in 1970, after Martha had turned down an invitation to serve on the National Endowment for the Arts Dance Panel. Martha had said, "Agnes is on the panel. She likes power. I have no interest in power." Actually, Martha needs power, just not the kind shared with a panel. She wields charismatic power over her dancers, her audiences, producer Alexander Pantages, composer Aaron Copland, esthete Lincoln Kirstein, gangster Frankie Fay.

After the tour, Craig Barton comes to New York City with LeRoy Leatherman, whom Martha introduces as a "southern writer."[3] They become her managers for the next twenty-plus years, giving Martha the devotion she needs. And being minimally concerned with management, their blundering incompetence only occasionally intrudes on the lives of the dancers.

March 21, 1949, Milwaukee, Wisconsin

After the final performance, Helen McGehee and Dorothea Douglas take a plane to New York. Joan Skinner disappears into Chicago. The others stay with the bus, demanding extra rest stops. Once we pull over and disperse into a cornfield until able to endure the bus again. Martha sits by her window, reads, watches the landscape, makes notes, chats with Erick, never naps.[4] When a dancer shows signs of cracking, she administers brandy, spreads her Persian lamb—a cloak of forgetfulness—over the afflicted one, who, succored by Martha's ministrations, may remain huddled for an hour or more. I never allow myself to fall under her power in that way.

Back in New York City, she berates us. "You allowed yourselves to be defeated. On the next tour, the men will shave every morning and wear ties, even the musicians. It will be in their contract or they will not be hired. And the girls will wear skirts. No slacks."

She tells about being allowed to watch her father's business meetings in their house. In midsummer, temperature near one hundred, not even an electric fan, the men doff jackets, loosen ties, and slouch in their chairs, while a nun, the only woman present, sits stiffly erect in her black habit.

"She didn't even perspire." said Martha. "When that meeting ended, the nun was in command. And you may be sure she got whatever she came for. I never forgot it."

March 23, 1949, New York, New York

We've traveled over 8,000 miles and played forty-three cities. I'd arrive somewhere I'd never been, walk strange streets to our theater, give myself a deep warm-up, lose myself in performance, eat heartily, sleep like a baby, have a big breakfast, then set out for the next adventure. Back home, I'm eager for technique class.

June 1949

No summer residence at Connecticut College. Martha goes west, but the school stays open. The hot months are great for muscles. I take one modern and one ballet class a day, squeezing in tap with Paul Draper and Jerry Ames.

I see a sublet near the Graham Studio, old-law tenement with hot water but no heat, bathtub in the kitchen, toilet in the hall, forty-six dollars a month, furnished. I'm drawing on army savings so ask Eugene Lester to share. He's glad to get out of his furnished room. Fresh from Yale, where he'd majored in music composition under Paul Hindemith, he's playing for technique classes, soon becomes second rehearsal pianist, eventually Martha's conductor.

September 1949

The Graham Studio at 66 Fifth Avenue is my artistic home, but I earn nothing there. That changes only slightly when Erick asks me to be his demonstrator, four dollars a class. All classes have them except for the company/professional in the morning. After a few months of demonstrating, Erick asks me to teach the Saturday actor's class that meets in his personal studio.

"What do I do with actors?"

"Teach them technique."

I'd always sought images for Graham moves and actors, my first students, are eager for them. I make it part of my teaching. Martha speaks fondly of her actor students, who include Gregory Peck and Marian Seldes. I soon understand why she does not want to give up teaching actors.

A male dancer is needed for the second Green Tour. Martha had met Bertram Ross at Connecticut College in the summer of 1948 and he's the obvious choice, yet she seems unsure. She has us teach him the opening from *Diversion of Angels* and he learns quickly, except for cartwheels which he'd never done. After the showing, sans cartwheels, Martha says, "Do a cartwheel. *Now!*" Bertram steels himself, does a wobbly cartwheel but enough to reassure Martha. She invites him into the company. Soon Bertram produces the following to the tune of "Arthur Murray Taught Me Dancing in a Hurry":

Martha Graham taught me dancing in a hurry
I learned Contractions with ease
To Martha I'm beholden
My spiral thrust is golden
But I can't get off my knees.

Martha needs still another man. Irving Burton is five-foot-seven, so she isn't considering him. Bob and I suggest she should. She has us teach him "The Party" from *Letter to the World,* and after we dance it for her she takes him into her private dressing room. Afterword, she said, "Irving is a fine dancer, but his specialness draws the eye." (See the photo on page 139.)

Years later, he recalls Martha taking him into "her little private dressing room" and saying, "You are a fine dancer, and will do something important in dance . . . but not in my company."

"Did she really say that?" I asked.

"She might as well have," he replied with a grin. "I knew she'd never take me. She was only interested in Greek gods." Irving went on to a notable career. I saw him in Doris Humphrey's troupe, in his own striking solos. (In *Thus Spake Sarabelka* he is bawled out by his mother, also a solo about masturbation that I recall vividly except for the title), as an actor, and as a founding member of the Paper Bag Players.

I inherit Sasha's role in *Lear,* the villainous Edmund, the Bastard, and teach Mad Tom to Bertram. Although Edmund is a bigger role, I'm sorry to relinquish Mad Tom, created with me and my own my personal stamp.

Greyhound slogan: "Discriminating People Go by Bus"

Bertram Ross: "But why oh why oh why oh did it happen to happen to us?"

October 31, 1949

Green Two opens in New Britain, Connecticut, then New England, upstate New York, Pennsylvania, Ohio, Minnesota, Illinois, Wisconsin, Indiana, West Virginia, New Jersey, ending in Reading, Pennsylvania, a day short of six weeks. Then five weeks rehearsing in New York City for a week at the 46th Street Theater. Then Green Three.

With the exception of Helen McGehee, all the women are new. The men are Erick Hawkins, Bob Cohan, Bertram Ross, and me. Eugene

Lester doesn't want to conduct from the piano so Martha hires a stand-up conductor, Irwin Hoffman.

I buy a Dance Notation correspondence course but by chapter 2 know I'm not meant to be a notator. Helen McGehee teaches me and Bertram to knit. I knit red socks, helped through the heels. Bertram works on tights for the whole tour, stuffing the mass of wool out of sight when we arrive at a hotel. On long bus trips, if we start to sing, the musicians dig out their instruments. Martha always sits in the first row by the window, talks quietly to Erick, reads, sometimes writes in a notebook, never nods or objects to the rumpus behind her. Mostly we play colleges, sponsored by a dance department or dance club. Dance had seriously entered academe at the University of Wisconsin, which in 1924 had the first dance major. Yet few professional dancers come out of colleges because college is too late to start dancing, and those who start as children are unlikely to go to college if they hope for a dance career.

Furthermore, colleges are suspicious of "training" ("animals are trained, people are taught") and so grandly offer "Dance Education," which includes music, dance history, kinesiology, academics, and "dance theory" (the college term for choreography). But many students get only two or three technique classes *a week*. "Fat, wobbly college dancers" show up at the Graham School to go into the elementary class. Yet Jean Erdman came from Sarah Lawrence. Ethel Winter, Dorothea Douglas, and Patricia Birch are from Bennington; and soon Mary Hinkson and Matt Turney arrive from Wisconsin.

November 2, 1949, Cambridge, Massachusetts

Margaret Lloyd, dance critic of the *Christian Science Monitor*, likes *Diversion of Angels* but not *The Eye of Anguish*. She writes:

> Apparently a starring role for Mr. Hawkins (now Miss Graham's husband), the result is a travesty. Mr. Hawkins in a fearsome wig and appalling costume does not even tear passion to tatters. He simply dissipates it.

This coincides with our opinion, not shared with Martha, of course. After Cordelia dies, Erick staggers around with her in his arms and we hear him muttering, "Oh my poor Cordelia." His utter sincerity makes it hopeless.

Bob Cohan and Barbara Bennion on bus after rest stop. Photo by Stuart Hodes.

Martha is not happy with *Lear,* but, ostensibly preparing for her own performance in *Every Soul Is a Circus,* never watches.

Barbara Bennion, new in the company, dances Red in *Diversion of Angels.* Alabaster-skinned with slightly frizzy blonde hair, wash-blue eyes, and what in my family we called a "milk face," dances with joyous abandon. To Bertram Ross, Martha says, "Barbara always dances in the sun." To me, "Barbara is a big cat."

During a streaking crossover, a nail sticking out of the stage floor gashes Barbara's foot. When the curtain comes down, the stage is covered with bloody footprints. A local doctor wants to stitch the gash, but when told she'll have to stay off it for a week or the stitches will pull out, she makes him bind it with tape and dances the next night.

A few weeks into the tour we're in a college theater with almost no wing space, crowded with a gaggle of hulking male undergrads. Worse than useless, but we can't ask them to leave.

"We are in *their* school dancing on *their* stage," says Martha. "They're probably members of the drama group and being backstage is their privilege."

In fact they are members of the football team there to gawk at the women. With only three feet of wing space, Barbara needs someone to backstop her streaking crossover at the end of *Angels*. The Graham men enter on her exit so she asks one of the college guys.

"What's your name, Miss?"

"Barbara."

"I'm Titus."

"Really? Titus?"

"Sure."

"All right, Titus. We'd better practice. Be sure to brace yourself."

Titus smiles. She goes at him half speed and slams him into the fly ropes. "If we can try that again."

They do it a couple of times before Barbara hits him with performance force. Seconds before curtain, Titus is gone, someone else standing there.

Barbara asks for Titus. "I'm taking over. Name's Jeff." He's huge. "Can we practice?"

"There's no time," says Barbara angrily. "I hit you *very* hard."

"Little girl," says the hulk, "I'm a tackle."

"Okay, but please be ready."

Before my entrance, I spot him, weight settled comfortably in his heels, hands slightly apart as though to catch a bean bag. Barbara slams into him, staggering him back into the fly ropes. When she pushes off to reenter for the bow, he loses his footing and crashes to the floor. After the show Jeff accompanies us to dinner and sits next to Barbara. The next day, Barbara says, "He said he could get me a football scholarship."

Conductor Irwin Hoffman heeds Martha's musical demands but ignores everything from the dancers, except for the one he's having sex with. For her, he makes egregious tempo changes, at one point doubling a ten-second solo in order to draw out her moment of glory. No one would give that more than a thought if Hoffman didn't obviously despise his job. After a performance of *Diversion of Angels*, he says, "What with dancer's tempos to worry about, the best I can do is play the notes. I don't even try to conduct it as music."

Bob: "It was written for the ballet. Dello Joio worked from Martha's scenario."

"So what?"

Bertram: "It was conceived as dance music and should be interpreted as dance music. If it is wrong for the dancers, it's musically wrong, too."

"Bullshit. Have you ever heard Koussevitzky's recording of *Appalachian Spring?*"

Me: "An abomination!" I did not know then that Hoffman had been a protégé of Serge Koussevitzky.

Hoffman: "It's the only musical version of that piece."

Bob: "I'll bet Martha wouldn't think so."

Hoffman: "She's not particularly musical."

Bob: "Are you serious?"

Hoffman: "Of course."

Bertram: "You think *Appalachian Spring, Hérodiade, Cave of the Heart,* and all the other great scores she commissioned were just luck?"

"She has more bad scores than good. *Deaths and Entrances* is bad music, and *Letter to the World* is worse."

"All her scores work as part of the dance," says Bob.

Whether a score that works for a ballet must also succeed as pure music is an old question. The arguments follow predictable paths until Hoffman says, "Conducting ballet isn't much of a job for a conductor."

"You think it's beneath you?"

"Frankly, yes."

Bertram: "Doesn't it make any difference that you're conducting for a genius?"

"You mean Martha Graham?"

"Yes," says Bob, dryly, "He means Martha Graham."

"She may be a genius, but she hasn't got rhythm."

We give up on Hoffman, assuming that when the tour ends, he'll be gone. But he isn't quite.

November 1949, Minnesota

Martha always arrives at the theater early, spending two hours or more on her warm-up which is both physical and sort of mystical. No one approaches unless invited. Her performances are always riveting. I conclude that her secret is the ritual of preparation and decide to try it myself. I arrive well before the others, do a floor warm-up onstage, grab a light stand or radiator to give myself a long hard *barre,* then go over all of my roles. While putting on makeup and costume, I keep to myself as much as I can.

I soon tire of austerity but, although I feel no improvement onstage, stick with it. Finally I mention it to Eugene Lester: "It feels like I'm danc-ing underwater. Maybe I'm not meant to be a dancer."

I observe Martha, redouble my effort, deepen my long, isolated warm-up, keep to myself before performance, shun the eager college dance ma-jors who hang around backstage. It gets worse.

After two weeks, I decide that when the tour ends, I'll quit dancing. A weight flies from my shoulders. That night, I join the group warm-up. Backstage is lively with coeds, a ravishing sophomore posted where I make several entrances. I tell her I'm thinking of going back to college and she tells me all about her school. Seconds before an entrance, I say, "'Bye now," leap on, and with her eyes upon me, dance like a tornado. Next day, on the bus, I tell the whole story to Martha.

"We must each find our own way to the source of energy," she says seri-ously. "My way is not everyone's way."

"Before last night, I had decided to quit dancing."

"Then this is an important day for you. We must celebrate."

She and Erick take me to lunch.

December 8, 1949, Friday

After a show in Wilmington, Delaware, we bus to New York City and sleep in our own beds. Saturday, a day trip to New Brunswick, New Jer-sey, Sunday off at home, and Monday, December 11, a day trip to Reading, Pennsylvania, the final performance of Green Two. On Tuesday, our first full day at home, Martha calls rehearsal. In five weeks we open at the 46th Street Theater.

January 22–29, 1950, 46th Street Theater, New York, New York

Three New York premieres—*Diversion of Angels, Eye of Anguish*, Erick's *The Strangler*—and a world premiere, Martha's new solo, *Gospel of Eve*.[5]

Gospel of Eve is a comic portrait of a vain woman, cousin of the dreamer in *Every Soul Is a Circus*. At curtain rise, Martha is at an enormous pink vanity with a curving mirror that extends high overhead. It gets a laugh. But after that, Martha mostly preens. *Gospel of Eve* doesn't work. I've learned enough about making dances to be amazed that so many of Mar-tha's do. She's earned the right to fail.

Audiences and critics love *Diversion of Angels,* and it's a joy to dance. As far as I'm concerned, anyone who doesn't love it is a dimwit. *Lear* is not a complete failure, but Erick's *The Strangler* is a disaster. What had made me avert my eyes at Connecticut College makes me want to slink out of the theater in New York City.

My personal high is the "Creature of Fear," in *Errand into the Maze.* The Minotaur's role is a physical tour de force, and at the climax, Martha climbs his thighs, forcing him slowly to earth in a controlled back fall. It's an audacious metaphor for defloration plus lots of sexual symbolism: a reverse—female on male—mounting, an umbilical cord, a giant vulva, an erection, a frenzied orgasm, even afterglow. The Minotaur bears his erection—a carved "bone" by Noguchi—across his shoulders like a yoke, does 100 or so pounding jumps, then falls, writhes, rises, and bearing Martha on his back, does pounding heel-beats across the floor. After a performance at an Ivy college, a female student delighted Martha saying it is her favorite dance, "Because I go through that every morning."

After the climax, Martha instructs me to turn the bone loose and relax in a posture of satisfied sleep. *Of course.* Years later, when Martha, no longer dancing, is not paying close attention, I am astonished to see a Minotaur end up in a position of writhing torment, still clutching his erect bone. Perhaps no one told him what was going on, yet how can he have missed it? Still later I am dismayed to see a trumped-up publicity photo of the Minotaur in a split jump above Ariadne. The monster is *smiling.*

The first Minotaur's costume was a black union suit crowned with a beautiful bull's head sculpted by Isamu Noguchi out of wire and black fabric. It was worn by Mark Ryder in the premiere and became my costume when I got the role in 1949. The bull's head rode on my shoulders and was strapped under my armpits, steadied by my jaws which bit down on a slab of tape-covered metal welded to the frame. It was hard to keep my jaws clamped when out of breath, but that is not why Martha got rid of it. The face had a sweet Ferdinand-the-Bull look, and its eyes, which appeared to be ping-pong balls suspended on threads, peered mildly out at the world.

Martha sent me to Woolworth's to buy fabric snakes called rats, used for big hairdos. She wound a couple around my head, sewed them into place, and topped them with a blocky balsa wood horn carved by me. It lasted one season. I carved double horns, which Martha encased in a black cowl, making the Minotaur look like a horned monk. Later Minotaurs

Stuart with Martha in *Errand into the Maze*. Stuart wearing Martha's revision of the Noguchi costume with Stuart's construction of a horn. Photographer unknown; from the author's personal collection.

painted their faces, went bare-chested and bare-legged, and bore graceful spreading horns.

In the middle of the 46th Street Theater season comes news: after Green Three, the company will go to Europe. I recall Martha's words: "The day you get a starring role, the world will fall."

The Minotaur is fine but one-dimensional. I want the Seer in *Night Journey* and the Preacher in *Appalachian Spring*. I ask Eugene Lester what he's rehearsing as he is leaving for rehearsal. He hesitates—"Well, nobody said I can't tell you"—and reveals that he's rehearsing Bob Cohan for the Seer in *Night Journey* and the Preacher in *Appalachian Spring*. I'm instantly seething. That day I tell Martha I need to speak with her. "Not now," and dashes into the studio. Next day: "I can't talk to you now." This goes on throughout the 46th Street Theater season. With one week before the start of Green Three, as she whips out of the studio, I yell, "I think you should know that I won't be going on tour." Stops in her tracks and without a word leads me back into the studio, sits on a bench, and waits for me to speak.

"I want two roles: the Seer in *Night Journey* and the Preacher in *Appalachian Spring*."

"When you're ready, you'll get roles."

"I will not wait for the *world to fall*." No reaction. "In Tallahassee, you said the day I get a starring role, the world will fall. I do not intend to wait that long."

"Nothing has been decided."

"Bob is rehearsing both the Seer and the Preacher."

"If you wish, you may tell Eugene to schedule time for you."

In the week before Green Three, I learn both roles.

John Martin, in the *New York Times*:

MARTHA GRAHAM SCORES IN RECITAL
Receives Ovation After Two-Year Absence
Novelty, "'Eye of Anguish" presented.

A frantic fantasia on themes from King Lear. It does not altogether succeed. Erick Hawkins fairly knocks himself out as King Lear, but not to any great effect . . . Yuriko as Regan and Bertram Ross as Edgar are also excellent.

Pearl Lang as Cordelia gets a good mention. *Errand into the Maze* gets a squib:

Miss Graham and Stuart Hodes made a stunning contest out of this curious personalization of the myth of the Minotaur and the labyrinth.

"Stunning contest" is fine but "curious personalization" seems another example of John Martin dismissing Martha's choreography by claiming the power lies in her performance. It also implies that once she stops, the dances can be scrapped. I had by then detected that very fear in Martha herself and concluded that Martin knows and that his insinuations are deliberate and vicious. *Errand into the Maze* enthralls audiences to this day.

Bad reviews have nothing to do with Martha's doubts about *Lear*. She and Louis are in the studio, I on the other side of the bamboo partition in the men's dressing room, overhear:

Martha: "Maybe I'll never make another good dance."

Louis: "Beethoven had to write the sixth symphony before he could write the seventh."

No one ever approached Bertram Ross's twenty-five years as Martha's partner, or the number of roles he created. In World War II, the army discovered that he could draw so assigned him to a mapping unit in Europe. One day he brought in one of his army sketches: a European village street, each cobblestone perfectly drawn, getting smaller and smaller as the street wound into the distance. "You have to be schizophrenic to draw like that," said Bertram.

Bertram's mother, who'd given up her own concert pianist dream, would listen to Bertram practice and, when he made a mistake, set a deck of playing cards left of the keyboard. Each time Bertram played the passage correctly he could move one card to the right until he'd moved the whole deck. One mistake and he had to start over.

Late one night, we exit 66 Fifth Avenue to see a full moon in the clear black sky. "Uh oh," cried Bertram, "My mother will be riding by on a broomstick any minute."

Bertram's blend of talent and mischief flavored his own dances. He made a solo titled *Trio* and a trio titled *Solo,* not gimmicks either, as he explored identity in subtle ways.

When my daughter Catherine turned seven, Bertram gave her a painting of Jack and Jill tumbling down the hill. Daughter Martha got a painting too. Today these hang in their adult homes, talismans of Bertram's revered "godfather" status.

One day Bertram mentions that he is related to Bethsabée de Rothschild. "My mother says we're third cousins twice removed, or something."

Left: Jack and Jill, painting by Bertram Ross. Courtesy of Catherine Hodes.

Below: Girl and Worm, painting by Bertram Ross. Courtesy of Martha Hodes.

"Tell Bethsabée," says Bob Cohan dryly. "I'm sure she'd like to know."

Bertram does. "I said we were cousins, and I never saw anybody disappear so fast. Probably thought I was going to ask for money."

Bertram has thick black hair. One day, Linda, Catherine, age eight, and I are in the back of a taxi, Bertram in the front. Catherine says, "Uncle Bert, from the back you look like a girl."

Bertram: "From the back, I am a girl."

Graham Technique is too demanding for a young woman in Tel Aviv, who tells Bertram, her teacher, that too much emphasis on technique spoils the natural instinct to dance. Bertram asks if she likes Chopin.

"I love Chopin."

Bertram points to the piano, "Okay, play me some Chopin."

"But I can't play the piano."

"That doesn't matter. Play me some Chopin."

"You think it's like that?"

"Yes," said Bertram. "It's like that."

Bertram owns a Steinway studio grand, stored with an aunt in Brooklyn. When we start Dancers' Studio, our group's private dance studio that we also hire out to others, Bertram wants his piano there but the aunt is reluctant. "She doesn't even play piano," says Bertram. "She just likes it to impress her friends." Finally a date is set. The piano is in a sunporch up a narrow two-flight staircase. The movers arrive.

"They'll never get it out," says the aunt.

"Someone got it in," replies Bertram.

Four huge men stand silent while the aunt threatens lawsuits if they so much as brush the wall. They make measurements, pick up the piano, thread it down the stairs, and take it to Manhattan, where it goes beside my $100 "player" with the player mechanics removed. The Steinway is used for two-piano scores and by luminaries like John Cage and David Tudor. When Dancers' Studio closes, the Steinway goes to Bertram's apartment.

January 29, 1950

For Green Three,[6] Yuriko returns to the company, joined by Patricia Birch, plus Judith Janus, Marie-Louise Louchheim, and Sara Aman. Irwin Hoffman does not return, and again Eugene Lester conducts from the piano.

February 7, 1950, Washington, D.C.

We dance in George Washington University's Lisner Hall, designed by an architect who knew nothing about theaters. The star dressing room is three flights above the stage, *no backstage elevator,* other dressing rooms above that. Our stage manager creates a curtained-off cubical on stage level for Martha. I mention this to someone who works at the theater and she says that on the day it was dedicated, Frank Lloyd Wright was guest of honor, and with the architect sitting front center, used the theater as an example of incompetent theater design.

February 9, 1950, Lynchburg, Virginia

Helen McGehee's home town. Martha sends her out for a solo bow. Dancers stand in the wings applauding.

Judith Janus dances Goneril, one of King Lear's evil daughters. I play Edmund. At one moment she crouches at my knees, springs up, I catch her around the waist, heft her high, and set her on her feet. Slipping my arm under her hips is easy if she is rising. But if she jumps too soon and I catch her on the way down, she weighs a ton. We practice before every show.

Martha lets partners work out individual problems, and we are tinkering with the lift at a clean-up rehearsal when Martha calls the women to do Lear Falls. These come out of a stride, and are sometimes called Stride Falls. The body must not bend at the hips which would make the butt stick up. After a dozen or so of the looping, bone-jarring falls, Martha dismisses the women to work with Erick. Judy and I go back to our lift but our timing is terrible. I whisper, "Judy, you didn't jump into the lift. Let's try it again."

She answers loudly, "I'm sick and tired of that lift. You can't lift me, that's all." Martha hears, turns toward us.

Voice hard. "Judy, come here please. Do Lear Falls."

Judy's butt sticks up. Martha reaches out and slams her into the floor. Judy stops, rises slowly, but does not look Martha in the eye.

"Again, Judy. This time, don't stop after one fall." As Judy falls, Martha slams her down, follows, slams her down again, and again, and again, until they've crossed the whole stage. Without a word she turns back to Erick.

"Judy," I call brightly. "Can we practice that lift now?" Judy is willing.

Fifty-nine years later, 2009, Judy and I are in *From the Horse's Mouth*. Devised by choreographers Tina Croll and Jamie Cunningham, it brings veteran dancers together to tell stories. This edition is for ex-Graham dancers and plays New York City's Joyce Theater. After the show, Judy and I are interviewed by a *New York Times* reporter, and remembering our arguments about that lift, Judy says, "You threatened to throw me off the stage and into the audience."

"I couldn't have . . ."

"Oh yes you did, and like a fool, I believed you."

It appears in the paper next day. Judy knew I would never have done it, but I certainly remember wanting to.

February 15, 1950, Rock Hill, South Carolina

Hometown of my World War II copilot, John Edward (Moe) McMurray, and navigator, Ardrah (Ike) Buddin. A drugstore in the center of town seemed like a good place to ask about them.

"Sure I know Moe and Ike," said the fountain clerk. "Moe's up to Charlotte. Flew with 'em, did ya? Sure remember the day y'all buzzed Rock Hill. I'll call Moe's brother, Mac." He went to the telephone.

The clerk was referring to a day we diverted a training mission from Tampa, Florida, to Charlotte, North Carolina. Charlotte is forty miles from Rock Hill so Ike suggested we fly over his and Moe's hometown, and, being navigator, he can fake the log. Two other crews come along, tightening into a "V" formation as we near Rock Hill, drop from 5,000 to 500 feet and fly over the town, engines roaring at high revs. Ike pointed to his girl's house and I led the formation over it. Nearing the house, our right wing man *peeled off* (we're at 500 feet, remember), I felt obliged to follow and we buzzed the rooftops at 50 feet.

"Emily!" screamed Ike at a waving pillow slip in a backyard. Departing, we shot flares into the gathering dusk. It's a flagrant violation, and we could have been grounded, even court-martialed, but Ike had called the

Rock Hill newspaper editor, who wrote only that "local boys" had been in "the big B-17s that flew over Rock Hill yesterday." He didn't identify us or say we'd buzzed the town.

The clerk returned. "Mac's on his way."

"I have to get back to the theater now."

"He'll find ya."

A few blocks from the drugstore, a black Mercury pulls up and a man who looks like an older heavier Moe gets out, introduces himself, and says, "Glad it was me spotted you. Every police car in Rock Hill is lookin' for ya."

He drives to a small house where I meet Ike and Emily, now his wife. I'd met her when she visited Ike in Tampa, shy and delicate, a real southern belle, now with babies and a harried look. She serves lemon Cokes and stays home when Ike, Mac, and I leave for the theater.

Backstage, the women are warming up. Ike leans close and whispers, "I *knew* when the war wuz over, you wuz gonna get y'self into somethin', and ya sure got y'self into *somethin'*."

Mac's gaze is riveted on Barbara Bennion. "I'd right appreciate having your troupe be my guests for steaks after the show. Got us a fine new restaurant, best in this part of the state."

"Who would you like to invite?"

Eyes glued to Barbara: "Ever'body."

"Well, let me introduce you to Barbara," I pointed her out, "and she can pass on the invitation. That all right?"

"That will be all right," he says carefully. The company accepts and, during the meal, I see Barbara and Mac sharing a lantern-lit table for two. When ready to leave, Barbara says Mac will drive her to the hotel.

Next morning in the bus, "What kind of people are these?" And at my alarmed look, "Oh, nothing *happened*."

"Something must have."

"He proposed. Asked me to quit dancing here and now and when I said I couldn't, he asked if could I quit by Easter. I'd stay with his mother for two weeks and he'd stay with a friend on the other side of town. I'd have the car. Ceremony in June."

"I knew you'd conquered him two minutes after he walked into the theater yesterday."

"You did?"

"The whole party was to get you to go out with him."

"You mean he paid for steaks for everybody . . . ?"

"Just so you'd have dinner with him."

"But he doesn't even know me."

In 1995, I emailed Moe about Barbara and Mac. "Sure sounds like Mac," he replied. "He was the black sheep of the family. Married four times and has a dozen kids all over the country. He's dead."

Eugene Lester is again feeling the strain of conducting from the piano. One night, Martha tries to speed up the tango in *Every Soul Is A Circus* by stomping it out from the stage. After, Gene says to me, "I'll play any tempo she wants, but I won't take tempos from her during performance."

The next day, backstage, I become aware that Martha and Gene, speaking softly, are having an argument. Gene stalks away, Martha stares stonily at his back, then turns a furious gaze to me. "You can always tell when someone masturbates!" I do not relay this to Gene. Soon a pianist is hired so Gene can concentrate on conducting.

February 23, 1950, en route to Tahlequah, Oklahoma

Leslie Anne Hooke is from a southern Mayflower family. Elegant, strong, she dances so passionately she often seems on the edge of disaster. Martha describes her as "very highly geared."

Mostly she is quiet but will sometimes make a remark that elicits discussion. One day at lunch: "Negroes have superior rhythm."

Bob Cohan rolls his eyes. Bertram Ross asks, "Do you also believe they love watermelon and fried chicken?"

"Is there anything wrong with superior rhythm?"

"It has nothing to do with race."

"You don't think anything has anything to do with race."

"Exactly," said Bertram.

In a troubled voice, "I don't know if that's true."

"Because you're a bigot," states Bertram not for the first time.

"I'm not."

One day on the bus, Bertram, sitting directly behind Leslie Anne, peers over her shoulder, shouts, *"What?"* Leslie Anne looks up. "Let me see that book!"

She snatches it out of sight. "You have no right to look over my shoulder!"

"Show me that book!"

"You are invading my privacy!"

"Well, I saw it. Leslie Anne is reading about anti-Semitism Tell us about anti-Semitism, Leslie Anne."

"I'm reading psychology," she says levelly.

Bertram stands up in his seat. "All right, go ahead and read."

She thrusts the book at him. He reads the title: *Anti-Semitism and Emotional Disorder.*

What keeps it from deteriorating is that Bertram is harmless and Leslie Anne is resilient. One day, heading west in Nebraska someone cries, "Indians!"

"Where?"

"There!" A dozen people are walking single file beside the road.

"Are those Indians?" cries Leslie Anne. "I thought they were human beings."

"OH MY GOD!" shouts Bertram.

"I didn't mean it like *that,*" wails Leslie Anne, and tries to explain she'd meant "*ordinary* human beings."

Bertram's gibes gradually diminish and after the tour she is not seen taking classes at the Martha Graham Studio.

March 5, 1950, en route to Tucson, Arizona

As we enter the western desert, Martha calls the men together. "This road passes the camp where Yuriko was interned during the war.[7] I want one of you with her at all times."

I am sitting beside Yuri when she says, "Those mountains! I recognize those mountains. This is where we were." All peer out at empty desert. "But our camp is gone, all gone."

March 10, 1950, Los Angeles, California

Yuriko recommends a Japanese restaurant and half the company, including Martha and Erick, go for an early dinner. We sit at a large circular table, Bob Cohan to my left, Martha on his left, serving ourselves from large platters in the center. I'm reaching toward the platter when a waiter places a bowl of rice on the edge of the table and bring my arm back, flipping the bowl onto my lap, rice side down. I want no more Freudian cracks from Martha so feigning intense interest in the conversation, snake a hand into my lap, remove first the bowl, then the rice, handful by searing handful, until I can brush the remaining grains with my napkin. Bob Cohan watches but doesn't give me away.

Movie star Gene Kelly comes to the performance in Los Angeles and goes backstage to see Martha. They leave together. Next day she comments on Kelly's intense charm. "He's the most important dancer in America."

"No, Martha! You are."

"His dancing sets a high standard and is seen by millions, so he is more important."

March 11, 1950, Santa Barbara, California

Martha had been born in Pittsburgh but grew up in Santa Barbara, a picture-postcard jewel on the Pacific Ocean. We arrive Sunday, don't dance until Monday night. Strolling toward the ocean, Bob Cohan and I pass flowering trees, pastel homes, gardens with plants I'd never seen, coming finally to the waterfront and a long pier. At the end is the Pacific Shell Shop. Bob picks up a huge scallop and holds the scooped-out glistening pink in front of his solar plexus. "If only I could do a Contraction like this."

"I'm going to buy Martha a shell!" I pore through whelks, abalones, sand dollars, and starfish, to find a dramatic beauty. Out of a creamy white body the size of my fist poke long black spines like crooked witches' fingers. The tag: *"Black Murex."*

"It looks evil," says Bob.

I have it gift wrapped. The clerk says, "A card inside tells all about the *Murex.*" That evening before giving it to Martha, I take it out to admire.

Bob reads the card. "You can't give it to her." Reads: "The Black Murex is a predator and the only member of genus *Murex* that eats other mollusks. It is also a cannibal, killing and feeding upon its own kind."

I decide Bob is right and don't give it to Martha. It kicks around until it gets lost.

Working our way back east, we are in a town whose unpaved main street and wooden sidewalks are like a Wild West movie. Heading for a local

Black Murex shell.

five-and-ten, I pick my way across a muddy thoroughfare and on the opposite corner, trying to cross back, are Martha and Erick. With a dark look, she says, "I ask myself, what we are doing *here?*"

March 29, 1950, Decatur, Illinois

The huge theater has enormous wings. For my final entrance of Green Three, I back off a dozen steps, take a running start, soar out, and land like a sack of dirt. Next morning I limp into the bus and after the two-day ride home, go on limping for a week. The Green Tours are over.

Two stunning dancers arrive at the Graham Studio, Mary Hinkson and Matt Turney, both from the University of Wisconsin, Madison.

5

. . . .

TKO'd in Paris and London

April 1950

When in Italy as a soldier, I was an occupier in the Army of Occupation. If I go as a dancer, I'll be an artist in the land where art as I know it began. Rumors are flying but no date, and Martha isn't even rehearsing so I audition. Hanya Holm, whose *Kiss Me, Kate* is standing-room only on Broadway, needs dancers for her new musical, *The Liar*.

Holm's audition has an unusual move; we stand in second position, and on sixteen counts of piano arpeggios, slowly raise arms while rising to half toe. The quick-study hotshots don't know what Holm is after. I know that she wants to see if we can "sell." I give it my all. Holm asks where I'd danced.

"Martha Graham."

"In her company?"

"Yes."

"Will Martha let you do a Broadway show?"

"We're not rehearsing."

She tells me to return for the final.

I inform Martha, who says we are about to start rehearsing for Europe. At the callback, I try to explain. Holm interrupts. "I knew she wouldn't let you."

Martha's rehearsals don't begin until *The Liar* had opened on Broadway—and closed.

The role of the Seer is mine, but Bob Cohan rehearses the Preacher daily. At a run-through for lighting designer Jean Rosenthal, I watch from a corner. The Preacher's big moment is the thundering hellfire sermon. Bob does it well but, to me, does not thunder. After he's danced, Martha peers into my corner. "Stuart, do you want to do it?" Like, "Think you can do better?"

I leap to my feet and hurl every denunciation straight at Martha. I get the role. But before *Spring* is performed, Martha injures her knee and the tour is canceled. When she is able to dance again, Erick Hawkins is gone, and I get his role as her partner, the Husbandman. I never danced the Preacher except in rehearsal.

We hear that our conductor in Europe will be Irwin Hoffman. Bob, Bertram, and I decide we must speak. It demands formality so we make an appointment with Martha and Lee Leatherman in the company office. Bob begins: "We're worried about the conductor in Europe. We heard you're planning to take Irwin Hoffman."

"Nothing's settled," says Leatherman.

Bob: "We don't think you should take him. He doesn't respect Martha."

Leatherman: "Why do you say that?"

Bertram blurts: "He said Martha doesn't have rhythm."

"And that she's not musical," I add.

"He said that?"

Bob: "All of us were there."

"Well!" Leatherman stares out of the window then turns back. "We can't have a conductor who thinks Martha doesn't have rhythm."

Martha stays silent. Ted Dale becomes our conductor for the 1950 European tour.

I have a serious girlfriend, Carla McBride, whom I'd met at a party thrown by her sister, Pat, a principal in the New York City Ballet. Carla and I are immediately drawn to one other yet get into fights over nothing at all. We are both scheduled to depart for Europe on the same day, she to Ireland to visit relatives, I to France with Martha. I am helping Carla fix up her new apartment and leave my tools there.

Martha and Erick cross the Atlantic on TWA, sleeping in a berth on a Lockheed Constellation (to me, the most beautiful airliner ever made!).

The troupe flies Youth Argosy, a low-cost charter with old four-engine Douglas DC-6s, four rows across, aisle in the middle.

The airport bus depot is in a midtown Manhattan hotel, and when I show up, there, to my amazement and to hers, is Carla. We're on the same flight! I introduce her to the Graham dancers, and we sit together on the plane, Carla by the window, me on the aisle. The instant we're airborne, Carla starts flirting past me to a guy sitting across the aisle. He's disgustingly pretty with a head of blond curls. He gets out of his seat and stands in the aisle talking to Carla over my head. Five minutes, I'm in a rage.

"Maybe you two should sit together." Neither notices my biting sarcasm. I take an empty rear seat and steam all the way to Newfoundland where we land to refuel, passengers exiting onto the sprawling tarmac. I ask Carla to accompany me to the refreshment shack a quarter of a mile away.

At the counter. "When we land in Shannon, you go your way, I go mine. I don't care who you see or what you do. But on this airplane, you're with me."

When Carla rejects this demand, I clamp my fingers viselike around her wrist, yank her off the stool, and start toward the plane, hauling her by main strength, she digging in her heels saying I need a shrink. Suddenly I'm disgusted—with Carla and even more with myself. This is not me, or how I am with women. I stop, open my hand like I'd noticed something nasty in it, say slowly, *"Good-bye, Car-la."*

On the transatlantic leg, I sit as far from her as I can get. The dancers are transfixed by the melodrama, but when Ethel Winter tries to speak to me I return a furious glare.

Carla deplanes in Shannon. I walk her into the terminal where she digs out the electronic exposure meter I'd given her as a parting gift. "I can't take it now," and presses it into my hand. I toss it into an open trash can and stalk off, glad however, to glimpse her burrowing for it.

The train from Luxembourg arrives in Paris at night, and we taxi straight to L'Hotel West End, ending a 21-hour trip. I wake at noon, famished. Louise Vincent (Claude), the French actress I'd met at Connecticut College, arrives and guides me to a restaurant where I become the zillionth American to discover the delights of dining in France.

In the top floor studio of Théâtre des Champs-Elysées, conductor Ted

Dale begins leading the orchestra through *Every Soul Is a Circus* while Martha and Erick mark their moves. Erick is fussy about tempos. "Ted, that's too fast." Dale slows down. "Now it's too slow."

"Make up your mind, Erick."

Erick is prickly, but Dale's rejoinder is unjustified; tempos can be too fast or too slow. But Martha's withering attack—"What do you *mean*, 'Make up your mind, Erick'?"—before the whole orchestra is shocking. Dale looks like he'd been clubbed. Somehow, we make it to opening night. Program:

Errand into the Maze—Errance dans le labyrinthe
The Eye of Anguish—Les yeux de l'angoisse
Cave of the Heart—Les arcanes du coeur
Every Soul Is a Circus—Toute âme est un cirque

June 27, 1950

In her biography, *Martha*, Agnes de Mille describes the Paris opening: "Finally the program did start, with *Errand into the Maze,* based on the story of Ariadne and the Minotaur, danced by Graham and Hawkins." *Nope.* It was Graham and Hodes.

De Mille writes that Martha was carried offstage after *Cave of the Heart. Nope.* She was fine after *Cave.* But in *Every Soul Is a Circus*, the last dance on the program, I saw her come down from a lift and her left leg buckle. Yet she completed the dance, took bows, and left the stage under her own power.

According to de Mille, the Graham troupe went to a party at the Bethsabée de Rothschild mansion, and on leaving everyone was "politely but thoroughly searched." *Nope.* The party was cancelled. It was feared that Martha had been seriously injured.

Next morning a message directed me to Martha's suite in the Hôtel Plaza Athenée. She was on the bed, left leg atop the coverlet, knee badly swollen beneath layers of wrapping. Bethsabée stood at the head on Martha's left. At the foot of the bed were Gertrude Macy, Lee Leatherman, and Craig Barton. Later it hit me that Erick had been absent. I had no idea why I was there.

"I have been examined by five doctors," said Martha quietly. "Insurance doctors. They say that if I dance tonight, I can damage the knee so badly

I may never dance again." In the shocked silence, "As it is, I may never dance again."

A gasp escaped Bethsabée. "Martha," she quavered, "Your dances will be danced forever."

Martha turned her an icy gaze. "If I can't dance, I don't care if they are *never* danced again."

"Oh, Martha."

I was indignant. How dare Martha doom her dances to oblivion because *she* cannot dance? But Martha is in despair and my anger vanishes. That night the show went on without her: *Diversion of Angels, Eye of Anguish, El Penitente.*

Agnes de Mille's book puts Martha backstage: "talking loudly to herself as she limped back and forth, and every few seconds she'd bang the cane on the ground like a divining rod. 'Yuk' she called out with a guttural cry of horror." *Nope.* This is pure fiction. Martha was as likely to say "Yuk," gutturally or otherwise, as swear in Yiddish. During that grim second performance, Martha remained in her room unable to stand. We gave it our all, but performances were canceled. Next day I went to the theater to collect my things, people standing disappointedly under the marquee. A crushing sight.

The London opening was a month off and hoping Martha would heal, we go to London. The New York City Ballet is there, and I attend the sixteenth birthday party of Jacques d'Amboise. He sits on the floor opening gifts, surrounded by adoring women.

We meet Robin Howard, Martha's London sponsor. A member of the Scots Guards in World War II, he'd been wounded and lost both legs. On prosthetics with two canes, he led us on a late-night pub crawl. Owner of the Gore Hotel in Bloomsbury, he offered Graham dancers rooms at rock-bottom rates. But I opt for a tiny central London hotel called Ryder Street Chambers, where a stairway winds around an ancient caged elevator and my windows overlook streets that could have been prowled by David Copperfield. Or Jack the Ripper.

Signs on the Piccadilly Theatre read "Martha Graham," but when it is certain she cannot dance the tour is over. In the wee hours, Patricia Birch and Barbara Bennion hear Erick bellowing on a sidewalk outside of the Gore Hotel. He needs cash, which they supply. He disappears.

Next day Leatherman calls a meeting. Not a word about Erick. He informs us that we are booked to fly back to New York in two days. I want to

Piccadilly Theatre, London. Photo by Stuart Hodes.

stay in Europe and ask for my airfare in cash. Lee refuses, saying he is responsible for getting us home and has obtained a group rate from BOAC. Aggrieved and accusing, he tells us that Bethsabée has lost $75,000.

"But she won't have to collect unemployment insurance!" I say. "Are you going back?"

"Of course."

I give in. Bob and Bertram, too. We leave the meeting, walk London's fascinating and uncommonly sunny streets, depressed at the thought that in two days we'll be back in New York City, out of work in the July doldrums.

I stop. "No! I won't go back." Bertram and Bob immediately agree. I telephone Lee, tell him that if he will not give us our fare, I'll pay my own way, and so will Bob and Bertram. Considering Martha's devastated condition, I'm appalled when he draws her into the dispute. She calls a meeting. Begins, "This tour has cost Bethsabée $75,000."

Then Gertrude Macy, the one really responsible and innocent of the fracas, appears and convinces Martha it is okay to give us our fare in traveler's checks.

Bertram writes a lyric to the tune of "Besame Mucho":

Bethsabée, Bethsabée Rothschild,
There's been a rumor that you lost mazuma on us.
Bethsabée, Bethsabée Rothschild.
You took a lickin' when Martha got chicken, don't fuss.
She cracked her knee cap, it sounds like to me crap,
We've all heard that story before . . .

That was all I remembered so asked Bertram for the rest, but he repudiated his lyrics as an abhorrent blunder.

I book a Youth Argosy flight leaving Luxembourg in six weeks and buy an English bicycle for a tour of my own. This intrigues Bob, Bertram, and Virginia Krolick, a sort of Graham groupie, so they rent bikes and we bike to Hampstead Heath, Stonehenge, St. Michael's Mount, Mousehole, Penzance, and Land's End. After goodbyes in London, I take a night ferry across the Channel, next day bike to Paris and there, at a sidewalk table of Les Deux Magots, sipping frosty glasses of yellow Pernod, are Lee Leatherman and Craig Barton.

I bike out of Paris with no plan except to be in Luxembourg in four weeks. Expect easy going in flat Holland, only to learn that pedaling into a strong wind is like biking up a mountain road that never descends. At a jazz concert in Amsterdam, I meet a cute girl who speaks adorable English. She's wearing a dress she'd designed and made herself. Same for a crocheted purse that expands like a concertina. I walk her home through softly lit streets. When I say something she likes, she says, "Mochta!" (Mighty!) She's sixteen. Momma and papa are waiting at the front door. Elderly for parents of a sixteen-year-old, I wonder how they'd fared in World War II.

Next day, pedaling out of Amsterdam, I think about making a U-turn, going back, pursuing my destiny.

I relish being alone and free in battle-scarred Europe but have no wish to enter Germany, erstwhile enemy. But the road to Luxembourg passes through a sliver, and I decide to spend the night in a German *Jugendherberge* (youth hostel). I cross the border, see odd German bicycles. Unlike Luger pistols or Messerschmitt fighter planes, they are neither elegantly designed nor well-made. Germans had melted down prewar bikes for bullets, and these are quickies knocked out to satisfy pent-up demand.

Early afternoon, forty miles to the *Jugendherberge*, pedaling easily, I pass a German cyclist. Ten minutes later, he passes me. He looks about my age. I speed up, pass, pump hard, then forget him. Half an hour later he zooms by. It's a race! He's on a German clunker and although my bike is only a three-speed, it has an English racing frame, and I have 2,000 miles of cycling in my muscles. I bear down, pass, and pedal full-out all the way to the *Jugendherberge*.

I check in, go to an outdoor basin with Arctic-temperature water, and am wondering how much to splash over myself when he pulls in straight to the basin. I watch as he scoops up double handfuls to splash over his body. After showing me that he is impervious to cold, he gestures to me. I fill the basin to the brim, climb in, and sink to my neck in water so cold I can't breathe.

Next morning, I buy sausage, cheese, *brötchen* (rolls), two bananas, and a candy bar. I still have two packs of American cigarettes, what's left of cartons brought for gifts and tips. It's sunny, the road to Luxembourg shaded by trees. I swing out to pass an elderly woman, and then stop in a field for lunch. I'm relaxing in the soft grass when she toils by, sees me, stops, and utters what sound like sad sighs. I don't understand a word yet realize she's saying I'd scared her when I'd passed. I take out the banana, candy bar, what's left of the cheese, two packs of cigarettes and hold it toward her. "Bitte, bitte."

"Anglish?"

"American."

She points to the cigarettes. "Pour le monsieur?"

"Pour *vous!*" and press the items into her hands. She toils on down the road. After a time I mount my bike and soon pass a tiny cottage to see her standing among sunflowers taller than she. Her gaze follows as I pass.

World War II ends.

Luxembourg Airport

The Youth Argosy plane is filled with people my age, but I sit beside a graying Air Force lieutenant colonel. When I mention I'd been a World War II bomber pilot, he says that the Korean War, just started, has upped the need for pilots. "If you want to go back in, you'll get an immediate promotion to first lieutenant."

I tell him I'll think about it and do, many times over the years, trying to imagine life in the military. But I know that, for better or for worse, I'm a dancer now.

6

· · · · · · · · ·

Drink the Sky

August 1950

Sports medicine and its poor relative, dance medicine, don't exist. A dancer with a minor injury is told, "Stay off it." A serious injury can mean an operation or an order to "stop dancing." Martha's insurance doctors had wanted to operate but she held off until she saw her own trusted doctor in Santa Fe, who prescribed weight-lifting. Back in New York, she demonstrated atop the office desk. Feet dangling, weights wrapped around both ankles, she lifted her right knee a few inches, straightened the leg on eight counts, held it extended for eight counts, lowered it on eight counts, dropped the knee, rested. She did this eight times on each leg, three times a day. She began with three-pound weights, soon upped it to five. A couple of months later, "I'm lifting twelve pounds now," and in about a year, "I lifted twenty pounds today."

Most dance solos last under ten minutes. For her first Louisville Symphony commission (before Europe), she had made *Judith* (the Biblical heroine who cut off the head of marauding general, Holofernes). A twenty-four-minute solo. After her injury and a year of weight-lifting, she made *The Triumph of St. Joan*. A twenty-seven-minute solo. She performed them on successive days. Knee proven, she turned *The Triumph of St. Joan* into *Seraphic Dialogue*, a dance for the ages.

When Martha taught technique, images illuminated the moves:

"Be complete in your skin, like a grape."

"The foot bears the miracle of the small beautiful bones."

"The arm connects to the spine for love."

"Your arms move from the back, like wings."

"Let a gentle waterfall flow down your body."

"When we dance, the body raises little flags of celebration."

"Contraction is a movement, not a position."

Of the floor position that begins every class: "Place the soles of your feet together, as if for prayer."

To a dreamy student: "You think dance is lovely. It's not. It's life."

Some teachers urge dancers to "Keep your focus," but none say where or on what. Martha says, "Present your gaze," which works for me.

"Drink the sky!" urged Martha. A powerful image and, to me, personal. Piloting an airplane, I felt part of that sky. In *Letter to the World,* Emily Dickinson supplied images:

"Inebriate of air am I, and debauchee of dew."

"*I will eat evanescence* slowly."

"I'm nobody. Who are you? Are you nobody too?"

Angela Kennedy told of rehearsing her lines offstage, repeating "I'm nobody," until a small boy who'd been listening said, "Lady, ya gotta be somebody."

In Martha's "self-embrace," the dancer reaches arms front, shoulders slide forward in their sockets, arms cross each other over the chest and reach behind the back until each hand touches the opposite shoulder blade.

"Drain the cup" begins with an imaginary goblet held in both hands, face lifted, neck stretched, body hollowed in dynamic receptiveness.

Martha uses three words with a Contraction-Release combo taught sitting on the floor.

"Sky." The body contracts, the face lifts, the gaze shoots straight up.

"Earth." Body pitches forward, the gaze bores into the ground.

"Man." Release, body lifts upright, gaze front.

When I become aware of sexism in language, I make it "Sky Earth *Human.*" Martha never happened to hear, but if she had I suspect she wouldn't have liked it much.

Faculty invent their own images. Yuriko, giving low slinky runs, says, "Feel as though molasses is running down between your thighs." Vivid, if a bit yucky.

Another Denishawn alum, Jack Cole, who admired Martha, used images too. Teaching a torso press up from the floor: *"Fuck the moon!"*

When Martha can no longer dance and teaches from a chair, imagery keeps her classes vital. In the late 1970s, I return to take classes. During floor work, she stops the class. The move begins with a Contraction Spiral, in which the body twists along the spinal axis from floor to face. "Open your throat," says Martha. "When two wolves contend for leadership of the pack, they fight. When one knows he will lose, he submits by opening his throat to the other's jaws. You must submit," says Martha, ultimate she-wolf. "Open your throat. Offer me your life!"

She sometimes says, "Be loose in your skin, like a cat." Yet about cats Martha is ambivalent. "I admire cats. But I don't trust them. They're too much like me." Describing one cat: "He was young but he knew exactly who he was."

Some make a distinction between dancing in class and onstage—class is for learning, stage for performing. To Martha, dancing in class *is* performing. Across the floor we must dance all the way "into the wings." At the end of a sequence we must "hold until the curtain comes down."

A floor position, the Sitting Fourth, begins many moves, legs splayed like half a swastika, forcing movement to begin in the upper body. One sequence begins in the torso, extends into the arms with a horizon-sweeping gaze that ends focused at the audience. Martha always watched for that gaze. "The next time you're at the movies watch the MGM lion. After he roars, he gazes at you, and in that gaze is intensely lion."

Auditions

Martha found company dancers in her classes. She did not audition outsiders until long after I'd left. As I become experienced at auditioning for paying jobs, I start to think of each audition as a free dance class. To arm myself against rejection: "I will not work for any choreographer who rejects me at an audition." (My take on Groucho's "I won't join any club that would have me as a member.") In *Once Upon a Mattress*, Carol Burnett tells me her secret: "I look at the VIPs out front and think, 'They're all sitting on the toilet.'"

I buy *Actors' Cues,* a crudely printed sheet that announces auditions and sells for twenty-five cents when the *New York Times* is a nickel. Dance auditions are in four categories: ballet, modern, commercial, and "exotic." The last includes strippers and anything African, East Indian, or Hawaiian. It seems to cover everything until I ask Eddie Roll if he's a ballet or a modern dancer. He looks at me quizzically. "I'm a tap dancer."

In 1954, George Martin hired me for *Kismet.* No audition. He hoped that a Graham-trained dancer could learn Jack Cole's "Broadway Hindu," which *set* Bharatanatyam moves to African rhythms. But Graham and Cole's moves are fundamentally different. Graham engages large muscle groups to create the powerful impulses typified by Contraction, while Jack Cole articulates separate muscle groups: shoulders, hips, torso, arms, and the side-to-side head slide (Greeva Bheda). Indian dance, with its subtly shifting rhythms, seems to bear the dancer on a divine flux. Jack Cole's jazz adaption generates an impression of impersonal mechanical power.

Anita Zahn and her Duncan Dancers performed at the 92nd Street Y, my first chance to see anything termed "Duncan." Martha and most of the troupe were there. The next day we asked her what she'd thought.

"I never actually saw Isadora, but if she had danced with so little passion, the world would not have noticed, no matter how many lovers she had taken."

Anna Sokolow, in the Graham troupe long before I arrived, choreographed Broadway musicals. In the mid-1970s, I chaired a discussion at NYU that included Sokolow, Charles Weidman, Valerie Bettis, and Jeff Duncan. At one point, Sokolow turned to me and said, "Stuart, why didn't you ever audition for any of my shows?"

"But, Anna, I always auditioned. You never took me."

"Oh. Sorry."

The creative spark I feel with Martha could not exist in any commercial setting. When people are paid, time is money so choreographers must spin out moves quickly, dancers must learn immediately and execute perfectly. Martha's unpaid rehearsals go on for months.

On Broadway, the dancing chorus is something to *rise out of.* One can aspire to principal roles, or dream of following Shirley MacLaine and Chita Rivera into stardom. One can also become a choreographer. In every chorus there's at least one dancer watching the choreography thinking, "I can do better."

On the first day of rehearsal, a choreographer establishes "Alpha" status, issuing tricky moves to keep the dancers busy. Agnes de Mille, not good at inventing, took her regulars to her country house where, for room, board, a dollar a day, and the promise of a job, they helped her devise moves.

Jerome Robbins, a fearsome Alpha in the two days before he fired me from *Two's Company,* hired more dancers than he needed, all on three-day clauses,[1] giving them good reason to be nervous. Puffing a cigarette, he worked out complex combinations while the dancers watched, called a name, and that one had to do it. He had novel ways of finding moves. Once he started four dancers running toward each other and stopped them when about to collide. "Now find a way through." Then again at full speed.

Merce Cunningham, a deep inscrutable Alpha, stayed more avant-garde than any of his alums. His first studio showing of *Suite by Chance* happened at my own Dancers' Studio, no audience except a few friends and a man with a 16-millimeter movie camera who included shots of the hat with slips of paper from which dancers drew, read, then danced what the slip instructed. In an art form dominated by control-freak choreographers, the idea of making dances by chance upset every rule in Doris Humphrey's book on choreography,[2] eventually leading to Yvonne Rainer's "No Manifesto,"[3] which threw out all else.

Some post-Martha avant-gardistas pretended to abolish Alpha status. Pilobolus listed *everyone* in the original cast as "choreographer." Yet it was mere gesture. The founding "Pils" (Moses Pendleton, Jonathan Walken, Allison Chase, and Martha Clarke) were all Alphas, and if they disagreed among themselves, as ex-Pil Austin Hartel told me, the dancers did whatever moves the Alpha in the audience that day wanted to see.

Steve Paxton's *Contact Improvisation* had people falling and leaning and hanging on one another so that every move depended on another. That Paxton went on to trademark his way of improvising reveals that he wasn't about to relinquish Alpha status.

Martha Graham's Alpha status was never in doubt, no matter how many moves she "stole" from her dancers. When she took your move and put it into her dance, you felt ennobled.

Work party at the 8th Street loft. *From left*: Bertram Ross, Irving Burton, Stuart (*hidden*), and Linda Margolies. Photo by Harold Lowe; from the author's personal collection.

John Cage and Merce Cunningham. Photo by Stuart Hodes.

Sign on East 8th Street: "Loft for Rent." One hundred dollars a month and great space although the building will be demolished in three years. Nine of us get together (Patricia Birch, Irving Burton, Rebecca Cappell, Miriam Cole, Ellen Green, Linda Margolies, Jack Moore, Bertram Ross, and me), put down second-hand maple flooring, install gas-fired radiators, paint the walls, tack plastic under the skylights, and partition off dressing rooms. We name it Dancers' Studio and rent it to ourselves for fifty cents an hour, a dollar for outsiders.

At the front overlooking 8th Street is a 10 by 14-foot room with a walk-in closet. I put in a cot, hot plate, half refrigerator, my clothes, and, as resident manager, live rent-free. Our first renters are John Cage and Merce Cunningham. I offer a freebie but Cage hands me a dollar. "Tape it to the wall."

Sunday, February 4, 1951

We hold an "Open Rehearsal" before a 92nd Street Y concert. Dances by Linda Margolies, Miriam Cole, Jack Moore, and me. The concert, December 27, 1952, gets great notices. I want to tour like Mark Ryder and Emily Frankel, but no one else is interested. Linda says, "Oh, let's just go on to the next thing."

When I'm hired for *Paint Your Wagon,* out-of-town tryouts in Philadelphia and Boston, Linda manages Dancers' Studio. A ballet teacher takes most of Saturdays, paying fifty dollars, half the monthly rent. The Graham Company rents the unused front section to store sets, another fifty dollars. The rent is paid.

I make a solo for Linda, *I Am Nothing,* from a news item about a mute child rescued from a blitzed London house. My program note is a depressing quote: *"I am nothing and nobody. My house went bang. My cat was stuck to a wall. They wouldn't let me have it. They threw it away."*

Linda was the child clutching a doll, which she rejected at the end. To me, rejecting the doll projected the child's lost ability to love. But it must not have been clear or maybe I needed a bigger doll, because Louis Horst in *Dance Observer* described it as a dance for a child with a *dead cat.*

After Linda's *Curley's Wife,* which every critic dubbed "the best dance on the program," she made a duet for me and Jack Moore, *The Ringing Down,* based on the English movie, *Dead of Night,* in which a ventriloquist and his dummy have a falling out. I play the ventriloquist Jack, plays the dummy, and after stomping the dummy—Jack—to death, the dummy's personality takes over. I stalk stiffly to my chair, sit, stare at the audience, and stretch my mouth into a dummy's mad grin. Another "best dance" for Linda.

Then *Reap the Whirlwind,* a trio for herself, Bertram Ross, and me. A girl whose father wants to keep her from marrying tries to scare off a suitor by claiming his daughter is a witch, whereupon daughter and suitor cast a death spell on the father. I play the father, and, after being dispatched, Linda and Bertram kick my body around in a bizarre dance of victory. Another "best" for Linda.

The going rate for an original score is ten dollars a minute. Morton Feldman, a composer known for long rests, composes a score for Jean Erdman; it turns out to be mostly rests. Erdman says she wants sound not silence and proposes to pay only for the notes. Feldman sues. The judge rules that if any rests are allowed, it is up to the composer to decide how many. Erdman loses but tells the story with glee.

In 1952, John Cage creates 4′33″ (4 Minutes and 33 Seconds) which is *all* rests. Not one note mars the silent purity of that historic composition. Cage told about submitting the score to ASCAP. The clerk had to sign it. After searching vainly for notes, she began to sign in the middle of the first page. Cage stopped her. "What are you doing?"

"I have to sign your score."

"You were about to sign in the middle of the music."

Any live performance is by its nature once-in-a-lifetime and, if missed, is missed forever. I see performances by Ronne Aul, Valerie Bettis, John Butler, Janet Collins, Merce Cunningham, Jean Erdman, Erick Hawkins, Pauline Koner, Pearl Lang, Iris Mabry, Marie Marchowsky, Helen McGehee, Donald McKayle, Daniel Nagrin, Natanya Neumann, May O'Donnell, Vol Quitzow, Bertram Ross, Herbert Ross, Sybil Shearer, Anna Sokolow, Tao Strong, Glen Tetley, Norman Walker, Ethel Winter, Yuriko, Anita Zahn, and (many) others. I forever regret missing Paul Taylor's astonishing debut.

Pauline Koner, Doris Humphrey's permanent guest star, calls me for a television show: *Alice Through the Looking Glass.* TV screens are mostly six inches wide. I don't yet own a TV, hardly know Koner, and wonder why she called me. Alice is played by Bambi Linn, with Herbert Ross as

Pauline Koner at Jacob's Pillow, 1966. Photo by John Lindquist. ©
Houghton Library, Harvard University.

the Knave, and Arthur Treacher as King of Hearts. The TV director tells
Koner that her moves are too small for a six-inch screen. She balks. "No
one can choreograph for a six-inch screen. It must be ten inches, at least."

Lewis Carroll's croquet players use upside-down flamingoes for mal-
lets. Koner has each man except me hold a woman upside down. I become the croquet ball curled up on the floor, and when smacked by a female head roll lumpily toward the camera.

To Carroll's "Speak softly to your little boy and beat him when he
sneezes," there's a bizarre soundtrack of sneezing, thumping, and an infant
squalling, to which we toss a life-size baby doll like a medicine ball.

On the day of the broadcast, Koner asks if I know how much longer

Martha Graham intends to keep dancing. "She's fifty-six, you know," and tells me she is the best one to take over her roles. I suppose Graham and Koner look alike—short stature, sharp-featured dramatic faces, long black hair, looming dark eyes. But can Pauline Koner imagine that Martha will simply hand over her roles? Does she expect me to pass this uncomfortable intelligence to Martha? Is it why she'd hired me?

Linda is making a dance from Tennessee Williams's one-act play, *The Purification*. A brother and a sister, deeply bonded, ride their horses through the desert, but the Church, suspecting incest, destroys them. A meditation on a spiritual bond and metaphor for any forbidden relationship, Tennessee Williams cast it in poetic language. Linda and Bob Cohan are the brother and sister, I, the condemning priest. She begins to sketch out moves, commissions a score from composer Louis Calabro and a set from Wally Martin. Calabro returns a powerful score and Wally Martin a sleek model suggesting a church topped by a steer's horn. Martha offered to put Linda's dance on in her coming New York season. She called us aside.

> *The Purification* is an important dance and you must give it the time it needs. It wouldn't be fair to make you sacrifice time for my rehearsals. I can find other dancers for your roles for this season, leaving you free to concentrate on this dance.

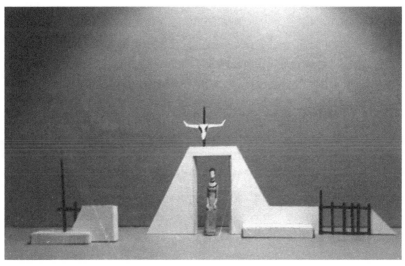

Set of *The Purification* designed by Wally Martin. Photo by Wally Martin; from the author's personal collection.

That night, Linda says she'd rather dance with Martha than make *The Purification*. Next day she tells Martha. Martha says, "Are you sure?" Linda's *The Purification* is never made. A year or so later, Mary Anthony asks to hear the Calabro music, then to use it for her own dance based on the same Tennessee Williams story. In a small way it assuages the guilt we feel at having left a fine score unplayed. But when Mary Anthony invites us to the performance, we cannot bring ourselves to go.

Ellen Graff, in *Stepping Left,* her history of modern dance and politics, wrote that Martha Graham was criticized by the leftist press "for subject matter that is too personal, too mystical, and too divorced from contemporary social issues."[4] She noted that as late as 1953, Martha and Louis Horst walked out on a New Dance Group concert whose overtly political dances offended Horst. In *Dance Observer,* he wrote: "as crude and illiterate an example of bad taste as could possibly degrade a great and powerful art."[5]

I didn't see that concert, yet saw such a dance, *Partisan Journey,* by Sophie Maslow. Bad guys dance menacingly. Underground fighters spring out, guns blazing, kill the bad guys, and celebrate with a chirpy folk dance. I also saw such a dance in China, in 1980, ridiculing the imprisoned Gang of Four. Both dances were creepy.

I enjoy batching it on 8th Street, eating at midnight in a 24-hour Bickford's whose night cook knows me by name. My refrigerator holds only snacks, cold drinks, and ground coffee. If I work up a sweat in the studio, I dash to my refrigerator for a gulp of cold canned grapefruit juice. I have a space heater turned off at night, and the studio is so frigid I sleep in soft chino pants and an old fleece-lined army bomber jacket. Yet a trek to the john is still bone-chilling, so I urinate into an old grapefruit juice can, which I empty in the morning. If I sleep late, I dash off to class, not picking up dirty socks or anything else. Linda, who'd relinquished management of the studio, still keeps it clean, and extends this service to my room. One afternoon after a hard warm-up, I dash in, throw open the door of the refrigerator and take a deep slug from the half-full grapefruit juice can which Linda had found under my bed and thoughtfully placed back in the refrigerator.

August 1951

Agnes de Mille is choreographing a new musical, *Paint Your Wagon*. I'm not in Chorus Equity so go to the "open" call. De Mille tells the men to do high kicks. I copy the ballet boys whose legs rise waist high.

"Forget classical ballet," yells de Mille. "You!" She thrusts her whole arm at me. "Can you kick over your head?" Abandoning form, I let go a series of kicks like when I tried to out-kick Mark Ryder against the Graham Studio wall.

"You see?" says de Mille loudly. To my surprise, I'm hired. After contracts are signed, chorus dancers and singers are ordered to let their beards grow.

"Is that a must?" asks a singer.

"It's a must," says stage manager Ward Bishop.

"I can't grow a beard," complains dancer Bob Morrow.

"Do you shave?"

"Just a little wisp on my chin."

"Then let your wisp grow." A month later he looks like Fu Manchu.

At the first rehearsal, Alan Lerner and Frederick Loewe sing all the songs and by lunch I'm sure we're in a hit.

I'd thought that de Mille's dancers would be superior and stuck-up and that I'd feel like a stumble-bum, but they are just as nervous as I. Agnes de Mille plays at being fierce. "Bob Morrow!" she trumpets, "if you do one more *pirouette,* I'll break both your legs."

Rehearsals are chatty and good-natured, like a quilting bee, different from Martha's, which are quiet and charged, like a chess match. Assistant Dania Krupska teaches steps, and in no time a can-can takes shape. De Mille is all over the place, changing steps, fixing formations, making cracks. She loves getting laughs.

The second day, she announces, "Pick a partner. We're going to waltz." I stand rooted until Mavis Ray, de Mille's dance captain, says, "Can you waltz?"

"No."

"I'll show you." Grabs my left hand, yanks my right arm around her waist, presses against me, and in two minutes we're whirling around the room.

After *Wagon* opens in Philadelphia, Alan Lerner calls a meeting. "The show needs work. We can do it quickly or we can do it creatively. We want to do it creatively and creatively takes time, so we'll stay out of town four more weeks." Nobody groans.

Wagon is neither smash nor flop. Many would feel jittery with a job unlikely to last more than a year, but to me, it's "security." Also, my initiation into the freemasonry of dancing "gypsies." (The word "gypsy" is frowned on these days as being disrespectful of the Roma people. So they are seeking a new word to designate Broadway dancers who go from show to show until they grow old and vanish. If you find that word, please substitute it for gypsy. Thanks.) Broadway dancers are as dynamic as Martha's and some have astonishing skills. But they dream about their careers, whereas modern dancers dream about art.

Paint Your Wagon breaks every night at 10:30, after which I stroll through Times Square, have a bite, go to Dancers' Studio, and get to sleep around 2:00 a.m. Rousing myself at 8:00 a.m. to light the gas radiators is a pain so I'm delighted when a dancer with a shining face says she'll light them if allowed to stay for an hour to do a barre. From then on, when I wake around ten, the place is toasty. One morning, up early, I see her hard at work, swathed in sweater and woolen tights against the slowly diminishing cold, face flushed and shining with sweat. Enchanting! I think about rising at nine to invite her for coffee. Luckily, I never did wake early. That part of my life is complicated enough.

I take in a stray cat which has kittens, and since people know I like cats, they bring others. Soon I have a dozen. Two litter boxes are changed daily but little used in the icy winter, and although there's no odor, I suspect that the cats have found an alternative in the freezing storage loft.

In March, the crates are removed, revealing an incredible amount of freeze-dried cat shit. I stuff it into two large shopping bags, making me late for ballet class, snatch up my dance bag plus the cat shit bags, and run toward Broadway looking for a trash can. There on the corner is my bus, no telling when the next will arrive. I jump on to meet a dancer also going to ballet class.

"Have you been shopping?"

"No."

"Costumes?"

"No."

"Well, what is all that?"

"Cat shit, actually."

After that I get a feeling she's avoiding me.

In *Paint Your Wagon,* I understudy "Pete," played by lead dancer, James Mitchell. On a Wednesday morning about two months into the run, the telephone rings at 9:00 a.m.

"James Mitchell broke his ankle last night."

I'd seen him stagger in "There's a Coach Comin' In" but am shocked to hear it's a break.

"Do you know the part?"

"That's what you pay me for," wondering if I really know it.

"Be at the theater by eleven to work with Gemze."

Gemze de Lappe, a de Mille stalwart, is the female dance lead. Her duet with Mitchell is not technically hard except for one flying catch. She throws herself into the air feet first, her right foot lands on his hip at the same instant that they catch hands. She is held horizontal for a double spin then set softly on her feet. In rehearsal it goes well. I call Martha to tell her I'm going on for James Mitchell.

"Can you get me a ticket?"

"Yes!"

House seats are held until a half hour before curtain, first few rows dead center, best in the house. I get one for Martha.

As the romantic lead, Mitchell was exempted from a beard, so I shave mine. The costume mistress offers me Mitchell's costume, but it seems ghoulish so I dance in my baggy roughneck pants with shirt and vest of mismatched plaids. After the matinee, Martha sends a note backstage:

Stuart,

You are dancing the romantic lead and cannot appear in baggy pants. Tonight, you will wear pants so tight, everyone in the theater will be able to count your buttocks. Martha

Next day Agnes de Mille says, "It's fine, Stuart. Now just relax."

I feel perfectly relaxed yet she says it again, "Stuart, relax." After six weeks it is certain that Mitchell will not return. He's a Broadway principal with "billing."[6] I'm in my first musical. Yet as I see it, no one can dance Pete as well as I. One night, Ward Bishop hands me a message to meet de Mille in the Astor Bar next day. *(Uh-oh!)* Were I getting the part, he'd hand me a contract. Sure enough, de Mille is saying I do the role well, yet she wants a dancer with more Broadway experience.

"Miss de Mille. Can I ask one question?"

"Yes."

"Is it a matter of looks?" James Mitchell, a cross between James Mason and Gary Cooper, is one of the best-looking men on Broadway.

"No."

"In that case, nobody you get will be as good as me."

"I'm glad you feel that way. And I hope you'll stay on as understudy."

She hires Scott Merrill, whose Broadway credits include Curly in *Oklahoma*. He's a confident dancer with a breezy style and smiles a lot. De Mille's words come back: "Stuart, relax." I'd been dancing Pete like the Dark Beloved in *Deaths and Entrances* (think Heathcliff in *Wuthering Heights*). No one (except Martha) could have made me understand that one does not dance like that on Broadway. But when Graham had her 1951 season, de Mille called producer Cheryl Crawford, who gave me an unprecedented week off to dance with Martha.

August 1952

Martha had helped Juilliard start its dance division and is now rehearsing there, a new work based on St. Francis of Assisi, "the nature saint." Bertram Ross and Yuriko are Brother Sun and Sister Moon.[7] Helen McGehee is Sister Water, Mary Hinkson, Sister Earth, Pearl Lang, Sister Death. I'm Brother Fire. Bob Cohan with Helen McGehee are Stars, and in a separate duet, he and Matt Turney are Wind. A star cluster is danced by Patricia Birch, Miriam Cole, Dorothy Krooks, and Linda Margolies (soon to be Linda Hodes).

Scattered around the stage are abstract wooden flats, curves, steps, and a hinged door in a frame. They were designed by architect Frederick Kiesler for student operas, and Martha uses them. *Canticles* begins with the Sun/Moon dance, an adagio duet. As Brother Sun, Bertram Ross dances in a curved standing Kiesler piece. Yuriko, Sister Moon, is at his feet, reflecting his moves. Mary Hinkson as Sister Earth, bears a flowering branch, sits cross-legged, rises to circle the stage with soft leaps.

The score is by Tom Ribbink, a talented musician with a desperate need to dance but wracked by physical tension. When he plays for classes the tension explodes in crashing chords and smashing arpeggios. At top volume, which is all of the time, he drowns out the teacher. It's like having a ravening wild animal at the piano, but no one asks him to quiet down. One day at the Neighborhood Playhouse, he's too fast. I stop, give him the tempo, to have him say tightly, "That exercise should be taught faster."

Canticles for Innocent Comedians, opening performance, Juilliard. Photographer unknown; frame capture from the author's personal collection.

Tom knows that tempo is the teacher's prerogative and has deliberately crossed the line. I stroll over, whisper into his ear. "As soon as I finish speaking, get up and leave. If you don't, I will yank you off this bench and throw you out in front of everyone." Tom leaves.

Tom's *Canticles* score starts with the Sun/Moon duet. But Martha does not regard it as an opening. One day, she has us shove all the set pieces into center stage, places us among them, and, on her signal, has us push them silently off the stage, except for the piece used in the Sun/Moon duet. It's striking and needs music, but Tom likes his musical opening and refuses to write another. A week before the premiere, a Juilliard professor, Paul Goodman, suggests a timpani beat, demonstrates, and Martha likes it. Ribbink is infuriated by what he sees as violation of his score and is further enraged when Bertram Ross, with whom he shares a loft, tries to explain Martha's side. While Bertram is rehearsing, Ribbink takes Bertram's suits, sweaters, slacks, and sport jackets to a dry cleaner, then moves out leaving the slips. To get his clothes, Bertram has to pay a huge cleaning bill.

Antony Tudor sometimes watches while Martha is making *Canticles*. One day, "Do you take ballet classes?"

"Yes."

"Why have you never taken my class at the Met?"

"Don't you teach only advanced?"

"You won't have a problem."

The Met's huge studio has a two-story ceiling with a high balcony where people watch. Bambi Linn takes Tudor's class, a flashing figure despite thunder thighs that can't be reduced by dieting. But in September she'd appeared with thighs slender as reeds. A gossip column gushes, "Bambi Linn, back in New York City with elegantly slender legs." No one knows how she did it.

The first day I take Tudor's class, after the *barre*, students arrange themselves for center work, women traditionally in front. He approaches a woman.

"My dear, I can't possibly teach the rest of this class with you under my nose, so move to the rear." Sobbing, face buried in her hands, she moves to the rear.

Inspired by Tudor's presence, I uncover unexpected resources. He gives a combination that ends with "free" *pirouettes*—time to do as many as you can. I'm usually good for three to the right, two to the left, but somehow I'm doing eight to the right, five to the left. A few days later, at Juilliard, he says, "I didn't know you could do twelve *pirouettes*."

It's a partial dig because he knows exactly how many I did.

"Only in your class, Mr. Tudor," which, unfortunately, is true. *Pirouettes* beyond four were never dependably mine. Also, in Tudor's class I achieve my first *double tour en l'air*.

One day I meet him in my neighborhood on his way to the Zen Institute. He tells me he is timekeeper.

"What's a timekeeper?"

"I tell people when to stop meditating."

"How long do they meditate?"

"An hour."

"Do you use a clock?"

"No."

"How do you know when an hour is up?"

"When I decide it is."

"Do you ever run over?"

"Only when I notice that they want to stop."

One day he asks if I take ballet class every day.

"You only teach Monday, Wednesday, and Friday."

"Margaret Craske teaches Tuesday and Thursday."

He's head of the Met school so I show up in Craske's class. She ignores me so thoroughly that when she approaches after class, I know it is trouble.

"Who gave you permission to take my class?"

"Mr. Tudor."

"Your placement is wrong. You are not ready for my class."

"Sorry. I won't take it again."

"Take Mr. Corvino's class. He will tell you when you are ready to return to mine."

Eventually I do study with Alfredo Corvino, a great teacher, but I will not be caught in a turf battle between ballet dreadnoughts and never do take another Craske class.

A movie is being made about Helen Keller, and the director wants to show how she perceives dance. Martha sets a rehearsal of moves from *Canticles*. Keller and Martha appear at the studio door as timpanist Paul Goodman is tuning with evenly timed beats. Keller can feel the vibrations and marks them with her hands. Martha guides her to the drums and places her hand on a drumhead.

Martha steers Keller from one dancer to another. She places Keller's hand upon Helen's McGehee's at the *barre*, Keller moves her hand up Helen's arm to her shoulder, over her head, down her back, to her leg. When Helen and Bob dance together, Martha carefully inserts Keller into the action. My entrance as Fire is a leap up onto a set piece, thence into the air. Martha places Keller by the curving flat where I land, and in the two seconds I hold, her hand brushes my foot before I leap into space. When we speak to Keller, her interpreter translates our words into her kinetic hand language, to which Keller replies in her own voice. She radiates glory into a world she has never seen or heard.

At the start of *Errand into the Maze*, a woman stands wracked by fear, evoked by shattering Contractions. Almost all Martha's falls begin with

Left to right: Miriam Cole, Patricia Birch, Linda Hodes, Martha, Helen Keller reaching toward me as I balance on a set piece of *Canticles for Innocent Comedians*. Courtesy of Helen Keller Tribute Channel.

a Contraction, which strikes before the body sinks to earth. Contraction can go into almost any move or context; Bisons first appeared as a Contraction at the top of a Stag Jump. (I vividly recall it because I was the one who had suggested putting a Contraction there.) The Pitch Turn of *Night Journey* became a Cave Turn when a Contraction was added for *Cave of the Heart*. It is called a Cave Turn because it is done in *Cave of the Heart*, not because the upper body is "caved." *New York Times* critic Anna Kisselgoff, pretending to expertise, got it wrong criticizing Christine Dakin for not doing a Cave Turn in *Night Journey*, when she was correctly doing a Pitch Turn.

Martha Graham does onstage what great preachers do in pulpits—stir emotion, inspire revelation, generate rebirth. It's said that she disliked being called the "high priestess" of modern dance, but I wonder? Her idol was always Ruth St. Denis, farm girl Ruthie Dennis who set out to become a goddess and made it. Martha, too, projects mystery and relishes those who say she's changed their lives. It is said that Miss Ruth almost rejected Martha because she wasn't a long-legged sylph. Ted Shawn became Martha's champion, yet it is Miss Ruth whom she loves.

Martha does not have the statuesque beauty of Ruth St. Denis, Doris Humphrey, or Helen Tamiris, or the sleek gams for which dancers are admired. She always covers her legs with a skirt. But she has a powerful back, soaring leg extensions, and extra-long tendons allowing her to slip easily through the rigorous moves of her technique. And a great jump. Sasha says it wowed audiences at Radio City Music Hall when she was the Chosen One in Léonide Massine's *Rite of Spring*.

She also has "attack," the dance equivalent of a cymbal crash, the sprinter's "fast twitch," called "burst" in football. Pauline Koner is also noted for attack. I once hear Doris Humphrey say, "She has bite, that one." Yet Koner is simply not as interesting as Martha, who also has depth, complexity, humor, and charm. Many deem Martha beautiful (me too!) yet not pretty. In any case, looks are not why people, including me, love to be around her. That doesn't change even after I learn she can be impossible, as Edith Piaf must have been impossible, and (I imagine) Amy Winehouse or Carrie Nation.

I like everything about the Graham Studio: dancers, classes, rehearsing, yet it is Martha who binds me. Even after I start ballet classes, I cannot imagine *dancing* ballet or with any other modern troupe. I very much admire tap dancing and take tap classes, knowing I'll never be as good as I wish.

In 1958, I was hired by The Latin Quarter, a nightclub, which required fingerprinting at police headquarters. They listed my occupation: "Entertainer." I don't hesitate to tell people I'm a dancer although I would have felt pompous calling myself an "artist." As for entertainers, they sing, tell jokes, and single-handedly keep audiences happy. I'm flattered.

The studio at 66 Fifth Avenue is surrounded by Mills College of Education, where young women study to become elementary school teachers. Classrooms above and below, their locker room on our floor across the hall. Between classes, Mills students outside make a huge racket. One day the hall erupts with laughing and shrieking. Martha waits. At last, after repeated slamming of doors, they are gone. Martha says, darkly, "They can't be loved. They can only be petted."

In the Graham Studio's tiny foyer office, Martha is on the pay telephone. "Well, if I ever do a musical, Guthrie, I promise it will be for you," hangs up, goes into the studio.

I shoot a questioning glance at Sasha who says that Broadway producer Guthrie McClintic is trying to get Martha to choreograph a musical.

"She should. We'll all have jobs."

"And who will dance in her company?"

A similar dilemma comes up after three national tours booked by Charles E. Green. She refused a fourth, saying that touring leaves her no time for creative work. Green suggested a separate road company while she stays in New York doing creative work.

"Do I send out my best dancers and keep my second-best to work with? Or do I send out my second-best for audiences to see?"

This is hogwash because there are enough dancers at the studio for two companies *plus* a Broadway show. The real reasons are (1) Martha cannot abide anyone else dancing *her* roles, (2) she doesn't want her dances being performed where she cannot personally oversee them, and (3) on Broadway, choreographers work under directors and Martha works *under* no one.

November 1950

I audition for a shared concert at the 92nd Street Y, showing a solo to Doris Humphrey. Before dancing, I hand her a program note:

FLAK
FLAK is the acronym for *fliegerabwehrkanone,*
German for anti-aircraft gunfire.
Music by Bela Bartok

Doris Humphrey likes it but says I'll need two more dances.

"I have two more ideas," I say. She puts me on with Nona Schurman and Midi Garth.

My opening dance is titled *DRIVE.* Then *Surrounding, Unknown,* with three sections: "Star," "Earth," "Life in a Water Drop." *FLAK* is last.

Martha and Erick come. I don't expect nor do I get a formal critique, but both are approving and Erick says he'd particularly liked my star dance.

FLAK. Multiexposure photo by Alfred Gescheidt.

One day after rehearsal, some company dancers admit that they take ballet classes. "José Limón takes a ballet class every day," says Pearl Lang.

Martha, hotly: "He should not waste his precious energy competing with little boys."

"Oh Martha, he's not competing. He just wants a workout."

When the Ford Foundation announced a multimillion-dollar grant to the New York City Ballet to help it establish satellite troupes all over the U.S.A., we ask Martha why it is ignoring modern dance, an indigenous American form.

"They believe classical ballet can be sold to the public."

"Do you think it can?"

"Yes."

Erick Hawkins and Martha Graham at Bennington College, 1941. Photo by Hans Knopf. Courtesy of Jacob's Pillow Archives.

According to Agnes de Mille,[8] Martha met Erick Hawkins in 1936 at Bennington College where he'd arrived with a classical troupe called Ballet Caravan. De Mille describes Martha as helplessly smitten by the arrogant male who is instantly hated by her all-female troupe. Erick did provoke resentment, but it was because Martha gave him authority once exclusively hers, and over dancers who knew her work far better than he.

But if the early troupe begrudged Erick's emotional hold on Martha, those who followed were put off by his blundering style. The instant the curtain comes down, he blurts out corrections, although one may need to get ready for the next dance, or, if the night's work is over, get away and let down. Martha is never brought into it. Any hint of a problem with Erick would cause an explosion, although explosions happen anyway. From Barbara Bennion's memoir, circa 1950:

Sometimes company members worked in Erick's studio a few blocks up Fifth Avenue. One day several of us were there helping him make masks. He loved masks. His enthusiasm could be irritating but that day he was so happy I could forgive him. Erick asked me to stay for a few minutes after the others left for rehearsal. I didn't think anything of it. He was the boss. Perhaps I remained fifteen minutes to help pack up. Then I walked back down to Martha's studio. Rehearsal had already begun. Martha heard me come in and marched into the dressing room, confronting me in a rage.

"Where have you been?"

"With Erick," I answered innocently.

"What were you doing?"

She looked crazy and began pacing like a caged leopard.

"We were making masks," I said, my throat going dry.

"I won't have a girl like you in my company," she yelled, baring her teeth. "Get out! Get out of here!"

I suddenly realized she thought something personal had been going on between Erick and me. How preposterous. I felt sorry for her. I wanted to put my arms around her.

"Why Martha, I never thought of Erick as anything but my teacher and your husband." (I wanted to say that most of us thought she'd married a horse's ass.)

"I won't have it. Don't come back," she snapped and swept out of the room.

I stood for a moment, heart pounding, then picked up my things and walked out to the elevator. Martha was there. She didn't look at me. We waited together—a bit of unplanned drama—both stepped into the elevator and didn't look at each other. Silence. I walked down Fifth Avenue and Martha hurried in the opposite direction.

I decided to disappear for three days. Later I heard that Martha asked Marjorie Mazia to replace me, but Marjorie had refused. On the third day I received a call from Martha asking me to meet her for lunch at an uptown restaurant. Dancers were "downtown people," so I assumed she was trying avoid us being seen. It was an awkward meeting and we both were nervous. She told me that Erick had been embarrassed, and had convinced her it was all a misunderstanding. Then she asked me to rejoin the company and I said yes.

After Erick Hawkins bolted from Martha at the end of the disastrous 1950 European tour, he, too, started to build his own technique. With Martha, his choreography had her imprint, but on his own, his dances gained distinctive character. Both he and Martha placed the human being at the center, but where Martha made the body a *source* of energy striking outward, Erick made it a *receiver* of energy flowing from the universe. It yielded a completely original style and gave his dances their own "Hawkins" character.

While performing, Hawkins might suddenly hold up his leg or forearm, peering at it with a startled expression, as if to say, "How amazing. What a miracle!" Martha strove to capture the extraordinary, while Erick strove to reveal the ordinary as extraordinary.

Beverly Brown, ex–Hawkins Company, taught a distinctive gliding Hawkins walk. One of her students, Bill Kleinsmith, was cast as an automobile in a student dance about cars.[9] To the sound of a speeding auto engine, he did his Hawkins walk around the stage.

"Look" said another student, "A Hawkins car."

For its annual Christmas Course and Summer Intensive, the Graham School attracts college dance majors and teachers. On the first day, forty or so collect in the studio, Martha enters and asks each student's name and hometown. Years later, one may show up backstage after a performance, and, before she can introduce herself, Martha will say quietly, "Jane Smith" (or whomever), leaving her deeply flattered. She tosses off this little gift with casual ease.

In 1972, heading dance at NYU School of the Arts, I ask every incoming student to send a headshot, mount them on my office wall, and study the faces all summer so that in September, like Martha, I can greet each by name.

Martha tells about an eight-year-old girl in her children's classes, a lovely child with extraordinarily beautiful feet.

"When I complimented the mother on her child's feet, she said that her daughter had been born with club feet. Doctors said she could be operated on when older, but from the day she was born, the mother massaged the tiny feet for hours each day. By the time the child walked, they were perfect."

Martha spoke of her Victorian grandmother who forbade her to sit with her legs together. To her grandmother, the only proper condition for a young girl is utter innocence, so she had to keep her knees naively apart in polite company.

She also told about a performance at an exclusive women's club in the Deep South. At the front door, a butler told her to go to a rear entrance.

"I returned straight to my hotel, called up the best limousine service in town, and asked for two drivers in full livery. When I returned, I rang the front doorbell, and when it opened, marched by the butler without giving him a glance, and straight through their party, liveried servants in tow. Those southern aristocrats understood exactly what I was doing and didn't dare stop me."[10]

Martha never raised her voice. When very angry, she seemed to hiss. Once in rehearsal, two men carrying women about to crash, she uttered a sort of croak, the loudest sound I ever heard her make. Yet at any party or gathering there would come a moment when every voice was hushed, every ear straining to hear her words.

In some ways, Agnes de Mille was like Martha: brainy, with looks that turned no heads. But where de Mille tried to bowl you over with clever cracks and outrageous hyperbole, Martha mesmerized with subtle insights and revealing metaphors. Both enjoyed center stage, but de Mille always seemed to be listening to herself, while Martha focused on her listeners. Both believed in the ennobling act of performance. One of de Mille's quotes:

> When you perform you are out of yourself—larger and more potent, more beautiful. You are for minutes heroic. This is glory on earth. And it is yours nightly.

De Mille was describing "magic time," likely speaking to dancers in one of her long-running shows. The Graham troupe seldom performed enough to call it "nightly."

In the dancing chorus of *By the Beautiful Sea,* as our cue neared, dance captain Arthur Partington heaved himself out of his chair, shouted, "Magic time, children!" Conversations, chess games, reading, knitting, etc., stopped. Hearts sped up and we dashed onstage for "magic time."

Magic time, an all-consuming blaze of being, can happen to pilots in the air. I believe that for most creatures—butterflies to eagles, earthworms to elephants—something akin to magic time is how they live their entire lives. (I will not claim it cannot happen to plants. In the words of Walt Whitman, a live oak is "uttering joyous leaves of dark green.") Only in humankind is it vanishingly special. In its place we have another miracle—sentience, which generates self-awareness, also self-consciousness. We spend our lives desperately self-conscious, yet sometimes aware that a world entirely beyond our little selves exists.

I once heard Martha say, "There are no roles for virgins in my company." Another time, "Virginity is a state of mind; it has nothing to do with sex." This seems to be two entirely different kinds of virginity.

The evening rehearsal begins at 8:00 p.m., and usually breaks before 11. But one night it goes to midnight. Martha sets her schedule book on the floor and begins to figure out the next day. Suddenly she looks up, reaches out a hand, and makes small whispering sounds. A tiny mouse crouches by the wall. It moves toward Martha, stops, turns back, reaches the wall, and in no hurry, heads for the dressing rooms.

"He can't understand why we're still here," says Martha. "It's his turn now."

We were discussing Martha's onstage focus. She never quite looked you in the eye, but didn't look past you either. One day Dorothea Douglas asked where she focused when dancing with another.

"Well, I don't take a bead on you. What I do is envision my world with you at its center."

A "Wow" answer, but I never try it.

One day Dorothea Douglas asked Martha how she felt about her imitators.

"I want to be first and I want to be best. After that, the world can take what it pleases."

First and *best*. As an enthusiastic competitor, I recognize a fierce one. But Martha also said, "A dancer competes only with the image of the ideal dancer she wishes to become." Competing with an ideal, there is no way to win.

Merce Cunningham was the most virtuosic male dancer Martha ever had, and considering the roles he created—March in *Letter to the World*,

Revivalist in *Appalachian Spring*, Pegasus in *Punch and the Judy*, Aerialist in *Every Soul Is a Circus*—Martha liked to exhibit that virtuosity. Mark Ryder said that Merce did not like it. After leaving Martha, influenced by ideas of John Cage, chance, "aleatory" music, and the *Book of Changes*, among others, he rejected virtuosity. *New York Times* critic Anna Kisselgoff once told me she heard Martha say, "Merce was the best male dancer I ever had, until he got *theories*."

Bonnie Bird, in the Graham Company in the 1930s, told me that Martha respected Isadora Duncan but disdained college courses termed "Duncan Dancing." When *New York Times* dance critic John Martin was at Bennington writing about college dance, he came to breakfast one morning with a letter from a dean saying that her college should be included, and to prove it, sent a catalog that listed "Duncan Dancing." Among the sweaters, socks, and underwear the girls had to take to school, was "three yards of chiffon for self-expression."

"That was the kind of thing Martha hated," said Bonnie.

Whenever I am asked about the difference between modern dance and ballet, I flounder. Tony Charmoli's "In ballet you do two and three turns, in modern dance you only do one turn" has a kernel of truth. Paul Taylor, in his biography, relates the answer he gave in Tokyo: "You know ballet? Well, modern dance is just the same, but uglier."[11] Bob Cohan told me that he overheard Paul saying to a rapt young woman in Manila: "There's no difference. Modern dance is just 'more grotesque.'"

In the early 1900s, a young woman with beauty, talent, and no dance training could don a sari, grass skirt, or houri pants, call herself an "exotic dancer," and dance in vaudeville. Ruthie Dennis, born on a New Jersey farm, became Ruth St. Denis who made dancing into a sacred art. Dance "technique" existed only in imported forms, so when she and Ted Shawn created Denishawn, they brought in teachers of Spanish dance, East Indian forms, and classical ballet. Martha Graham boasted that she'd mastered every ballet move except *entrechat*. Graham is said to have broken away from classical ballet, but I believe she really broke away from Denishawn and its adaptions of exotic forms when she started to build the rigorous discipline termed Graham Technique. Like ballet, her dances had structure and virtuosity, separated performer from audience, told stories, and aroused emotions. The moves, of course, were her own and excitingly original.

In 1933, Martha was speaking in a seminar at The New School in

Manhattan when a man in the audience rose. "Miss Graham, you must admit that modern dance is ugly." It was famed classical choreographer Michel Fokine.

"Yes, it is," she replied, "if you're living in 1890."[12]

Paul Taylor made *The Rehearsal*, to Stravinsky's Rite of Spring, entirely out of "archaic" moves. This flattens the body toward the front, like figures in an Egyptian frieze. I saw its first performance from standing room at the back of the theater; Paul was a few feet to my left. When it ended, he turned to me. "Now I think I'll make a pretty dance. You know, instead of an ugly one."

Defining archaic as "ugly" is just Paul being a tease. I deem *The Rehearsal* to be the greatest dance made in the twentieth century.

Bodies come in three types: ectomorph—reedy, like Merce Cunningham, Lucas Hoving, and Robert Cohan; mesomorph—regular, like José Limón, Erick Hawkins, and me; and endomorph—stocky, like Carl Roemer and Betty Osgood of the Humphrey-Weidman troupe, and Irving Burton, famously of the Paper Bag Players.

Martha herself, small, with rounded thighs, always starving herself, would be an endomorph were she not Martha Graham. Photos of Martha's early troupe show women more voluptuous than later.

In 1949, Ballet Theatre's *corps de ballet* was dubbed "the beef trust" but soon slimmed down, likely not wanting to suffer comparison with the New York City Ballet, whose cadaverous *corps,* reflecting the not-so-sublimated hankerings of George Balanchine, became a standard. Lincoln Kirstein boasted that the New York City Ballet had "one body."

Merce Cunningham, after starting with Graham mesomorphs Natanya Neumann, Joan Skinner, and Anneliese Widman, built a company as gaunt as Balanchine's. Martha's troupe also slimmed down in the 1950s. But by the 1970s, a new generation of choreographers was rebelling against the mainstream, which included a grudging Martha Graham. The new generation used dancers once disdained because of their body types. Bill T. Jones used Lawrence Goldhuber, a clean, powerful dancer in his linebacker's body. Others break the age taboo, putting elderly dancers back onstage, including this chronicler. Perhaps they influenced Stephen Sondheim, whose 1971 musical *Follies* puts a dance team nearing fifty— Victor Griffin and Jayne Turner—into a number that brings down the

Lawrence Goldhuber. Photo by James Schreibel. Courtesy of Lawrence Goldhuber and James Schreibl.

house. Revived in 2001, two septuagenarians, Donald Saddler and Marge Champion, stop the show.

The Baroness Bethsabée de Rothschild, of the French Rothschilds, is Martha's patron. She bought a building at 316 East 63rd Street and in a dazzling act of Old World patronage, presented it to Martha. Before the sale, Martha asked Bob, Bertram, and me to meet her at the ivy-covered, three-story brick building. On either side were overgrown gardens enclosed by high wrought-iron fences. We entered a warped wooden door, passed through a long foyer cluttered with broken furniture, entered a large room where Martha and Bethsabée were waiting. Along one wall was a jumble of steel tables, wash basins, and battered pots and pans.

Exterior of 316 East 63rd St. in 1952. Photo by Stuart Hodes.

Bethsabée murmured that the debris would be removed and the column in the middle of the room replaced by a beam. We were not asked for advice or opinions, there simply to help Martha imagine herself in the space. Presently she said, "I can work here."

The big room was quickly cleared, new flooring laid where the kitchen had been. The rest, varnished rock maple, needed only scraping. Bob Cohan and I volunteered. We rented a sander and an edger, started at dawn and finished around four. Martha arrived, startled to see us covered with wood dust. Next day we put down penetrating seal and when it dried, Studio One was ready.

Studio Two was on the third (top) floor, narrow yet long, with windows on three sides. Its sturdy green battleship linoleum floor needed only a good washing. Studio Three, on the ground floor, smaller than the others, was left unfinished for a few months. With my own Dancers' Studio about to feel the wrecker's ball, my sturdy old upright piano was trucked to 63rd Street and put into it. There were also spacious dressing rooms with showers, offices, closets, a kitchenette, faculty lounge, costume room, and a tiny private room for Martha.

Martha showed neighborhood police around, including the kitchen, a pot of hot coffee always on the stove, above it a cabinet with a bottle of whisky, saying, "It can get very cold in this neighborhood."

Studio One was a generous forty by fifty-five feet, but just off-center was a weight-bearing column. Martha gave combinations that circled it. One day she cried out: "It *draws* like the pole of a magnet! Everything is forced to radiate from it!"

Bethsabée waited until we were in Europe, and when we returned, a huge I-beam was on the floor, soon hoisted into place, the roof rebuilt, and the beam plastered over. The ceiling was lower at the beam but not enough to endanger even the highest jumper.

A tiny walkway across the ceiling, reached by a vertical wall ladder, got half a dozen stage lights, and, with the addition of Noguchi benches three to eight inches high, and Nakashima chairs and stools, three and four feet high, fifty people could watch as though in a raked theater. Studio One was now worthy of the powerful creative spirit that reigned there.

Luckily the garden was large because half was owned by the city, and soon a high wall is built for a feeder road from the 59th Street Bridge. Yet the remaining half, carefully tended, offers leafy peace, and graced receptions for honored guests like the Peking Opera dancers on their first visit to New York City.

The garden at 316 East 63rd St. Photo by Stuart Hodes.

A bookkeeper at the Graham School gets it into her head that I owe the school eighty-five dollars. She sends a bill. After two weeks, a second bill, then a call saying I have to pay up. "Okay, I'll put it in the mail."

I make out a bill to the Graham School, $150 for the player piano I'd given to Studio Two, minus the $85 I supposedly owe. Balance, $65. *Please remit.* Never hear another word.

Theater for a Voyage, 1952

A mansion sits on the edge of a desert. On its terrace a man and a woman, escaped from a partying throng within, face one another. The dance is for Martha, Bertram Ross, Bob Cohan, and me, and as it unfolds, time melts.

Martha often manipulated time: the whole of *Night Journey* takes place in the instant Jocasta takes her own life. She also manipulates contexts, once telling us about a performance of *Deaths and Entrances,* "after which a society matron berated her: "A woman in a taffeta evening gown does not roll on the floor."

"Yes, that is true," Martha replied. "But have you never heard something said, at a party or by someone you love, that makes the very soul within you reel and fall, as though to the floor? The woman turned pale, excused herself, and left."

Soon each of us has a character, Bob a creative principal, Bertram a beloved, I a demon. I liken us to the Hindu trinity: Bob as Brahma, the Creator; Bertram as Vishnu, the Preserver; I as Shiva, the Destroyer. I don't mention this to Martha, not that I couldn't have.

Martha commissions a set from Isamu Noguchi, and it arrives in two parts. Center stage is a high arch, portal of the house, perhaps. But the other is unmistakably a ship.

Bob Cohan: "Why did he build a ship when you asked for a desert?"

Martha: "Isamu sees the sea as a kind of desert."

Me: "But one represents life, the other, death."

Martha: "To the Japanese, life and death are the same."

Soon we're clambering all over the ship, which to me, resembles a deck chair. Progress is slow. Martha says, "If I've done my work outside of the studio, I never have a problem finding movement. When I seem to be having trouble with movement, the *fallacy* was there before I entered the studio."

Noguchi set, *Theater for a Voyage*. Photo by Kevin Noble. Courtesy of the Noguchi Museum.

Sometimes Martha will arrive to say, "I think I've found the *fallacy*," and return to some earlier point, there to seek a new way toward her powerfully felt yet shrouded vision.

Years later when Martha's *Notebooks*[13] were published, they reveal her thoughts:

> One—sees her as a Goddess to be placated and paralleled in all things—(Bob)
> One—sees her as one to do battle with (Stuart)
> One—sees her as part of his own being (Bert)
> Each man changes into a costume denoting his aspect of mankind—
> Bob—the Youth-
> Stuart—Don Juan pirate matador (if so he can use cape?)
> ?perhaps he also has dagger—& it is a duel—
> Bert—Orpheus?

I slam the book shut, not ready for a look into Martha's thoughts. Eventually I realized why I had not wanted to look. Martha had been trying to make a dance from our *actual relationships*.

Bertram "sees her as part of his own being." Apt, considering his selfless ability to give her concentrated attention every minute of long rehearsals. For years.

Bob's "goddess to be placated" intrigues me. When Bob left for England, he wrote Martha a letter to which she once referred: "Bob is very put out with me."

My role *as "one to do battle with"* is no surprise, considering our blow-ups. Yet I find battles disturbing, and eventually they are a factor in my departure. I certainly don't think of my relationship with Martha as *defined* by our battles. I tell myself that Martha's thinking is theatrical, or, to use an academic word, reductive. Our actual relationship is certainly more complex.

Progress is slow. Martha seems willing to try a hundred moves to find the right one. After a long rehearsal in which only one move is found, she'll say, "Well, we found one little treasure today."

She wants us in formal attire, so we're fitted for dinner jackets. Bob's is dark green, Bertram's midnight blue, mine maroon. In a primal moment each man removes jacket and shirt to dance in bare-chested savagery, donning the jacket again—a civilized veneer—at the end. The title is *Theater for a Voyage*.

April 23, 1952

Theater for a Voyage premieres at Juilliard. Reviews, from puzzled to disappointed, don't concern Martha. *Cave of the Heart*, *Errand into the Maze*, and *Diversion of Angels* had been deeply reworked after their premieres. She returns to the studio.

Rehearsals start at noon, after the 10:30 a.m. technique class. As before, progress is slow. One day Martha says, "The studio is so busy, it breaks my concentration."

Me: "Why don't we come in early?"

Bob: "You mean before the 10:30 class?"

Me: "Yes." I have nine o'clock in mind, giving us an hour and a half to work.

Martha: "All right, let's try it. Maybe it will give us a new perspective," and schedules rehearsal for eight.

"You and your big mouth," says Bertram.

"I never dreamed she'd call such an early rehearsal."

Next morning at eight Martha is there, coffee perking. The studio is quiet, sunlight a different color and from a different angle. For the second "premiere," she changes the name to *Voyage*, but again, the reception is cool. That alone would never cause Martha to abandon a dance, yet she puts it beyond recovery when the "deck chair" becomes a ship sailing the Aegean Sea commanded by Bertram Ross as Odysseus and Clive Thompson as Pilot, who reach the island of the Sirens where they fall under the spell of Circe—Mary Hinkson—reclining delectably on top of the *Voyage* arch. *Circe* is an immediate hit.

Yet I will always think of that arch and that "deck chair" as *Voyage*, and those months of rehearsals as one of the great adventures of my life.

April 14–26, 1953, Alvin Theater, New York, New York

Bethsabée produces a gala for eight troupes: Martha Graham, Doris Humphrey, José Limón, May O'Donnell, Nina Fonaroff, Pearl Lang, Helen McGehee, and Merce Cunningham. It's my first chance to dance the Husbandman in *Appalachian Spring*, as fine a role as I can imagine.

Canticles for Innocent Comedians, is scored for small orchestra plus baritone. Helen McGehee has a new trailing fishnet costume that evokes a mermaid and turns "Water" into a magical solo. *Canticles* is a success, and Frederick Kiesler is praised for a brilliant set. His units have been at Juilliard for years but not until Martha used them did the world notice.

Merce Cunningham gets puzzled respect for *Sixteen Dances for Soloist and Company of Three.* His dancing is stunning and so are his dancers, Graham stalwarts Natanya Neumann and Joan Skinner, with Anneliese Widman, (the fine dancer Martha irritably rejected because she wore tearose lingerie).

Helen McGehee presents *La Intrusa,* about Spanish gypsies to whom the fires of life are always close to death. Miriam Cole and I are the couple, and Helen is Death—La Intrusa. Her dance is brave and good.

Backstage is a modern dance convention. Martha does her bit, yet we all know she would have much preferred her own New York City season.

August 1953, Jacob's Pillow, Lee, Massachusetts

I'm there to dance in Gilbert Reed's *Shropshire Lad.* Antony Tudor had recommended me along with a brilliant eighteen-year-old named Sallie

Wilson. Ted Shawn invites Reed and troupe to dinner on a screened-in second-floor sunporch. We arrive in our summer best and after we're seated he appears, beefy in a white terrycloth bathrobe. He's distracted and seems vaguely annoyed.

I saw away at a slab of dry gristle, noticing that Shawn is just pushing his food around. He answers questions about Jacob's Pillow, sometimes referring to himself as "Papa Shawn," expresses no interest in Gilbert Reed, any of us, or the dance we're there to do. Before we leave the Pillow, we see him perform. In *Dervish*, he turns in place for about four minutes. In *O Brother Sun and Sister Moon*, the rear of the theater opens, making the moist greenery outside part of the setting.

Ted Shawn is a decent dancer but a very poor host.

September 1950

On the small dining table in my loft are lighted candles and goblets of wine. As Linda and I sit to dinner, there's a knock at the door. Carla Mc-Bride stands in the doorway holding the tools I'd left at her apartment. She looks past me at the candlelit scene to meet Linda's curious gaze.

"Here are your tools," hands them over, and flees. Months later I hear that she'd gone to Alaska, but never see her again.

Martha has a book of paintings by Leonor Fini. We gather round. Fini paints ominous women called *Sphingi* (Sphinxes). Martha pauses at a nude female with an exploding mane of hair, cradling the head of a nude adolescent male asleep at her breast, his flaccid penis lying limply between his legs. "You can see what she thinks of men," says Martha.

Martha, Bertram Ross, Bob Cohan, and I are in a taxi heading uptown on our way to rehearsal. Martha speaks about not dividing one's focus. I'm half listening until I hear, "for instance, one should not smoke while going to the bathroom."

Lincoln Center is only cleared acreage when *LIFE Magazine* decides to photograph artists likely to perform in its theaters. Martha returned from the shoot saying that among the notables was the Metropolitan Opera director, Sir Rudolf Bing, who spotted an idle tractor, climbed up, sat in the seat, and would not budge. Said Martha, "He was letting us know who will be in the driver's seat."

March 12, 1953

Linda and I marry at Temple Emanuel. Martha attends. It's Friday and in a rush of generosity she offers us the weekend off. On Saturday she calls to ask if we can possibly rehearse on Sunday.

Why, sure.

The Baroness Bethsabée de Rothschild, small, thin, with a slight stoop, always in a dark suit and sensible shoes, is as modest a multimillionaire as one can imagine. Her blue eyes bulge slightly, one a bit smaller than the other, and she has an occasional tic. Yet, if her expression had not held such a plea to be unnoticed, her pale face would be pretty. She speaks in a quavering voice, with a scuffling French accent that forces you to listen closely. Her marriage to Donald Bloomingdale ended after the birth of an afflicted child who lived only a few hours. Her response to that deep personal tragedy was to fund research to study birth defects.

It's a mistake to think Martha needed only Bethsabée's money. She also needed Bethsabée's need. "The only thing I can offer Bethsabée is success in the eyes of her friends. Money isn't success to them. They've had it for generations. But spending it well is difficult. If I have a successful season, Bethsabée is congratulated by her friends."

Martha also becomes Bethsabée's big sister. "I told her she simply cannot dress as she does. All her things are made for her and are of finest quality, but I'm going to get her to a designer. She must accept the fact that she's a de Rothschild."

She tells us how Bethsabée had escaped the Nazis by walking out of Paris in the dead of night. Some members of her famous family perished, but most survived and their property was returned.

Bethsabée often shows up at the studio after rehearsal to take Martha to dinner and was there on the day that company photos for the souvenir booklet arrived. Bob Cohan showed them to her.

"Dorothea," he said.

"Melancholy," said Bethsabée.

"Natanya."

"Mmm, romantic."

"Stuart."

"Dangerous."

"Joan."

"Far away."

"Helen."

"Mischievous."

"And here's mine," said Bob.

"Charming," said Bethsabée.

Robert Cohan grew up in Brooklyn but there is no trace in his speech. He is slender, sinewy, with dark curly hair, a sculpted poet's face, and a droll sense of humor. Once when I was living in the 8th Street studio, and after a late rehearsal, I persuaded the elegant dancer with whom I was working to spend the night instead of trekking all the way back to her apartment in Queens. She made it clear that I should not expect a night of glory because "I'm in love with Bob Cohan."

"It won't do you any good."

"I know, but I can't help it."

Bob wants a saffron-colored necktie so buys a white silk tie, spends a considerable sum on genuine saffron, brews it to a rich infusion, and dyes the tie.

Martha: "What a pretty yellow tie."

"It's not yellow," says Bob loftily. "It's saffron. I dyed it with real saffron."

Martha slips on her glasses, peers closely, takes off the glasses, and stares Bob in the eye. "It's *yaller.*"

Bob often carried a tome, philosophical or occult, by someone with an intimidating name: Ouspensky or Krishnamurti. One day, I too am carrying a tome. "What's that?"

"Science fiction."

I've been reading science fiction since age ten, and this tome, titled *Dianetics,* is by L. Ron Hubbard. Bob asks to borrow it when I finish. A week after I give it to him he says, "I'm half through that book. It's not science fiction."

"Sure it is. That's what L. Ron Hubbard writes."

"Not this time."

A week later Bob returns the book. "It's junk. But it's *not* science fiction."

Tired of drug store lunches, Bob, Bertram Ross, Natanya Neumann, and I try a deli a few blocks north of the Graham studio. On a raised perch near the door, sits a young cashier, her face, neck, arms, and torso so smoothly molded she had the contours of a Macy's Day parade balloon. But her pale skin is flawless, and her glossy black hair is coifed in a neat bun. Presently, we're all staring at her.

Me: "How can a young person let herself get that way?"

Bertram: "She had to have been born that way."

Natanya: "She looks healthy enough."

Bob: "She's beautiful"

Bertram, "Of course Bob would say that."

Bob, admiringly: "If people were raised for food, they'd all look like that."

In 1953, while working on *Ardent Song,* Martha discovered poet Saint-John Perse. She brought his epochal *Vents* to the studio and would embrace the book and say, "That man!" She thrilled to a line that ended "that face will be held by force, into the wind!"

"That man!" embarrassing pianist, Helen Lanfer. I get the impression that to Helen, Martha was being sexual. In Paris, 1954, we hear that she had met the poet but no sparks had flown.

7

· · · · · · · · ·

The Grand Tour

Fall 1953

Four years after her calamity in Paris, Martha announces that we will return to Europe. I have a reasonably steady job on *The Buick Circus Hour,* once a month in the slot of the *Milton Berle Show.* With teaching, I earn about $175 a week, enough to live on. One day, choreographer Edith Barstow says, "When the *Garroway Show* moves here from Chicago I'll be setting numbers and I'd like you to be a regular. They want dancing three days a week. I'll set two of the days and you can set the third. You'll be paid for setting numbers, of course."

"Edie, I'd love to, but I'm going to Europe with Martha Graham."

"Oh, pooh. When did you sign the contract?"

"I haven't."

She brightens. "Wonderful! So, you can do *Garroway.*"

"I haven't signed, but it's a commitment."

Like she didn't hear. "You'll earn $200 for each show you dance in, plus $600 for setting the number."

Twelve hundred a week is *great* money in 1954. "How much will you make with Martha Graham?"

"Two-fifty a week."

"But, Stuart . . ."

Edie Barstow's offer is the kind that can make a career. One dance number a week, plenty of time to make it eye-catching and attract other

Alan Hovhaness. Photographer unknown.

choreographic opportunities. Commercial choreography is where a financial future lies. Walking out on Martha would have been hard, but . . .

Martha's new dance is to a score by Alan Hovhaness. I have all his LP records, relish his mysterious melodies and forceful rhythms, and had made a duet with Patricia Birch to his piano piece *Achtamar*.

He shows up at the studio, tall, bone-thin, limp handshake, indrawn personality. But his wife, Serafina, is a quietly spectacular beauty. When I describe the pair to Frances Rainer, my *Buick Circus Hour* partner, she says, "He must be a tiger in bed."

Hovhaness quickly delivers a score, melodic, sensuous, meditative, exuberant, often with a powerful beat. Martha likes it but feels pushed by the beat.

"It drives and drives," but never asks Hovhaness to make changes.

The theme is love, not between woman and man like *Diversion of Angels,* but of all creation, like *Canticles for Innocent Comedians,* although not tied to St. Francis. There are five sections: Moon Rise, Moon High, Moon

Set, Deep Dark, and Dawn, with solos for Yuriko and Pearl Lang, and powerful group dances. Soon there's a title: *Ardent Song.* Yet the dance lacks focus, and Martha keeps making changes, leaving sections of music unchoreographed. So things remain until the premiere in London, when there comes, in a biblical phrase Martha favors, "a great weeping and wailing and gnashing of teeth."

Leatherman calls a meeting and informs us that Craig Barton, with enormous effort, has booked us into good hotels at the best possible rates, and reprovingly extracts our promise to stay where booked. The tour will include England, Holland, France, Belgium, Switzerland, Italy, and Austria. We sail on the *Queen Elizabeth.* The debacle of 1950 is unmentioned.

Martha turns repertory rehearsals over to senior company members. I learn the Dark Beloved in *Deaths and Entrances* from a 16-millimeter silent film, including duets with Martha, who schedules only one rehearsal for the two of us. Bob and I work on our fighting duet together. A few rehearsals are supervised by Pearl Lang, yet *Deaths and Entrances* is all bits and pieces because we don't have a single run-through.

Martha has new costumes for all of her roles. Working on costumes, she seems absorbed and content. One day she has me put on a new black unitard for *Errand into the Maze,* takes a roll of three-inch embroidered trim with a jagged silver pattern, and starts pinning it to the fabric. Holding one end at my shoulder, she pokes the pin into my skin. I twitch. She unrolls trim down my chest and sticks me again. At a second twitch she says, "Psshh, psshh, psshh," which I take to mean, "Don't be such a baby."

The next time she sticks me, I stand like a stone. When the trim is pinned, shoulder to ankle on both sides, she says, "Take it off and give it to Mrs. Hatfield."

"I can't."

"Why not?"

"You've pinned it to my skin."

She unpins and re-pins with exaggerated care.

The night before we embark, I make an alarming discovery. I'd not learned a fifteen-second transition in *Deaths and Entrances.* Never having had a complete run-through, I'd missed it, and if I make up something, Martha will know. She'd fix it, of course, and dismiss my lapse, but I'd feel disgraced. Heart pounding, I lug the 16-millimeter projector into the studio and load the reel.

"What are you doing?"

"A last check."

I run the entrance a few times, do the moves on my feet, make notes, put the projector away, and say nothing to anyone.

Second class on the *Queen Elizabeth* is luxurious, but March winds are high, seas heavy. Martha spends hours huddled in a deck chair, furious at her weakness, LeRoy Leatherman or Craig Barton always near. In the dining salon, crockery crashes to the floor. The maître d', glad to see anyone with an appetite, proffers the first-class menu.

We ask for a place to work out, are led to the deserted first-class gym. Adjoining is a swimming pool and once I'm in the water, all feeling of motion *disappears*. I want to tell Martha but feel certain she doesn't want to know.

The fourth evening at sea, we are invited to the show in first class. The ship is listing steeply so the singer plants her shoulder against the stage right proscenium and starts.

"*He's just my Bill . . .*"

The ship tilts, gravity dislodges her, and she stumbles sideways all the way to the stage left proscenium.

"*. . . an ordinary guy . . .*"

It is bizarre and funny but no one laughs. Before the ship can tilt again, she sits on the edge of the stage and completes the song to warm applause.

In London, all stay at the Cavendish Hotel on Jermyn Street. Martha has a suite. The front door is locked at night and after the first late rehearsal, Linda and I ring, to be admitted by an elegant woman who speaks directly to Linda, "Will med'm wish breakfast in her room tomorrow morning?"

"Yes."

"What time will med'm wish breakfast?"

"Nine."

"Does med'm wish a fire?

"Yes."

"Is there anything else med'm requires?"

"No."

As we climb the richly carpeted stair, Linda whispers, "I *like* being 'med'm.'"

We wake to a wood fire burning; in come eggs, kippers, broiled tomatoes, marmalade toast, and pots of tea. We eat at a window table overlooking Jermyn Street where people are bundled in scarves and coats. Rosa Lewis's Cavendish Hotel had been blitzed in World War II but not destroyed. I can sit in the window and imagine English lords and their ladies having cozy breakfasts at this very window in this very room. In 1962 it was torn down and replaced.

The Saville Theatre is icy. Lee Leatherman brings in an enormous pot of coffee, tar-black with an oily sheen. We load it with milk and sugar, finish the pot, and ten minutes later *everyone* is retching. After that, only tea in England.

Backstage on every floor is a bathroom with a six-foot tub and hot running water. Bob Cohan fills one, letting hot water run in and drain out at the top until he's startled by a loud banging on the door and a furious voice. Later, outside, he points to little pipes sticking out below each bathroom window. Each tub drains directly onto the sidewalk.

Notices come in:

Exhausting
The unceasing effort to deduce from these dance dramas even a hint of Miss Graham's abstractions and philosophies leaves one exhausted rather than entertained.

Cyril Beaumont, *The Observer*

Converted
She is one of the great creators of our time . . . I hope all thoughtful people will see her, for she has enlarged the language of the soul.

Richard Buckle, *The London Star*

Bare-Foot Dancers
The famous Martha Graham and her bare-footed troupe of dancers from America are giving three ballets a night at the Saville Theatre. In the intervals people walk around and ask each other what they are all about . . . In the first program she and Stuart Hodes dance "An Errand-Journey into the Maze of the Heart's Darkness to Face and do Battle with the Creature of Fear." Maybe that's what it was. Anyhow, the woman was certainly scared of the big bad ox of a man . . . *Diversion of Angels* was better. It expressed the angelic felicity of a poet's idea of Heaven: Just happy youngsters dancing. Pearl Lang, in red, was the personification of passionate energy. Helen

McGehee, in yellow, was as lovely a spirit as one could have wished to see . . . It was hard to stomach "Night Journey" showing Oedipus marrying and defiling Jocasta, his mother: The classical tale. Martha Graham's distressed Jocasta assumed the broader countenance of Epstein's *Genesis*. This mobile essay in incest made one wonder if the troupe's trip from America was really necessary, but the enthusiasm of the audience at the end was a categorical answer.

P. B.

Keeping pace with American Martha Graham as she winds barefoot through a maze of symbolism in her programme of futuristic dances at London's Saville might prove too much for those who prefer the more classical forms of dancing, but thought-provoking it certainly is. Miss Graham, known across the Atlantic as "high priestess of the modern dance," admits that "some like us, some don't, and some remain puzzled." But all will agree that she gives us something new.

News of the World

Table Talk
Words like "hungry-looking," "tragic," "soulful" figure frequently in descriptions of Miss Martha Graham, the pioneer of a modern style of ballet puzzling audiences at the Saville Theatre. Miss Graham is a warm, sensitive little woman with that rare combination of dignity and friendliness that one finds more often in small children than in grown-ups.

"I build the dance up out of movements based on ideas and images," she said. "Especially images drawn from childhood. I try to make all the movements dramatic and meaningful and beautiful to watch. Like children at play. Deep play." There are no formal movements, or set dances, as there are in classical ballet. I suppose this is why many of the ballet experts, though they sound impressed, write as though they were not on the same wavelength.

Pendennis[1]

Every night dancers from the Royal Ballet sit in the first row and cheer.

During that first week, Martha worked on *Ardent Song* every afternoon and all day Sunday. The premiere is Monday but gaps remain, the biggest during Yuriko's "Moon Rise" solo. Three couples downstage right—reverent moon worshipers—are supposed to weave a slow counterpoint to Yuriko's dance, but nothing is set. Also untouched is a fast-moving trio for Linda Hodes, Mary Hinkson, and Matt Turney.

Sunday night Martha summons us to her suite, announces grimly that there is no way to finish, and she must cancel the premiere. Into the leaden silence bursts Gertrude Macy, out of breath:

"Martha . . . I heard . . . you're canceling . . . the premiere. You . . . mustn't. The English are looking . . . forward. They feel honored. . . . To cancel . . . would be a slap. It would be . . . badly taken. Considered . . . unprofessional."

"I've been called many things but *never* unprofessional!" says Martha.

Pearl Lang breaks in, "*Martha*. We can do it. Ninety-nine percent of the dance is done. We'll get together in the morning and work out a way to get through. Then you can set it later."

Martha gives in. Next morning, Bertram Ross and Miriam Cole, the downstage couple, improvise a slow five- or six-second phrase. The second couple repeat it, then the third, then the fourth. This takes about thirty seconds, whereupon Bertram and Mimi ooze into a second sequence, and so on until Yuriko's solo is over.

There is no easy solution for Linda, Mary, and Matt's demonic trio, but they assure Martha they can work it out.

Ardent Song gets glowing reviews, but Martha never gets around to setting the trio. A few days later, Bob asks, "Have you been watching Linda, Mary, and Matt?"

"No."

"You should."

That night I see an astonishing melee. As Linda dashes off for two seconds, she spots me. "When is Martha going to finish this fucking dance?" and dashes back.

I've been keeping a European journal of sorts and lend it to writer Don McDonagh, who puts the incident into his biography of Martha.[2] When Linda reads it, she says angrily, "Where did Don McDonagh get such lies?"

The Saville Theatre stagehands treat us as though our comfort is their primary concern. This magnificent English theater tradition will never make it to the U.S.A.

Cyril Beaumont, *London Times,* remains crabby, but the *Observer's* Richard Buckle loves Martha. I meet him at a party: slender, thoughtful, articulate, the kind of person Martha considers her own. I tell him how much I'm enjoying London.

"Yes, London is lovely, but I dream of New York."

"You've never been?"

"Never. I hope to go next year."

"It's not like London."

"I'm sure it's not. But I have a dream of New York. I see it floating at the edge of America, like Venice, but all of light . . ."

"Venice? New York is nothing like Venice. It's jammed, hysterical, noisy, unglamorous . . ."

"Stop!" Martha materializes at Buckle's shoulder, a hand protectively upon his sleeve. "Don't you *dare* destroy his dream."

On the ferry ride to Holland, as though following a script, the cloud cover clears and we arrive in brilliant sunshine. The whole country feels cozy, the food so good I wonder why Holland isn't touted for cuisine, like France and Italy.

In The Hague, we are told that the Queen will attend "incognito," and that we must be ready for a backstage visit. Martha explains that everyone knows she is there but when incognito they pretend not to notice, a splendid system I doubt would work in the U.S.A.

We're in our dressing rooms removing makeup when a white-haired gentleman pokes his head in the door, turns back, beckons, and in comes a middle-aged woman—the Queen—and a beautiful young one—a princess. We leap out of our chairs and stand half-naked, Bob holding his dance belt (a dancer's jockstrap invisible under tights) in his hands. Our dishabille seems unnoticed. The Queen speaks softly, asks a few questions, listens to our answers, smiles, bids us farewell.

I am deeply impressed by the Queen of the Netherlands. Her loving sweetness reminds me of Helen Keller. I mention this to the white-haired Dutch gentleman who accompanies us throughout Holland. Next day, he tells me he'd passed my comment to the Queen.

Responding to a request, Martha gives an open class for Dutch dance people. She cautions us: "The arts in Holland receive royal patronage. Dance is changing and several factions are vying. You must make no statements that can be taken to support one or another."

Demo class in the Netherlands. Photographer unknown.

The smallish studio, open on three sides, is filled. Martha wears a new teaching dress and gives familiar class work, explaining each move. We end with Bison Jumps followed by Standing Falls, to enthusiastic applause. It is our first ever "lecture-demonstration." Today, the "lect-dem" is a staple of educational dance programs, but as far as I know the first ever took place that day in Holland.

Our promise to stay where booked had been easy to keep. The Cavendish in London was a delight, and from our pleasant room in The Hague, we bus to Delft and Amersfoort. But Amsterdam's grandiose Hotel Krasnapolsky dumps Linda and me into a creepy room never intended for guests. One tiny window opens on an airshaft. The walls are so close to a sagging double bed that we have to skooch in sideways to reach the head. Pipes snake across the ceiling. The bathroom is a dank closet with a rust-stained sink. The toilet looks like salvage from a tramp steamer, and a showerhead sprays the entire room. Creepiest is a wall between room and hallway of glass panes painted white. I go outside looking for pinholes in the paint through which people can peep. Only our promise to LeRoy Leatherman to stay where booked prevents immediate check out.

Next morning, in a dining room the size of a blimp hangar, we meet Bob and Bertram, who also hate their rooms. Bertram dubs the Krasnapolsky, one of Europe's grand luxe hotels, "the Stanley Kowalski" (brutish protagonist of *A Streetcar Named Desire*). A few blocks away is a modest hotel with large airy rooms that cost half as much as the Stanley Kowalski, whose miserable rooms nullify our promise to LeRoy Leatherman. We switch hotels.

Paris

French audiences are thoughtful if not as enthusiastic as the English or as generous as the Dutch, and French critics are not as wild for Martha Graham as for Jerry Lewis. The *International Herald Tribune,* printed in English, carries a piece by Thomas Quinn Curtiss: "few modern artists have captured the essence of our age as vividly as has this dancer from America."

After the first show, limos take us to Bethsabée's mansion, which seems to be in a Paris park. Brandy from a bottle whose label was inked with a pen. I dine under a Rembrandt.

Our impresario, Anatole Heller, is a Frenchman who drinks no wine. He holds up a bottle of Vittelloise sparkling water. "This is my wine. America is such a big country, there must be thousands of springs, but all you have is club soda."

Pearl Lang and Linda play the older sisters in *Deaths and Entrances.* Pearl's role is a shade more dominant, but Linda, a strong stage personality, holds her own. One night after the show, she fumes. "She changed her headdress. Didn't you notice?"

"No."

"Well, look tomorrow."

I see a slightly brighter spray of lilac flowers in Pearl's hair and mention it to Linda.

"Exactly."

Linda's headdress has three grape-sized maroon orbs, but before we leave London she finds larger orbs in a lighter red and makes a new headdress.

Amsterdam: "She's done it again!"

Pearl's lilac spray is thicker. But before we leave Holland, Linda finds what looks like a handful of strawberries.

The third attack comes in Geneva where Pearl's headdress blooms with large purple flowers. Linda looks grim when she goes out, and that night her headdress has three blood-orange dragon claws shot through with metallic gold. Pearl's headdress does not change again.

Martha had kept her distance, so I thought. Decades later, Linda told me that Martha had started it all, telling Linda to "get a bigger headdress."

Stockholm, Sweden

The opera house stage is steeply raked. A bowling ball released upstage would careen into the orchestra pit. Swedish dancers take ballet class in a raked studio. To my relief, my *double tours* in *Deaths and Entrances* are perfect. But in our next performance, Malmö, on a flat stage, my body involuntarily compensates for the missing rake and I lurch off center. It's a week before I'm steady again.

Florence, Italy

Teatro della Pergola is 298 years old. I ask a stagehand if anything backstage has lasted the whole time. He takes me to a stone floor in the flies. "*Ecco!*" I stand on the old stones, communing with commedia dell'arte players who'd trod this exact spot for three centuries.

We follow a comic opera, *Il Diavolo Nel Campanile* (The Devil in the Bell Tower). Plot: An Italian village has a law that all engaged couples must marry on the same day once a year. But the marriages don't become official until midnight. After a wedding mass with vino and dancing, the couples retire with chaperones until the longed-for moment when the clock strikes twelve. But the Devil enters the bell tower and strikes an hour early, so all the marriages begin in sin.

After such a bomboloni, the audience is not ready for *Dark Meadow*. Baffled silence when Martha, shrouded in dark fabric, starts across the stage with tiny little steps. An ominous swelling murmur, as if a huge sleeping beast is starting to wake. Martha's face emerges from the fabric to stare straight at the audience. The murmur dies. The next time the beast stirs, Martha's glare is followed by an arm, flung like a curse. The beast is cowed.

This audience knows it daren't mess with Martha, but I am worried about the Seer's staff-thumping entrance in *Night Journey*. Martha will be upstage roped to Bertram Ross. If the beast wakes, I'll have to deal with it myself.

I enter jumping sideways so I can glare straight at the audience, rotate as I pass center, jumping backward until the last jump, when I whirl and like a malediction, hurl the entire frenzied condemnation at the beast. It stays cowed. After the show Martha glows in triumph. "They are Italian and know the Evil Eye when they see it!"

Next day, the program opens with another comic opera: *Il Contrabasso*, about a bass fiddler who leaves his case by a river where a naked princess, whose clothes had been stolen while she was swimming, hides inside to be revealed at court when he opens his case to play. It is followed by *Diversion of Angels*, whose playfulness relaxes the audience, also providing a transition into the charged depths of *Deaths and Entrances*.

Florence, Italy

Day off. Linda and I, Bob with David Wood on the back, rent Vespa motor scooters. Florence ends abruptly. Instead of suburbs, we pass orchards and manicured farms.

"I love this!" Linda yells into the fresh breeze.

Bob chooses a fork heading up, and soon we are entering a village on the crest of a mountain. The road becomes crowded with pedestrians. Bob and I downshift at the same time but he has trouble re-engaging. Motor racing, the scooter bucks. David hops off backward but Bob is underneath. Passers-by rush to his aid. He gets a small scratch on one calf. Martha spots it, drags out the story, and bawls *me* out.

"Maybe you have the right to endanger yourself, but you have no right to endanger the precious instrument of another dancer—*I am talking about your wife!*"

I hang my head in shame.

Vienna, Austria

The city is divided into American, British, French, and Russian zones, but no walls. Our hotel is in the Russian zone. From our tiny balcony we can gaze down the boulevard into the American Zone, where the gloom gives way to bright lights, a telling metaphor for two systems already grappling in the Cold War.

We take a horse-drawn carriage around the Ringstrasse, eat pastries in whipped-cream cafés. Nine years after World War II, Vienna has recovered its *gemültlichkeit.*

Linda and I plan to buy a Vespa motor scooter and tour Europe, but again Leatherman tries to make us return immediately to New York City. Most refuse, so he complains to Gertrude Macy, who calls a company meeting where it turns out she has no problem paying us our airfare. That should have ended it, but Leatherman gripes to Martha who calls a third meeting in a studio of the opera house, accusing us of high crimes and misdemeanors. I respond by accusing Leatherman of dragging Martha into something already settled to everyone's satisfaction.

She's surprised but can't drop it. "Well, I know you've been rude to Gertrude Macy."

"I have never been rude to Gertrude Macy."

The dancers back me up. "We've never heard Stuart speak rudely to Gert," and turn to Macy, who is sitting quietly in the back.

"Stuart has not been rude to me."

I expect little of Leatherman yet am surprised he'd out-and-out lied to Martha. I accuse him of it, adding that, in case she hadn't heard, after the 1950 tour he'd tried to force us all to return to the U.S.A. so he and Craig could take a vacation. "I was biking through Paris and there they were, the two of them, sitting in a sidewalk table of Les Deux Magots, drinking Pernod."

With that, I charge out of the room, out of the opera house, and am striding away when I spot Linda behind me. I ask why she'd left the meeting.

"You're my husband, aren't you?"

Next day, Gertrude Macy, calm and reassuring, adds airfare to the dancers' pay.

In 1999, David Wood put his version of the incident into his memoir, *On Angels and Devils and Stages Between*: "As I exited, I heard Martha chastising Stuart with her full coquetry. 'Stuart, you naughty boy.'"

This is a false memory. Before she could say a word, I'd walked out. And she never *ever* called me a "naughty boy."

Two days later, Linda and I, Bertram and Cameron McCosh, are on a train to Venice, windows open to a hot sticky breeze. Linda wants her hair cut short. Bertram snips off tufts, tossing them out of the window. When she has a nice bob, we head for the diner a few cars back, passing people angrily picking Linda's hair off their sweaty arms and faces.

We reach Venice around 7:00 p.m., choose one of the clamoring twelve-year-old boys hawking hotels, follow him onto a vaporetto that chugs through canals, then walk dark streets to a small clean hotel. Next morning, leaning out of our window, we can see Piazza San Marco.

A week later Linda and I, also Bertram and Cameron, buy Vespa motor scooters in neighboring Mestre, and head south on separate itineraries. For the next six days it rains.

After a wet day we find a beach front *pensione* and spend the next day staring at the Adriatic Sea from a vine-covered veranda. Second day we must get moving. By mid-morning I see something ahead on the two-lane blacktop, like a flapping tent on wheels. We pull abreast of Bertram and Cameron covered by enormous slickers. We lunch together, don't meet again until Rome.

The rain stops when we reach Foggia, where I'd been stationed for ten months. I want to find Maria DiBari, bilingual secretary of *The Foggia Occupator*. The soldiers in our newsroom office had advised: "Whatever you do, Maria, don't marry an American."

At 12 Via Freddo, I learn that the DiBaris have moved to a new building on the other side of town. Maria's mother answers the door, listens to my broken Italian explaining that I know Maria from the war, and now want to introduce her to my wife. She bursts into tears and, weeping, beckons us in, picks up a framed picture of Maria wheeling a baby carriage down a tree-shaded street. *"Ska-nek-a-tah-dee!"* and wails that she has never held her own grandchild.

Greatly relieved, I stammer, "Perché no va lei a America?" hoping it means, "Why don't you go to America?" She replies in Italian, the meaning clear.

"And what about my other children?"

The bed in our Foggia *pensione* sags in the middle so at 4:00 a.m., when the crows start cawing, we leave, heading west into the mountains on the Foggia-Napoli road over which I'd jeeped nine years before. At 6:00, we stop at a café in a mountaintop village. Hot rolls fresh from the oven and huge mugs of glorious steaming café latte. Nearing the outskirts of Naples, the sides of the road fill up with thousands of people who stare at us as we putt-putt by. "I guess they heard we were coming," jokes Linda nervously.

A police officer frantically waves us off the road and seconds later a motorcycle zooms by, rider facedown legs stretched back. We are scootering directly into the Milano-Taranto motorcycle road race.

After lunch in Naples, Linda is in pain. American Express (which has tourist-friendly people in all its outlets), sends us to a clinic that diagnoses food poisoning, prescribes medicine and a night's stay. I get a cot in her room. Next morning, a nurse pushes in a wheelchair with a young actor named Don Murray, who'd come down with mononucleosis while doing volunteer work relocating the cave people of Napoli. Eight years after taking shelter to escape bombings, they are still there. He's so interesting, we spend a second night. A few years later, he marries Hope Lange, who'd studied at the Graham School, and we run into him at a party in New York City. Now a star, he disappears immediately after we mention meeting in Naples.

The clinic is on the Vomero, a high ridge south of the city, and from a window overlooking the harbor, I recognize the silhouette of Capri. I want to show Linda the five-star Hotel Quisisana where I'd spent a week at the army's expense, and the Marina Piccola, "Little Beach," (officers only) and La Grotta Azzura, the famed Blue Grotto. Deck hands pick up our Vespa and unload us on Capri.

The famous island is two mountains connected by a saddle. Every road is either steeply up or steeply down, but the sturdy Vespa putt-putts effortlessly. The Hotel Quisisana is now way beyond our means, so we find a *pensione* with a tiled patio and million-lira view. We scooter to Tiberias, the Marina Piccola, rent a boat, row to the Blue Grotto, and swim into it. Inside is still pure magic. We putt-putt to Anacapri, where army jeeps had never gone. On a sweeping hillside, grape vines are being torn out and replaced by villas. "Progress" has come to Capri.

After a day in the sun, Linda is burning. *Sunstroke.* Recalling an army manual, I soak a towel in cold water, slap it on her, her temperature drops,

Capri. At Marina Piccola, "the Officer's Beach," Photographer unknown; from the author's personal collection.

and she sleeps. Back on the mainland, we go to Herculaneum, dug out of Vesuvian lava, where I want us to see murals of men with two penises, one for day, one for night, and street signs—erect penises—pointing to the nearest brothel. Our elderly guide says my wife can wait while he and I go. I tell him that *mia figlia* will see everything and damn quick if he expects to be paid. Giggling, he agrees.

On the road to Rome, it is my turn for sunstroke. We find a *pensione,* and Linda wields the wet towel. We visit St. Peter's, the catacombs, the Pantheon, toss coins in Fontana di Trevi, stroll the Via Veneto, stare at another super luxe hotel that had been an army R&R, pass a sidewalk café where, like a glowing ember in a pile of ash, Anna Magnani sits surrounded. Her black dress is cut to her naval; exploding hair, eyes that effloresce in a deeply tanned face.

We meet Bertram Ross, Cameron McCosh, and, unexpectedly, David Wood, who is off to Spain. I telephone Ronne Aul, who invites us to dinner with his wife and four-year-old daughter. Aul and his wife were a sensation in their first Italian revue. She is not a trained dancer but an extraordinary beauty, which is enough for the Italians (and most producers anywhere). His new contract includes a babysitter.

In Cannes, France, the owner of our *pension* proudly shows me his auto, a Citroen Deux CV, canvas seats and a tiny motor. How I wish we were in it heading north into the *mistral*, a zephyr one moment, a gale the next. The wind that drove Van Gogh crazy. At Avignon, we collapse into a *pension,* air a-whine with mosquitos. At 4:30 a.m. there's a mighty thump in the middle of my chest. Linda had swatted a dream mosquito. Laughing too hard to go back to sleep, we roll the Vespa into the cool predawn street, head north, reach Lyon by noon, and hop a train to Paris, the Vespa traveling as baggage.

Linda finds ex-pat American artists with whom she'd sat whole days in sidewalk cafés when in Paris with her father. We spend one day at it, pleasant enough, although I can't imagine a second day, much less as a way of life. One artist invites us to his studio and offers any one of his paintings for $100. They're patterned like light on sand under water, but we don't much like them so pass up an early Sam Francis for less than a fiftieth of its worth in a dozen years.

In Le Havre, we meet Bertram and Cameron aboard *De Grotebar* (The Great Bear). We dock in New Jersey, collect our Vespa on the pier, zip through the Lincoln Tunnel to our basement apartment on East 8th Street, and park the Vespa in our garden.

8

· · · · · · · ·

Asia

July 1954   —

Newspapers announce that the U.S. Department of State will send the Martha Graham Company to Asia. But no date. So I go to a replacement call for a Broadway musical, *By the Beautiful Sea.* The choreographer is modern dancer Helen Tamiris, so I figure my chances are good. But she lets her dance captain run the audition. Down to me and a kid who'd taken my classes at Performing Arts High School.

"What size shoe do you wear?"

I'm 10, he's 8½, he gets the job. Beat out by my own student and a shoe size. Two weeks later I get a call, the job is mine.

"What happened to the kid?"

"He got a role off-Broadway."

I squeeze into the eight-and-a-halfs until the costume mistress sees me walking on eggs backstage and orders a new pair in my size. A few years later the dancers' union, Chorus Equity, forbids hand-me-down shoes.

By the Beautiful Sea stars Shirley Booth. I'd seen her, poignant in *Come Back, Little Sheba.* In *By the Beautiful Sea,* she sings sweetly. Lead dancer Eddie Roll, a stringy five foot nine, has an eccentric solo in which he dives—fish flops—into the stage, rocks on his stomach, arches up like a porpoise, barks like a seal, flaps his arms like a penguin, and gapes like a goldfish. Helen Tamiris may have hoped to evoke Coney Island's beachy ambiance, but the dance is just goofy. Martha surprises me by coming.

Afterward, she says, "Your lead dancer [pause], dances without expectations."

Eddie and I are in three more shows together: *Milk and Honey, To Broadway with Love,* and *Sophie!* What Martha meant, I decide, is that Eddie Roll is too good for such macabre choreography.

November 1954

On the 22nd, a one-off performance of *Appalachian Spring* in Philadelphia, a Monday night. I contact producers Fryer and Carr asking to be released. *By the Beautiful Sea* is playing to half-empty houses and they are busy with new shows so say okay. On the Friday after Philadelphia, closing notice goes up, and on November 27, my thirtieth birthday, *By the Beautiful Sea* closes. On final bows, the women weep, tears mixed with mascara running down their faces.

I get a call from the dance captain of *Kismet,* George Martin, who asks me to come to the Ziegfeld Theater. It's an immediate job offer. I see the show that night. Jack Cole's "Broadway-Hindu" dances glisten like cut diamonds.

Kismet has two male dancers, both principals. One had already been replaced by Ronald Field. I am to replace the other. There are no Cole-trained dancers in New York City, so George Martin had suggested that a Graham-trained dancer might do. Instead of the usual two-week notice, *Kismet* has six, so I have more than a month to learn three short numbers.

There are two ways to teach a dance. One is to quickly sketch out the entire thing, then clean up. The other is to clean as you go. George Martin works the second way and wants each move perfect before teaching the next. We work thirty minutes on the *first four seconds.* I wonder if a month will be enough.

Ronald Field was not Jack Cole–trained but can do anything and is a lightning study with the astonishing ability to watch a long combination just once then jump to his feet and reel it right back. A steel-trap kinetic memory is rarer than perfect pitch. Ronnie says that he remembers every step of every dance he's ever learned, and as a June Taylor dancer on the *Jackie Gleason Show,* he'd learned dozens. I tell him that this huge storehouse of moves will be a fine asset when he choreographs.

"Choreograph? What makes you think I'll be a choreographer?"

"You will be. I guarantee it."

Ronnie goes on to choreograph *Applause* and *Cabaret* on Broadway, *Baryshnikov on Broadway*, the Academy Awards, and many nightclub acts.

I'd been in *Kismet* a month when the stage manager pokes his head in the dressing room to say that Jack Cole will be out front. George Martin nervously repeats the message. He's on the spot because hiring me had been his idea.

"Are you nervous?" Ronnie asks.

"Should I be?"

"No. Jack will probably fire *me*."

After the show, a head pokes through the door. Field says, "Uh, hi, Jack."

I leap to my feet. "Mr. Cole?"

"Yeah, mmm, yeah. Um-hmm. Okay. It's earnest, not exactly Indian, we'll fix that tomorrow." The head disappears.

"He loved you," says Ronnie.

After Denishawn, Jack Cole had gone to Hollywood and persuaded Columbia Pictures to put a small troupe on salary. It included Gwen Verdon, Carol Haney, Rod Alexander, Matt Mattox, and George Martin. With them he developed his unique jazz style, now worldwide yet rarely credited to him. He and Martha Graham were not in Denishawn at the same time, and although he admires her, I get the impression he doesn't really know her work. Or does Martha know his. When Cole's musical *Magdalena* was on Broadway, Bob saw it (I, alas! did not) and when he enthusiastically described it to Martha, she snapped, "If you like him so much, why don't you just *dance* with him," which Bob did, in Cole's nightclub act.

Erick Hawkins, back in New York and on his own as a choreographer, strove for a direct relationship with his audiences. One of his dances is titled *Here and Now, with Watchers*. His titles have a sensuous poetry: *Naked Leopard, Sudden Snake-Bird, Early Floating, Classic Kite Tails, Dawn Dazzled Door, Geography of Noon, Black Lake, Summer Clouds People*. His main composer, Lucia Dlugoszewski, adorns her music with poetic titles too: *Disconsolate Chimera; Goat of the God; Eros, the Firstborn*. These reflect a clean break with Martha and her dramatic titles.

Martha is making a full company piece from her solo, *The Triumph of St. Joan*. She divides Joan into four characters: the Maid, danced by Patricia Birch; the Warrior, danced by Helen McGehee; the Martyr, danced by Matt Turney; and Joan herself, danced by Linda. Bertram Ross plays St. Michael, with Lillian Biersteker and Carol Payne as Saints Margaret and Catherine, Joan's "voices." The set will be by Isamu Noguchi.

I'm earning a living doing musicals, nightclubs, cabaret shows, industrials, and TV. Enjoying it more than I'd expected. The dancing is fun and the people are funny.

In a beer garden scene, Ernie Kovacs is handed a beer stein with a lid you flip up with a thumb. He says, "Get me a can of beer to put into this thing."

In the *Esther Williams Aqua Spectacle*, live and on the air, I am swimming just behind and right of Esther Williams, yelling counts. But she ignores or can't hear me, swims off in her own direction, leaving the swimming chorus in confusion.

Rehearsing for the Milton Berle show, I lose my *double tours* and fall to the ground. *Four times in a row.* After the first two, Berle looks puzzled. On the third and fourth he breaks into a grin.

"He falls down! That's funny!"

In June 1954, I'm hired to understudy Buzz Miller as lead dancer in *Arabian Nights* at Jones Beach Marine Theater. He gives notice the first week, leaving me with the lead for the rest of the summer. The theater is on a manmade island in Zach's Bay with a twenty-yard moat between stage and audience. During intermission, bathing beauties do their routine in the moat. Klieg lights on the water attract thousands of crabs which roll, exposing claws and white underbellies, through which the beauties swim while gondolas full of showgirls, poled by musclemen, sail through. One muscleman, a good-natured giant—think Burt Lancaster as Mangiacavallo in *The Rose Tattoo*—rocks his gondola from side to side, ogling the bathing beauties and yelling, "I love yez! I love yez all!"

In the opening number, the men are costumed as gladiators with swords, bare-chested in red trunks and gold Roman sandals. Howard Jeffrey studies himself in the full-length mirror, sword held high. He doesn't like his hairy armpits so carefully removes the hair with Nair.

Stuart Fleming's comb-over doesn't quite cover his bald spot. Yells, "Anybody got something for the hair?" Jeffrey shoves over the Nair. Stuart massages the white goo into his scalp while reading the label. Suddenly

Public relations image of Milton Berle when he was "Mr. Television."

shrieks, *"Removes hair in ten minutes?!"* Laughing like maniacs, we hustle him into a shower before the Nair dissolves away what is left of his hair.

Paul Taylor reads quietly. In four weeks of rehearsal, he'd done everything Rod Alexander had asked, but with such profound disinterest Alexander dubs him "the absent one" and assigns him lowly chores like kneeling on all fours so Buzz Miller can jump on his back to start the Aladdin number.

"Five minutes," burbles the speakers. Paul reads on.

"Aren't you going to put on makeup?" asks Jeffrey.

Paul looks up. "Sure."

"It's five minutes."

"Okay." Paul puts down the book, takes a black grease pencil, and draws vertical lines through his mouth and the center of each eye. Dips a finger into a tin of lip rouge, reddens the end of his nose.

"You've put on a clown makeup."

"Well?"

Jeffrey turns to me. "Paul doesn't say much, but when he does . . ."

One rainy, gusty night, the audience plants itself under umbrellas like at a football game. Stagehands mop up puddles and the show goes on. Nirska and her sixteen butterfly dancers are slipping and sliding on the wet windy stage. A gust takes down an entire line of butterflies who stagger to their feet with wet bedraggled wings. I'm watching and laughing.

Exiting, one yells, "Wait till you're out there."

I join Kathryn Lee and two other men in a dance that follows a circus parade which ends with two elephants, a big one and a baby holding the big one's tail in its trunk. The elephants stop in the exact center of the stage. They are not supposed to stop.

"What's that dangling from the big elephant?" asks Stuart Fleming. A closer look reveals it is not dangling, it is *gushing*. The big elephant is urinating exactly where we dance.

"Magic time," sings Kitty, leads us out, and we follow, bandannas whipping, splash through puddles of clear rainwater to center stage where the puddle is foamy, drop to our knees, slash our bandannas into elephant urine, rise, whip each other with urine-drenched bandannas, exit into the wings where the butterflies are gasping and falling against one another, helpless with laughter.

On Thursday, August 17, Martha has a single performance at the Hollywood Bowl. By threatening to give notice, and supported by Kitty Lee, who says my understudy is ready, I get permission to miss one show, leave at dawn, do a run-through in the Hollywood Bowl in the afternoon, dance *Diversion of Angels* and *Appalachian Spring* at night, catch the red-eye to New York City, sleep all day, and am back at Jones Beach in time for the Friday show.

Arabian Nights catches the eye of Radio City Music Hall, which expresses interest in putting it on their "Great Stage." They invite the show's producers and principals to a cocktail party. On that very day and hour, Lee Leatherman announces a Graham Company picture call for the Asian tour.

Linda warns me that telling Martha I'll have to miss her picture call is sure to cause a blowup. She advises me to tell her about the cocktail party, offer to miss it, then wait for her to "generously" allow me to go. This I cannot do.

I present the conflict in the company office where Martha is conferring with Leatherman, Craig Barton, and four production people. I explain that I'll be a featured dancer, "Courtesy of the Martha Graham Company

Hollywood Bowl rehearsal. (*From left*) Linda Hodes, Bertram Ross, and Patricia Birch. Photo by Stuart Hodes.

will be printed in the program, and remind Martha that she herself had been featured at Radio City,[1] hoping she'll view it as me following in her footsteps. Martha explodes.

Me: "I knew it! The first thing that doesn't go exactly your way, you blow up at me. If this is how it's going to be, let's call it off. I won't go to Asia. Tear up my contract. I feel like I'm drowning in the emotionalism around here."

"I heard that," Martha hisses. "Oh, I heard what you said. Oh yes, it's been said and you can't unsay it." She points around the room at people agape. "One, two, three, four, five, six. Six people heard it."

Me: "I *will* attend this party. It may be important to my future. I have to think about my future because obviously I have no future around *here*."

"Your future is whatever you want it to be," and accuses me of caring more about dancing in *Arabian Nights* than with her.

"Ah-ha! That's what you hold against me, that I have to dance for a living."

"We'll not talk about it." She starts down the stairs.

I follow. "We've got to talk about it. Or end it!"

Down the stairs into the hall, through double doors into the big studio, quick U-turn and exit through the door into the kitchen, pass through into the faculty lounge where Martha locks herself in the bathroom. I stand outside. Her sister, Georgia, enters. Geordie is as gentle as Martha is fierce.

"Why are you upsetting Martha? Leave Martha alone!"

I exit the lounge and go into Studio Three. In less than a minute Martha emerges and the argument resumes. Again she storms out, me following. In the foyer near the front door, she stops.

"What do you want? What is it that you *want?*"

"What do I want? I'll tell you what I want. I want to walk around here holding my head up like a man, instead of lying flat on my face with your foot on my neck like everybody else in this place." Martha looks shocked. "I'm sorry Martha. I didn't mean that."

Quietly: "Yes, you did. You did, because it's *true!*" utters a sob, and plunges back into Studio Three, slamming the heavy door in my face. I shoulder it open.

I'm devastated, never having seen Martha cry. "Martha! Martha!"

"No!"

She dashes into the faculty lounge, slams that door. I yank it open. She's sitting on the couch, head in hands. I stand in the doorway not knowing what to do. The door to the kitchenette opens a crack, Leatherman peers at me—at Martha—at me. I think, "Get a good look, creep. Are you happy now?"

Leatherman shuts the door.

"Martha, what did I say that's so terrible?"

"Leave me alone."

She stands up, goes toward the kitchenette, opens the door, Geordie rushes through and lunges at me, beating her tiny fists against my chest.

"You . . . You . . . What have you done to Martha, you brute?"

Martha spins around and pulls Geordie away, saying, "No, Geordie, No!" in the tone she uses when Geordie's poodle, Roderick, chews a dance slipper.

I am in the mad scene of a very bad play. Martha and I play detestable characters. I hate my role.

After gently guiding Geordie out of the lounge, Martha exits the kitchenette, walking past me back into Studio Three, leaving the door ajar. I follow. We pass through and into the corridor where she stops and faces me.

Calmly: "Stuart, you are the only man in this entire organization who is not a homosexual."

What does that have to do with anything? And it's not even true. But the fight seems over. Martha tells Leatherman to reschedule the picture call. Rehearsal next day like nothing had happened. A few days later, Radio City decides not to produce *Arabian Nights* and the cocktail party is called off.

Martha's men include Bertram Ross, Bob Cohan, David Wood, Donald McKayle, and me. For Asia, one more is needed. Martha presents three candidates: Alvin Ailey, Gene McDonald, and Paul Taylor. Alvin has outstanding gifts but is brand new at the Graham School. Martha says that the tour will be sponsored by the U.S. Department of State, we will be cultural ambassadors, and that conditions will be harsh. "There is no room for a prima donna on this tour."

Helen McGehee: "I think we should take Gene McDonald." She lauds his character, how easy he is to work with, is seconded by Yuriko, Ethel Winter, and Pearl Lang. I'm fidgeting. Martha snaps, "Well, Stuart, what are you trying to say?"

"I don't understand how you can go on about Gene McDonald when one of the best male dancers who ever walked into the studio is available."

"All right!" hisses Martha. "We'll *take* Paul Taylor. But if he makes trouble, it will be on your head!"

Four dancers senior to me had spoken for Gene McDonald; one word from me, she grabs Paul Taylor. In his autobiography, Taylor reveals that when Martha had seen him in Doris Humphrey's class at Connecticut College, she'd said, *"I want him."*[2]

Martha always discussed new dancers with the troupe, and I believe she sincerely wanted us to agree. But the decision is 100 percent hers. Years before, in a flat-out rejection of Pearl Lang and Ethel Winter's advice, she'd turned down a fine dancer because she wore tea-rose-pink lingerie. This time I was her cat's paw. On tour, Paul gets the honeymoon treatment: lunch, dinner, tête-à-têtes. But I'm not jealous. Well, only a little.

Lee Leatherman hands me a contract for the Asian tour. "Sign this, please."

"Mind if I read it first?"

"Why bother? Nothing will change."

"I always read my contracts."

"Suit yourself. But I have to have it back today."

A few years after I'd left the Graham Company, Paul Taylor shocked Lee by demanding double the proffered $250 for a one-week Broadway season.

"That's ridiculous!" said Lee.

"Okay." Paul left the studio, contract unsigned.

Martha asked why Paul wasn't at rehearsal. Lee indignantly related Paul's demand. After rehearsal, Martha said, "What should I do about Paul?"

Linda, with a sigh, "Pay him the $500."

I was no longer in the troupe, but Leatherman called me at home. "Your wife is trying to destroy Martha Graham!"

Next day, Martha made Lee change the contract to $500.[3]

Asian Journal Entries

September 16, 1955

We feel headachy from anti-cholera and typhus shots. Linda hit hard. Martha feverish for four days. Today, fitting a dress on Ethel, she seems sullen. Bob says she is depressed and wishes there were no tour.

September 17, 1955

Company rehearsal without Martha. About 5:30 Martha walks in wearing a chic afternoon dress, looking rested and much better. She watches a lift, then excuses herself. "Tomorrow," she says, ominously.

September 18, 1955

Helped Bertram Ross bury Cedric. The cocker spaniel died yesterday after eating strychnine-loaded rat poison. Bob Cohan said it was Cedric's way of removing himself from Bertram's life now that he's an old dog. Committed suicide out of love for Bert. This upsets Bert. We drove to the Harrows' country place to bury Cedric beside Tessa, Ellen Green's cocker, Cedric's mate, who died last year. A lovely old house by two converging brooks. Bertram shed tears when we put the small blanket-wrapped body into the ground.

September 29, 1955

Signed AGMA contract with Iberian Attractions, Inc., 20 weeks, $175 a week.

October 21, 1955

The company leaves a day before Martha. She travels with Bethsabée, who will be along for the entire tour. We switch to Japan Airlines in San Francisco, stop for fuel in Hawaii and Wake Island. While refueling at Wake, we shower and have dinner. The women spot male faces at the shower room window.

October 22, 1955

We land in Tokyo at 8:30 a.m., greeted by people waving signs: "Martha Graham." Our sponsor, *Asahi Shimbun* newspaper, puts us on a bus full of balloons and takes a circuitous route to Tokyo with photo stops, ending at its editorial offices where we hang around wondering if we'll ever get into a room. Finally, the Imperial Hotel, Frank Lloyd Wright's marvel. Our bathtub is lined with tiny gold tiles and we have a private garden. When Tokyo razes the Imperial, it proves itself as barbaric as New York City, which had razed Penn Station.

On October 23, Martha and Bethsabée arrive at the Imperial Hotel met by the dancers. Pearl compliments Martha for looking chic and rested. She replies, "Why shouldn't I? I haven't had the company to worry about."

Imperial Hotel, Tokyo.

Opening night bows, Tokyo. *Left to right*: Ethel Winter, Bertram Ross, Martha Graham, Eugene Lester, Matt Turney, Stuart Hodes, Helen McGehee. Photographer unknown.

Linda snaps back, "Well, we haven't had a moment's peace since we arrived."

At our first press conference, we hear the speech Martha will make, with variations, in every country:

"We are washed by two oceans."
"We draw from the cultures of Asia and Europe."
"We must be true to our differences."
"They had no poets, so they died."
"The artist is an acrobat who walks the high wire of circumstance."
"Being before you is a challenge and a terror."

The "challenge and the terror" is sometimes the "terror and the challenge."

Japanese audiences have ferocious energy and there is no rule against taking pictures. Every show is a non-stop flash barrage. When the curtain comes down on *Appalachian Spring,* the audience leaps to its feet cheering and pelting flowers.

After a lecture-demonstration for Japanese dancers, Martha looks at their dances and offers scholarships. Those who show up in New York

City include Akiko Kanda, Takako Asakawa, Yuriko Kimura, and Kazuko Hirabayashi. The first three become members of the Graham troupe. Kazuko (Kaz) becomes a beloved teacher, and head of her own troupe, the highly regarded Kazuko Hirabayashi Dance Theater. Her dances are dreamlike and beautiful.

On a sightseeing trip to the great Buddha at Kamakura, Donya Feuer disappears. Our panicky hosts alert the police, cut short the excursion, and return us to the Imperial Hotel. Donya shows up for the performance. Next day, Martha tells us she'd gone off with an American sailor, adding, "She will jump into bed with anyone." Not sure whether Martha deplored or admired.

After Tokyo we are scheduled to play Seoul, Korea, but Korea is having a general strike so we get the week off. Some take a train to Osaka. Linda and I stay in Tokyo, spend a day at the Kabuki, another at Noh, see a show at Nichigeki Music Hall—like Radio City's *Rockettes* with twice as many high kickers. We take tea in a huge multistoried tea palace on a floor lit only by glowing tanks of tropical fish. Our table is tucked into a corner and shielded by screens. For the price of a pot of tea, one gets a bit of privacy in a society where privacy is greatly valued and hard to come by.

We depart for Manila on a Taiwanese charter airline, Flying Tigers. The pilot is American and when I tell him I'd flown B-17s in World War II, it turns out he had too. With thousands of ex-military pilots hunting jobs, he says he's lucky to be with Flying Tigers.

I mention that Martha is nervous because the plane has only two engines. He finds her and explains that they are the newest turbo-props, and the plane can fly perfectly on one. The copilot, "Smitty," also American, lives in Bali and shows Martha, then everyone, a photo of himself with a small bare-breasted woman and their three children. "My family," he says proudly.

An hour out of Tokyo, the pilot invites me to the cockpit, flips off the autopilot and offers me the controls. All I do is hold the plane straight-and-level, aware of dancers coming and going behind me. The air is calm until we run into some clear air turbulence, updrafts and downdrafts that shudder the plane slightly. I thank the captain and return to my seat. Martha catches my eye.

Copilot, Smitty, and his Balinese family. Photographer
unknown.

"I flew for a while."

"So I heard," she says sourly.

"First time I've flown a large plane in ten years."

"We could tell that you're rusty."

Rusty? I'd like to explain about clear air turbulence but have a preposterous notion; Martha knows that I love flying. Is she jealous?

November 15–18, Manila, Philippines

Our first performance is a lecture-demonstration for students in Mapua
Memorial Hall. We dance on a raised platform, surrounded by 16,000 people. Martha puts us in a circle facing outward and stands in the middle.

In one of the first floor moves, when we extend legs and flex feet, there
is a crisp laugh. What's funny? They laugh unexpectedly during other
moves, and all through the *exercise-on-six*. Then I realize that they are
laughing for pure pleasure. The Philippines have their own dance forms
and also classical ballet, but no one had ever seen bodies take the shapes
we are making, and it delights them. Applause mixes with laughter and
when Martha concludes with Bison Jumps, they cheer.

At dinner we are ceremoniously served the Philippine national dish—roast suckling pig. It's the size of a dachshund, crouched on a platter, blank eyes open, tiny legs tucked under.

"He hasn't lived very long," says Martha sadly. But no more, not daring to offend our hosts. The waiter hacks it up, each portion a few clumps of soft bone, baby fat, and crusty skin. It's delicately spiced yet almost no one can get it down so the onus is on me with my reputation as a human garbage can. I don't like it that much yet fall to with exaggerated gusto.

"Look how Stuart loves it," says Martha, distracting attention from her own plate. I accept seconds. When we leave the table, Martha whispers, "Thank you."

At a demonstration by Bayanihan, a Philippine folkloric troupe, a woman holds a glass of water in each hand, a lighted candle floating in each, and dances, spilling nary a drop. A solo dancer jumps in and out of the shifting spaces between bamboo poles rhythmically pounded on the floor. When Bayanihan plays New York City, the bamboo dance is a hit.

November 20–25, Bangkok, Thailand

As we taxi toward the welcoming *panjandrums* to whom Martha will give her "terror and challenge" speech, Bertram says: "Okay, who's going to be the challenge and who the terror? In Manila I was the challenge, so in Bangkok I want to be the terror."

We are invited to the university to see a traditional Siamese combat dance. To drumming, two young men don elaborate garments. The taller bears a six-foot, red-lacquered staff, the shorter, thick black-lacquered clubs strapped to his forearms. They circle, lunge, parry. After a few minutes, they retire to opposite corners. Thinking it is over, we applaud.

They strip off the ceremonial costumes revealing white pants and bare chests and take up weapons of battered hardwood. No drums, just gasps, grunts, and the slam of weapon against weapon. Splinters fly. Good Heavens, they are really fighting! I'm appalled and angry. Someone is sure to be injured and for nothing more than our amusement. The tall fighter with the staff tries to keep his opponent at a distance, the short one with clubs tries to get close. Suddenly the small one is down and rolling away stalked by the other who smashes his staff on the other's spine. A death blow. In the hush, the fallen fighter rises, both face the audience and bow. *I've been had!* and applaud fiercely in admiration and relief. A student explains that it is an ancient dance.

"Does anyone ever get hurt?"

"By accident sometimes, but nothing like in boxing."

He means Thai boxing—kickboxing—which I'm half glad I never see. The demonstration gives me an idea for a dance:

Title, PUGILISMO
Scene: ropes suggest inside a boxing ring.
Music, rhythmic punching bag sounds.

Characters enter: Referee, Fighters, Seconds. Fighters wear silken robes, name on the back. Seconds remove robes, insert mouth protectors. Fighters go center, shake hands.

Round One (Danced). Bell followed by cadenced drumming like a punching bag. Dancers spar in slow-motion. Two minutes. Bell ends round. Boxers to Corners. Seconds, stools, buckets, sponges, etc. 30 seconds.

Round Two (Start choreographed, end improvised.) Boxing as before until a real blow lands, then another, fighters begin to fight, really fight, not fake real, real real. When I am bloody and down for the count, my opponent exits, dresses, and leaves the theater. No one is told in advance, not the stage manager or other dancers.

My concept is to invert what I'd seen in Bangkok—art pretending to be combat, and present combat pretending to be art. When the Asian tour is over, I find a worthy opponent, a Broadway dancer from Idaho, Chad Block. He outweighs me by twenty pounds. I describe it to him, and he's eager. But I lose confidence in the idea and never do make *PUGILISMO*.

In *Cave of the Heart,* after the Victim, played by Helen McGehee, runs off in flames, her body is dragged back under a shroud that falls from the shoulders of Medea, played by Martha. Under the shroud, McGehee lies on her back grasping Martha's ankles, to haul herself along as Martha takes one step, then another. When they reach center, Jason, played by Bertram Ross, staggers on, tears off the shroud, and falls on the dead body.

After the curtain, Helen is heard yelling at Umaña. "I don't care what the others say, I want a floor cloth on *every* stage from now on!"

"What's wrong?" I ask Helen.

"I'll show you what's wrong." She turns around, yanks down her pants, and under the skin of her lower back are long splinters like toothpicks. Each had been forced *slowly* into her flesh while Martha was dragging her across the stage.

November 26, 1955, Singapore

We look forward to Chinese cuisine, to learn that the cost of our room in the Raffles Hotel includes boring English food which we pay for whether eaten or not. The pretentious menu lists eight main courses, plus sides, cheeses, fruits, and beverages. At one meal, for spite, Paul Taylor and I order every dish.

November 27, 1955

My 31st birthday. Linda gives me a gold-and-black brocade vest copied from the *Appalachian Spring* vest, which she had secretly taken to a tailor in Bangkok. The shimmering brocade is made in China, thus contraband in the U.S.A.

We do a lecture-demo at 5:00 p.m., attend an embassy reception at 8:00 p.m. Then we are invited to the hotel's cabaret to see a husband and wife dance team. The man is about five nine, steely strong, and wears tails. His wife looks about sixteen, reed slender and as flexible as silly putty. Her costume would fit in a teacup. He folds her into pretzel-like shapes, wraps her around his torso, spins holding her over his head, then tosses her in the air to be caught inches from the floor. Her face stays blank except for an occasional sharp glance at the audience, like a cat alerted by a sudden sound.

Next day I say to Martha: "It was bizarre."

"Didn't you like them?"

"Yes. But she looked so disconnected."

"She is very young."

"She didn't seem to know she was performing."

"One doesn't always know."

One doesn't? "How do you judge something like that?"

"Maybe you shouldn't try to make a judgement."

"Is it as good as *Errand into the Maze?*"

"It's not worse. It's *different.*"

Kanbawza Palace Hotel. Rangoon.

December 2, 3, 1955, Kuala Lumpur, Malaysia

Martha and Bethsabée travel to a distant city where Bethsabée buys Martha a Chinese bridal bed. Eventually it becomes the central feature of Martha's living room on East 63rd Street.

After the performance, there is social dancing at the embassy. A pretty young matron is teaching me a Malaysian dance. "Look!" She indicates a slender gray-haired man. "Our greatest dancer."

"How old is he?"

"Sixty-eight. He's now a high government official."

I'm impressed that in Malaysia, a dancer can become a high government official.

December 7–11, 1955, Djakarta, Indonesia

Instead of a hotel, we're farmed out to homes. Linda and I stay with an embassy couple, the O'Sullivans. Servants bring breakfast, late morning tea, lunch, dinner (if there's no banquet), and a snack before bed. A female cook squats on the floor. Mrs. O'Sullivan says that preparing food on the ground is a folkway impossible to change.

At the opening night party, Donald McKayle converses with an important-looking man, who, I'm told, is editor of a local paper. They conclude with a handshake. McKayle said he'd been asked about being a black man in the U.S.A. Next day, the O'Sullivans tell us that the resulting piece is the first decent thing that that editor had ever written about the U.S.A.

We're invited to spend Sunday morning at an embassy retreat an hour from Djakarta, a rambling villa with a small swimming pool set in rolling hills planted with tea bushes. Our host points out tiny green shoots at the tops of each tea bush, explaining that tea for royalty is made from such leaves, and invites us to pick some.

David Wood and I are jumping in and out of the pool doing dance moves as we fly through the air. The lunch bell sounds and as I turn to leave, David yells, "Do a *bicycle* into the pool." I turn, dash toward the pool, skid on the wet concrete, hit my right foot against a concrete ledge, plunge into the water and jump out yelling, "I'm okay!" Then I notice that the end of my right big toe is sitting on top of the middle joint. A car takes Linda and me to what looks like a doctor's office in Jakarta.

After a two-hour wait, a Dutch doctor, tottering drunk, appears. He stares at my toe with watery blue eyes, takes a syringe, injects the toe, which goes limp. I ask what's in the syringe. Cocaine. He presses the joint back into place and leaves. A nurse pours on sulfa powder and wraps the toe. By evening my leg is swollen to the knee. Martha cuts *Errand into the Maze,* and the show goes on without me, *my first ever missed performance,* destroying my "iron man" image. I drown my regrets in Singapore Slings, becoming wildly elated when alcohol mixes with cocaine.

Next morning, my swollen leg makes dancing out of the question. I limp along when Martha and troupe tour the royal palace, accompanied by Mrs. Sukarno Number One. There are three Mrs. Sukarnos. President Sukarno lives with Number Three, but our hostess is still Number One, so we are highly honored.

The palace has half a dozen halls, each containing a complete *gamelan* orchestra. An old scholar accompanies us, explaining that the instruments *are* the orchestra, that each is hand-made by one master and tuned to the note that he selects. They can't be retuned, so must stay together. I'm staring at a huge gong when Mrs. Sukarno approaches. "Would you like to strike it?"

"I wouldn't dare."

"But you must." She points to a mallet the size of a woodsman's axe, then at a grapefruit-sized knob in the middle of a huge gong. "Strike it there."

The sudden *gwa-a-a-a-ang!* makes everyone jump. As we cross the sward, the old scholar falls in beside me. "We believe each instrument has a soul," he says softly, "and that we must ask permission before it is struck."

"I only struck that gong because Mrs. Sukarno told me to."

"Oh. Ah. Yes, I understand."

Later, I ask Martha if Mrs. Sukarno had known it would upset the old scholar. "Oh, yes. But she is mischievous."

December 13–18, 1955, Rangoon, Burma

Our hotel, the Kanbawza Palace, is the former mansion of a Chinese "kerosene millionaire." I discover that Linda and I are booked into a room *with* Bertram Ross and Cameron McCosh. I hunt down Craig Barton.

"But they have no more rooms."

"Does Bill Marlott have his own room?" Marlott is our paymaster.

"Yes, but he's an old man."

As to a half-wit: "Then put the *old man* in with *the two young men* and give the *married couple* the old man's room."

My toe is not healing. Severed tendons are growing out. I'm sent to an Indian doctor and with his first touch, know he's a *healer.* He snips off the protruding tendons and sews up the wound. The toe feels better immediately but I still can't dance and Martha wants *Errand* back, so I teach the role to Bertram Ross. The Rangoon stage, built to order in an open field, is the only place to rehearse. Burmese kids slip under the curtain to watch. Martha forbids snapshots, but I slip in among the kids and manage to get one.

Ellen Siegel's room has a mysterious closet within which a staircase rises into darkness. We ascend by match light, reach a door that opens into a huge octagonal room that fills the central tower, then up another flight to a room above that. Encircling windows offer a view of lush treetops and the city of Rangoon a mile away.

Bob says it is perfect for smoking the hashish for which Burma is famous, and that he'll get some. After the show we climb into the tower, stuff the supposed hashish, which looks like tea, into cigarettes, and light up. I'm a nonsmoker so maybe do it wrong because I feel nothing. Others claim to feel high but I think that they are fooling themselves.

Martha and Bertram Ross rehearsing *Errand into the Maze* in Burma.

Every country thus far has shown us their own dances. In Burma, nine- or ten-year-old children do a dance that never rises out of deep *plié*. Martha asks our hosts if it is danced by adults and next day we see a performance on the hotel lawn by women, the same dance, expertly done. The women have hooded eyes, never glance our way, and leave without being introduced. Later, Martha says they'd been recruited from brothels.

December 20–25, 1955, Dacca, East Pakistan

Limping better, I meet a young Bengali who offers to show me Dacca. We take a taxi to town where he points to men in ten-gallon hats. "American engineers, looking for oil. I hope they find it. It will help our many poor people."

He's delighted when I mention that I'd read the Bengali poet, Rabindranath Tagore. "The government tried to stop us from speaking Bengali, *our own language*. We refused. Soldiers shot at us. I ran toward them, tore open my shirt and shouted, 'Shoot me!'"

We eat lunch in a "people's restaurant" where I am the only Westerner. I've been briefed:

> If you are in a position where it will insult your host to refuse food, go ahead and eat. The local flora may make you sick but is not poisonous. Your leader will have medication to relieve the symptoms until your body rids itself of the offending material.

First, a tasty broth, then a savory stew. (I hope it is not monkey, which is eaten here.) Finally glasses of tea. My friend insists on paying. Change comes in a dish filled with seeds. He leaves the change but offers me seeds. "Good for digestion." We pop a few into our mouths. They have a sharp clean bite. That night my stomach is fine although my foot still throbs.

December 26, 1955–January 3, 1956, Calcutta

The usual swarm of officials, reporters, and dance people who meet us at airports include famed dancer Uday Shankar. (Older brother of Ravi, the musician.) Martha rushes into his arms. His star is fading, but Martha always does her best to honor local artists. She outdoes herself with Uday Shankar.

At the press conference, a slender young man asks, "Why are there no dances in your company about social justice and the dignity of man?"

"*Communist paper*," someone hisses amid a murmur of disapproval.

Martha quiets them with a glance. "If I did not believe in social justice and the dignity of man, I could never have made a single dance. If you come to my performances, you will see that all my dances begin with social justice and the dignity of man. But I want my dances to be art, not propaganda."

"Well answered!" says a voice, followed by applause.

From toes to knee my right leg is blue, but the swelling is down and I can put weight on it if I wear a tight shoe. I cannot dance barefooted in *Diversion of Angels*, but David Wood is fine in my role. I do *Errand* in ballet slippers and wear boots in *Appalachian Spring*.

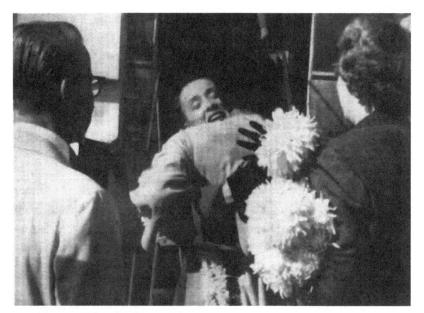
Martha greets Uday Shankar in Calcutta.

Our Christmas party is a day late, gifts exchanged after dinner in the dining room of Calcutta's Grand Hotel. Linda gives me fire opal cufflinks. I show them around, rewrap them in tissue, set them by my plate, and forget them until we're back in our room. I return to the dining room now cleared, tell the manager, stop him when he lines up waiters for body searches, ask to see the trash. He leads me to a yard with a pile of garbage the size of a beach house. In the moonlight, thousands of crumpled white tissues. Resigned, I kick at the nearest heap, catch a gleam, reach down, and pick up my cufflinks.

January 3–5, 1956, Madras, India

Rukmini Devi is head of the Martha Graham Sponsoring Committee. She famously rescued classic Bharatanatyam from India's brothels, taking one of the prostitutes for her guru, learned to dance, and began to perform, something no high-caste Brahmin had ever done. She made Bharatanatyam respectable. Something similar happened in Europe with classical ballet and in America with jazz, which got its start in New Orleans whorehouses.

The entire Graham Company is bussed to Kalakshetra, a gated community, where artists kicked out of princely palaces by the British Raj live and pass on their art. The theater is outdoors and begins with Kathakali, a dramatic form. The dancer is eighty-two years old.

Then, Bharatanatyam by a stunning seventeen-year-old named Sarada. When her guru comes onstage, she drops to the floor and places her forehead between his feet. She rises to be presented with a large floral garland, which she whips off her own shoulders and around the head of another dancer in a shower of petals. Everyone falls in love with Sarada.

After the performance, dinner is served on a leaf the size of a dinner plate, placed on an eight-inch-high table: vegetable mash, plain and green milk curds, nut and vegetable soup, saffron rice with ghee, hot lemon pickle and sweet lemon pickle, fried bread, and rice pudding. I consume every morsel.

Linda smiles. "What a good boy! You've eaten everything on your *leaf.*"

I accept an invitation to return to Kalakshetra the next morning. The grounds are verdant and sunny. Strains of music from thatch-covered cottages. Twelve-year-old boys learning Bharatanatyam slap their bare feet sharply upon the smooth concrete floor. An elderly composer is accompanied by a young musician whose job is to note down every melody the old man hums, a living tape recorder. I wonder; is it too late to hand over all my money and study Bharatanatyam until it runs out?

In New York City, fancy men's shops sell shirts made of Bleeding Madras, each tagged, "Guaranteed to Bleed." In New York it is something of a craze. Bob wants to buy the fabric in Madras and have it custom made into shirts by an Indian tailor. We go shopping but none of a dozen stores has the stuff. In a large shop, Bob carefully explains that the colors run when washed.

The proprietor is indignant. "We would never sell a fabric whose dye is not fast."

Bob explains it is the rage in America. The man turns thoughtful. "Yes, we do sell something like that to America. I have always wondered what they do with it. Come with me."

He leads us to the rear and points to a stack of bolts. "We make that for Africans who can't afford properly dyed goods. Why do you want such cheap stuff?"

January 7–12, 1956, Colombo, Ceylon

Day off. Linda and I sleep late in the Galle Face Hotel, breakfast in our room gazing at the ocean. From our travel brief:

> January 9 Mon. [Performance at 9:00 p.m. for the sole purpose of allowing Martha Graham and Company to take a trip to Kandy and return.] Kandy is 72 miles from Colombo and there are traffic jams because working elephants use the road.

On Monday we rise at 6:00 a.m. Reaching Kandy's central square, we are stormed by vendors. In his memoir, Paul Taylor described it as follows: "We're getting off a bus to stretch when out of the steamy forest a seer-like youth emerges, pauses as if having a vision, then floats straight to me. He's somehow known that of the twenty or so of us, I'm the one who'll go for what he's carrying."

I hope Paul won't mind if I reveal details. I couldn't spot the steamy forest from downtown Kandy. The "seer-like youth" first approached Bob Cohan, displayed embalmed insects, whereupon Bob pointed to Paul, said, "Him," and gave a gentle shove.

January 14–19, 1956, Bombay, India

A private concert by the great classical dancer, Balasaraswati. In her fifties with a thick midriff and heavy arms. Her dance portrays the mother of Shiva, the Divine Infant. Shiva is often represented as a baby holding the earth in one hand. But to his mother he is her adored infant, loved more than her own life, and when he smiles at another, that person, too, is smitten by love, making his mother proud and also jealous. The dance blends classical Indian movement and mime.

Afterward, "Bala" is introduced, accepting our thanks with quiet humility. I offer mine, knowing there is no way to convey that hers is the greatest dancing I have ever seen. Later, Martha speaks reverently of Bala. I nod but know enough not to overdo it.

After our own show, everyone including Martha and Bethsabée taxi to an outdoor arena to see another famed dancer, Shanta Rao, who dances a form known as Mohiniattam. After two riveting hours, she comes downstage center, tosses back her head, and sings. Our host explains that local

Balasaraswati, "Bala."

critics condemn Shanta Rao because her dancing is too powerful for a woman. I hope they stay the hell away from Martha.

January 20, 1956, Agra, India

The flight from Bombay to New Delhi takes us directly over Agra and the Taj Mahal. The U.S. State Department had not budgeted a landing so Bethsabée pays, which is how we come to see this wonder of the world.

Bethsabée, I note, needed an official job in order to go on the tour, so the Baroness Bethsabée de Rothschild is listed as wardrobe mistress. After the tour, Linda confided that large triangular burn marks began appearing on their *Angels* dresses, so the women took to ironing their costumes as soon as they got to the theater so it was finished when Bethsabée arrived.

Jawaharlal Nehru and Martha. Background (*l–r*): Ellen van de
Hoven and Ethel Winter.

January 21–25, 1956, New Delhi, India

During bows, Rukmini Devi strides onto the stage, plants herself on the
apron, and we're trapped while she speaks for thirty minutes. Later she
introduces Martha to India's prime minister, Jawaharlal Nehru.

It is Indian Independence Day, and we are invited to see the parade. India has some thirty cultures, and after the tanks and soldiers, come glori-
ously costumed dancers. Preteen boys do a male puberty dance with foot-
long batons. A troupe of jousting warriors is costumed to look like men
on horseback. Near the end comes a Manipuri dance troupe, less theatrical than Kathakali, less complex than Bharatanatyam, just rhythmic, sensuous, and breathtaking.

January 27–February 1, 1956, Karachi, West Pakistan

After dancing on a specially built stage in the atrium of the Metropole Hotel, we are taken to see the Uzbek Cultural Delegation. The women are ballet-trained and do fluttery-eyed "folk dances," while the men leap around doing Russian-style split jumps. A man beats a disk-shaped drum, spinning it on one finger and tossing it in the air. A basso profundo thunders into a microphone. It's a mindless variety show, the performers skilled but bored. We go backstage hoping to meet them, but they're gone. Martha Graham is America's answer to the Uzbek Cultural Delegation.

February 3–5, 1956, Abadan, Iran

The day after the show, we depart for Teheran in an ancient (first made in 1936) twin-engine Douglas DC-3, soon plunge into clouds and turbulence. Seasoned travelers, no one gives it a thought, or that our airplane is a museum piece. When we drop out of the clouds we can see the snowy tops of mountains. I ready my 8-millimeter movie camera.

The turbulence intensifies, forcing the flight attendant to cling to seat

Stage being built in atrium of Metropole Hotel, Pakistan. Photo by Stuart Hodes.

backs as she makes her way along the aisle. We climb back into the clouds and when we drop down again, I see that we are in a valley ringed by mountains whose tops disappear into the clouds. The service ceiling of a DC-3 is well below the peaks. An alarm bell sounds in my brain. When the pilot steeply tilts the plane, I recognize a "panic turn" (180 degrees, back where you came from), and ask the flight attendant if we're heading back to Abadan.

"No."

"We just made a 180-degree turn."

"No, we didn't."

She's lying! The plane is bucking like a jeep crossing a ploughed field, and snowy crags can be seen through the clouds below. It occurs to me that the film I am shooting may never be developed. I put the camera away and settle into my seat resolving to die well.

Ethel Winter, with a hopeful smile, "Did you ever fly through air pockets this bad?"

(There are up drafts and down drafts but no such thing as an "air pocket.") "Dozens of times," I lie.

Another minute and the pilot announces that we're heading back to Abadan. Forty minutes later we're on the ground. Cheerfully, he tells me we'd lost or gained fifteen hundred feet in a single draft. He spots Martha. "Miss Graham, as soon as I check the weather, we'll be ready for take-off."

"Not in *this* plane. I will not subject my company to another such flight. You will find us a four-engine plane. Call the ambassador. Call the U.S. Department of State. Until it arrives we will be *there*," and points to the terminal.

It is dark when an old, unpressurized, four-engine Douglas DC-4 arrives. But it can rise above the clouds, and a flight attendant goes from seat to seat offering breaths from an oxygen bottle. Later, Martha says that during the turbulence she was dancing *Errand into the Maze.* "I did it through three times, beginning to end. And then we landed safely."

February 7–12, 1956, Teheran, Iran

In the dining room of the Park Hotel, our women are the only females in the dining room. Men in dark suits, white shirts, and ties huddle at their tables shooting covert glances our way.

"What creeps," says Chris Lawson.

At a banquet, the Shah of Iran, slender in a finely tailored gray suit, greets us in cultivated English, points to the rug covering the banquet room floor, about eighty feet on a side, saying it is largest Persian in the world, that our meal includes Iranian rice, the world's best. Each grain is an inch long.

Teheran is our last U.S. State Department–sponsored booking, but Martha announces that Bethsabée will send us to Israel. To save Bethsabée money, she won't take Paul Taylor. The dancers have a meeting and ask Pearl to speak to her. Pearl does, Martha relents, but when she tells Paul he can go, he declines. In his memoir, Paul describes their verbal fencing match.

February 15–28, 1956, Israel

Israeli newspapers list the dancers, among them: "Sturat Hoodes," "Bartram Rose," and "Max Turkey." Matt becomes forever, *"Max."*

Sold out. Opening night in the basement dressing room of Tel Aviv's Habima Theater, I hear knocking on the casement window. A woman's voice. "I'm a soldier. I hitchhiked from the Negev. Can you get me in?"

"What's your name?"

"Nurit."

"My name is Stuart. Stuart Hodes. Go to the stage door, say you're my cousin."

"Stuart . . . ?"

"Hodes. Stuart Hodes."

"Stuart Hodes."

"You're my cousin. Okay?"

"Okay."

In a few minutes a man comes. "Your cousin is here."

"Nurit?" I jump up and follow him to the stage door, see a stocky young woman in an army uniform.

"Nurit!"

"Stuart!"

She rushes into my arms, and babbling happily we head toward the dressing room. In the shadowy cavern beneath the stage, "This is all I can do, Nurit."

"I'm fine now. Thanks."

Wild Israeli audiences bookend the enthusiastic Japanese at the start of the tour.

I ask an Israeli if I can brush my teeth in tap water. He's offended. "Our water is as safe as yours. And our streets are safer."

It's nice to be able to walk anywhere unaccompanied, but one night, leaving the theater hungry, no taxis, no nearby place to eat, Linda cries, "It's a whole Jewish country. Wouldn't you think there'd be one deli open late?"

The director of Cameri, a new theater company, visits Linda and me at our hotel. "Habima is a great traditional company, but we are the future of theater in Israel." He wants us to settle there and work with Cameri.

This is a surprise, but as much as I admire Israel and its heroic people, the U.S.A. is my country, my home, and where I need to be. I couldn't tell him that.

"If I stayed in Israel, I'd want to build houses and plant trees."

"Then you'd be wasted. We have plenty of people who can build houses and plant trees. We need people who can dance."

I'd never questioned the intrinsic worth of an actor or a professional athlete, and from that moment I never again question the value of a dancer, and my right or anyone's, to dance.

Linda and I plan to stop off in London and spend two weeks seeing theater, but the dancer's grapevine reaches all the way to Tel Aviv where I learn that Jack Cole will choreograph a new *Ziegfeld Follies*. I'll miss the first audition so cable George Martin, asking if I can show up for the second. By return cable: "You have job. Be at rehearsal March 9, 10 a.m." We cancel London and fly straight to New York.

On the bulletin board at the Martha Graham School:

—from U.S. State Department:
December 19, 1955. We have had nothing but good reports . . . Mr. Terry's article in Sunday's Tribune about her tour was considered a wonderful tribute to her and the work of this Program. Mr. Kirstein wanted to know if it would be possible to . . . have film clips made of these tours to be distributed to television news programs and newsreels?

December 22, 1955. In Japan there were 2300 people in a theater that seated 1700. In Djakarta, Indonesia they were sold out and added a special student performance. The leading nationalist newspaper blamed us for hiding our cultural prowess.

Mr. Martin [John Martin, *New York Times* dance critic] continues to think that there is something "phony" about the Program ... [He] must be made aware of the good the Program is doing. He ... never prints releases sent to him. We might consider going over his head, as this is improper coverage of the news. Mr. Martin is against the principals of the Program; he does not believe sending culture abroad does any good. Somebody should have lunch with Mr. Sulzberger and ask him why this subject is not being covered.

As I'd suspected, John Martin, dean of American dance critics, is a crank.

Back in New York City, Martha says that she'd accepted an invitation to visit the Arab sector in East Jerusalem because refusing would have been a slight. She'd kept it secret because the Jewish dancers had not been invited.

9

. . . .

Dancing Fool

Sings the Jester in *Once Upon a Mattress:*

> My dad was debonair, and twice as light as air,
> In his very soft shoes.
> How he could dip and glide and skip and slip and slide,
> In his very soft shoes.
> I used to love to stand and watch him ev'ry day,
> He was always smooth and cool.
> I used to love to hear the people say, "He's a regular dancing fool!"[1]

In Martha's *Lear,* I played Mad Tom, and Bob played the Fool. Martha explained that the Fool was powerless and no threat so dared speak truth to the king. Yet there was danger, so the Fool had to be wise. Mad Tom wasn't wise enough to be a Fool, so pretended to be mad. The Fool and Mad Tom, loyal to King Lear, follow him out of the castle onto the wild heath and into the storm.

Does Martha think of me as her Fool? Sometimes I'm sure she does although if I dare speak truth, she flies into a rage.

Anyway, "dancing fool" means one thing when applied to Donald O'Connor or Rudolf Nureyev, quite another when applied to me. I wasn't a dancing fool, just a fool, dancing.

Leo Tolstoy's *Anna Karenina* begins, "Happy families are all alike; every unhappy family is unhappy in its own way." But for dance troupes that

Dancing Fool photos by Alfred
Gescheidt.

reverses. Unhappy dance troupes are all alike; with inept artistic direction, incompetent management, pampered stars, and a demoralized *corps de ballet.* Happy dance troupes come together around creative polestars. Like Isadora Duncan and her Isadorables, Ruth St. Denis and Denishawn, from whence came Martha Graham, Doris Humphrey, and Jack Cole. Jack Cole went to Hollywood where he mixed Indian Bharatanatyam with African rhythms and produced jazz dance, independently co-invented by Katherine Dunham (Ph.D., University of Chicago), who found African and Indian influences in Caribbean culture and created a dazzling troupe that launched the careers of Alvin Ailey and Eartha Kitt, among others. Martha Graham and Doris Humphrey settled in New York and created American modern dance. When Hanya Holm showed up, an emissary from Germany's Mary Wigman, American modern dance embraced her. Then came Alwin Nikolais, Merce Cunningham, José Limón, and Erick Hawkins, in a flowering that made New York City the world epicenter of modern dance.

Sneered at by classical aficionados, disdained by careerist commercial dancers, ridiculed by critics, modern dance became an embattled avant-garde. Intoxicated by their visions, modern dancers dreamed of changing dance, changing art, changing the world. Their troupes became families, each different, each happy in its own way.

In 1956, near the end of the Asian tour, Martha had said, "When we get back to New York, you will all have a salary. I will make sure everyone in the company gets fifty dollars a week." A third of what I need, even that didn't happen. After nine years with Martha, the $14,000 I'd saved in the army is down to $2,000, so I can no longer endow the Graham Company with my unpaid labor. Linda and I never discuss financial matters with Martha, but somehow she learns that we need a bank loan and offers to cosign. She walks me to Chemical Bank, where the bank officer acts star-struck when making out the papers.

To afford Martha, I dance for whomever can pay. But can I do Martha justice, giving so much time and energy elsewhere? And how do I rise out of the dancing chorus if I leave every time Martha snaps her fingers?

Dancer's seeking their first job envy me, although at thirty-two, the dancing chorus is a desperate place to be. You can be discovered there, like Shirley MacLaine, write a hit musical there, like Nicholas Dante wrote

Bank loan cosigned by Martha Graham.

A Chorus Line, or use it as a credit for a teaching job or to open a dancing school. Most other ways out are *down.* James Tarbutton, who added zing to the chorus of *Paint Your Wagon,* took a job in a bookstore. Frank Derbas, who danced "Steam Heat" in *The Pajama Game,* tried photography while holding down a job selling art prints in Ye Olde Print Shoppe. I walk in one day and he approaches, grave and haughty in a vested suit, elegant salt-and-pepper hair, and a serious moustache.

"Frank, you look like a curator at the Met."

He breaks up. "You ought to see me with a rich bitch. I really lay it on."

David Neumann, five years older than me and still in the dancing chorus, tells a joke: "Two men work in a circus cleaning animal cages. A load of bad hay gives the elephants diarrhea. After three days shoveling elephant poop, one says, 'If this keeps up, I'm getting out of show business.'"

Martha Graham's David Wood teaches at the Graham Studio. His classes are demanding, his manner serious. Martha approves, saying, "David has authority." He also teaches at Performing Arts High School where his master's degree in something hikes up his salary. It is there that he choreographs *Country Style,* a dance worthy of professional repertory. David has his life under control and nails it when he marries Marnie Thomas, moves to his native California, and becomes head of dance at UC-Berkeley.

I see no comparable path for myself. Chorus dancing in Broadway musicals is a treadmill to oblivion. Yet I cannot afford to dance exclusively with Martha. Where am I going? Marlon Brando, in his biker movie, *The Wild One,* says, "You don't go no*where,* you just *go.*" I've been doing that for too long.

August 1956

Martha is rehearsing for a film. But there is delay after delay. By the time it's ready to shoot, Linda is noticeably pregnant, and I am in the *Esther Williams Aqua Spectacle*, $1,500 to Martha's $150. *A Dancer's World* is made without either of us.

December 23, 1956

Linda's time is approaching. I get a TV quickie, *The Stingiest Man in Town*, an adaption of Charles Dickens's *A Christmas Carol*.

December 27, 1956

Linda's contractions begin at four in the afternoon. We invite friends to a "labor party." The apartment is clamorous with laughing and chattering while I time contractions. Midnight, two minutes apart, we shoo people out and taxi to Beth Israel. Linda had declined natural childbirth after her pediatrician explained that its main use is getting overweight women to exercise. At dawn I breakfast in the hospital cafeteria with weary residents and interns until summoned to an upper floor, dash out of the elevator, almost collide with a nurse holding an infant in one arm.

"Hodes?" I ask.

She points to a picture window. I rush over to see her place the infant in a bassinet—Catherine Regina Hodes—out of the everywhere, into the here.

Dancers routinely add whatever scrap of voice they have to the singing chorus but don't have to audition vocally. This changes with *The Boyfriend*. My audition song is "For Me and My Gal," learned in the army as a marching song. Paul Taylor sings "Happy Birthday." Neither of us is hired. The alarming part is hearing big trained voices on dancers who'd never before given me competition. In less than a decade, all chorus performers must sing *and* dance.

I do TV musicals: *Steve Allen Show, Herb Shriner Show, The American Cowboy, Ruggles of Red Gap, Satins and Spurs, A Midsummer's Night Dream,*

Cinderella, Lamp Unto My Feet, also "industrials," in which manufacturers show their wares to buyers. *Esquire Fashion Forum* was written and directed by Burt Shevelove, who also wrote *A Funny Thing Happened on the Way to the Forum.* I'm hopping from job to job, in between drawing unemployment insurance, going to auditions, and taking classes while waiting for Martha to start a project.

> I ask Martha if she'll employ me.
> She says, "Stuart, please don't annoy me."
> When I say, "I insist."
> She really gets pissed.
> And screams, "I won't let you destroy me!"

> I do an audition for Fosse
> His combos are zippy and saucy.
> When he asks for a jump,
> I fall flat on my rump.
> He says, "Thank you," and looks rather crossy.

> Jack Cole can be very quixotic,
> When making up movement exotic.
> He combines tap with voodoo,
> John Martin says, "Doo doo,"
> Deborah Jowitt says, "Highly erotic."

A new portrait of Martha arrives in the school office. She's in profile wearing Noguchi's bone-like *Night Journey* jewelry. The photographer had caught her, head thrust aggressively forward upon her long neck. Lee Leatherman disapproves, saying, "He's made her look like a vulture." Bertram Ross differs: "It's not Martha, it's Jocasta."

Bob says, "It's not Martha's picture. Her *shakti* escaped and he took its picture."

Martha had found the word *shakti* in India, a Hindu female principle or the wife of a deity. I arrive at the studio without Linda to have Martha's sister, Georgia, ask, "Where's your *shakti*?"

Martha arrives and studies the new photo.

"I think he's made you look too predatory," says Lee. "Bertram says it's Jocasta."

Martha's "ominous" profile. Photo by Angus McBean. MS
Thr 581 (olvwork613752), © Houghton Library, Harvard
University.

Martha studies the picture "It's not Jocasta," she says slowly. "He saw
that in me. And he's right. It's *there*."

August 1957

Catherine is eight months old when I get a call from California to dance
the Wild Horse in *Annie Get Your Gun*. It is the era of live TV when mistakes are seen by millions, so *Annie* will begin as a stage musical, perform
four weeks in San Francisco, five in Los Angeles, and do the live broadcast
on November 27, my thirty-third birthday. I don't want to go to California
but instead of turning it down ask $250 a week, surprised that they say yes.

When choreographer Ernie Flatt hears I'd seen *Annie* on Broadway, he says not to expect his to be anything like it. Flatt is friendly and soft-spoken. His moves are standard showbiz, put together with verve.

The California chorus dancers work mostly in films. Unlike New York dancers, they own cars and homes. Like us, they are often between jobs. One says that if he has to be out of work, he'd rather be out of work in Los Angeles. He asks what *tribe* I am from, evidently assumes I'm a Native American.

"Oh. Uh, Zuni."

"Zuni? I don't know much about Zuni."

"We have Pueblos and are culturally related to the Navaho. But our rug designs are finer, more detailed, and so is our pottery and silver."

This seems to satisfy him.

In the *New York Times*, Linda reads that Martha is working on a new dance set in the Garden of Eden. Bertram Ross is Adam, Yuriko is Eve, Matt Turney is Lilith, and Glen Tetley is the Devil. The Devil is the kind of role Martha had always made with me. But I am no longer one of Martha Graham's "Little Crackers."

Mary Martin plays Annie Oakley and comes to rehearsal in a flouncy white princess gown. Her sixteen-year-old daughter, Heller Halliday, wears a beige sheath of raw silk. A dancer whispers, "Mary should let Heller tell her what to wear."

As a performer, Mary Martin can do no wrong, but as the premiere approaches she gets serious laryngitis. Opening night, she begins to sing:

Folks are dumb where I come from, they don't have any larnin'.
Still they're happy as can be, a-doin what comes nnnaaatttcchh . . .

Her voice conks out. A standby, fully costumed, steps from the wings, and the show goes on. Martin is back the next day.

The musical has a juvenile couple played by Kelly Brown and Susan Luckey. But the show is too long for TV, so the juvenile roles are cut. In her monthly column, "Looking At Television," *Dance Magazine*'s TV critic, Ann Barzel, wrote: "I missed most of *Annie Get Your Gun* (Nov. 27-NBC), but for the record can report charming performances by Susan Luckey and Kelly Brown as the young lovers."[2]

Back in New York City, I bump into Donald Duncan, now working for

Dance Magazine, and tell him Barzel's column should be renamed: "*Not Looking at Television.*"

January 1958

Dr. Rachel Yocum, head of dance at New York City's High School of Performing Arts, asks if I'd like to teach there and arranges for me to take the exam for an Emergency Substitute license. The written part is based on a book by *New York Times* critic John Martin. The oral exam is in the studio of the school where I am questioned by a panel. One asks me to improvise.

"Any particular way?"

"What you'll teach the class."

"I don't teach improvisation."

"But you need to improvise."

"Why?"

"So you can make up combinations."

"I prepare my combinations before class."

"Well, can you improvise?"

"Of course. But I make combinations out of technique," and illustrate by stringing together skips, skitters, leaps, prances, pull-backs, tilts, falls, chugs, and whatever else pops into my mind. It occurs to me that that is what she had *meant* by improvising, and that she knows nothing about dance.

David Wood and I take part of the test together and when they ask for a show of technical skill, we dance a section from Martha's *Ardent Song.* That and an observed class are the only meaningful tests. We both get licenses. Department head Rachel Yocum says she was sure I'd blown it when I'd gotten testy with the panel.

Performing Arts High School brims with talent, but sometimes I give them hell. One day, Jane Kosminsky dances by and says, "You can yell if you want, but we know you love us."

One day they're dancing badly. "What's the matter with everybody? You look like you're sleepwalking."

"We are," says Kosminsky. It is October 27, 1962, the day after President Kennedy had given Khrushchev a missile ultimatum.

"Cuba?"

"We thought the atom bomb was going to drop, so we were up all night on the telephone saying goodbye."

I call a halt to technique and we sit on the floor discussing why dance is needed in this screwed-up world.

Helen Tamiris, choreographer of *Annie Get Your Gun* on Broadway, offers me the Wild Horse in its New York City Center revival, a run that closes before Martha's season. City Center musicals pay minimum even to stars. They don't attract the likes of Ethel Merman, but great roles attract stars, and Annie Oakley attracts Martha Raye who signs a contract but never shows up. Betty Jane Watson, who does Annie Oakley in summer stock, takes over.

Helen Tamiris had promised me "billing," which means my name in advertising. An assistant hands me a contract and when I point out it says nothing about billing, assures me that as a featured dancer, billing is a matter of course. Like an idiot, I sign. When a *New York Times* ad appears without my name, I show it to Tamiris, who acts surprised and sends me to producer Jean Dalrymple.

"It's not in your contract," says Dalrymple.

Tamiris tells me I should make a formal complaint to Actors' Equity and she will back me up. Fuming, I go to the *barre*. One hour later, sweating from every pore, all I want to do is learn the moves.

Helen Tamiris, tall, blonde, and statuesque, must have been a wow in her prime. In *Annie*, one of her best moves is the Wild Horse's flying entrance, a stag leap that reverses in the air like a karate kick, although in 1957, few know about karate. After *Annie* opened, Brooks Atkinson, *New York Times* drama critic, was lukewarm in his review. About me: "Stuart Hodes, as the Wild Horse (it says in the program), invokes the gods ferociously."

I like "ferociously," but what does "(it says in the program)" mean? And I was not invoking gods. I was a wild horse, like it says in the program.

I attend one rehearsal of my understudy, a promising lad named Edward Villella, who gives the role a polished classical look instead of the slashing rawness I think it should have. Nevertheless, I resolve that if I can help it, Villella will not show his stuff to the world in this production.

April 1, 1958, Adelphi Theatre

The B. de Rothschild Foundation presents Martha Graham and her Dance Company. Two stunning premieres: *Clytemnestra* and *Embattled Garden*. I feel more than a twinge of regret watching Glen Tetley as the Stranger, a role I imagine would have been mine.

There's a passage in which Glen slaps his thighs, and after the show he sits in his dressing room proud of his raw broken-veined skin, evidence of his dancing ferocity. When Tetley leaves, Paul Taylor inherits the role and "pulls" each slap, hands barely contacting his thighs, to create a creepy, ominous Stranger. In 2003, the Stranger is danced by Christophe Jeannot, who could be the dancer Martha meant when she said that if she ever staged *Swan Lake*, the villain, Rothbart, would be beautiful and irresistible. With Jeannot as the Stranger, I can believe that Eve would do anything he asks. I can't help but wonder how the Stranger would have turned out if he'd been created by me.

Merce Cunningham is so stunning I watch whenever I can, although I seldom follow his creative drift. And I don't even try to understand explanations that invoke Zen, chance, the *Book of Changes,* or other philosophies. In 1958 Merce creates a scandal. In a dance titled *Winterbranch* at the New York State Theater, a stage light shines straight into the eyes of people in the orchestra. Some shield their eyes waiting for it to go out, but it never does. Afterward, people argue what Merce was up to. Some say grandstanding. Some say that light cues had been chosen by chance. That the cue to turn it on had come up but not one to turn it off. Bertram Ross said Merce wanted to force people to strain past the light, to actively seek out the action on the stage. Makes as much sense as any.

Martha is rehearsing for a spring season at the Adelphi Theater with two important premieres, *Seraphic Dialogue* and *Clytemnestra.* I'm mostly working commercial jobs outside the troupe, but Martha asks me back to dance the Husbandman in *Appalachian Spring* and Dark Beloved in *Deaths and Entrances.* The season opens on April 1, 1958. It is my last appearance in the Graham troupe.

June 1958

A film of *Appalachian Spring* is supposed to start shooting. I'd missed *A Dancer's World* for the far better paid *Esther Williams Aqua Spectacle* so am anxious not to miss *Spring*. It was scheduled right after I returned from California, when Linda was invisibly pregnant. She is barely noticeable now and Martha wants her in it. She refuses. "Twenty years from now, I don't want people thinking Linda Hodes was fat."

Bertram Ross disagrees. "If you look pregnant you *have* to be in it. Those revivalists were always knocking up the women in their flocks."

Shooting is further delayed, and she is nine months pregnant when it finally starts. On the second shooting day her contractions begin. At dawn we go to the hospital, but I must be on the set at 8:00 a.m. The hospital calls around 9:00. When I tell Martha Graham that our daughter is her namesake, she says, "Be careful. Martha is a very strong name. It means 'mistress of the house.'"

Sixteen years later, Martha Hodes goes backstage after a performance, to be warmly greeted by Martha Graham. When they part, she takes my daughter's hand in hers. "You have a very dangerous name."

Before contracts for *Appalachian Spring* are signed, I learn that producer Nathan Kroll had obtained a "dispensation" for me from Screen Actors Guild. I won't have to join the union, and he will not have to pay scale. Dispensations are mostly for documentaries, letting people appear once without joining SAG. But this is my second film. The first was *Diversion of Angels,* never released. A second dispensation violates SAG's rules. When I call, SAG threatens to kill the film if I don't keep quiet. So I agree to Kroll's pittance, $250, but demand a royalty if the film is ever shown on network TV. Kroll refuses so I don't sign. When shooting is finished, I still haven't signed. The film is "in the can" but cannot be released without my signature. Two weeks later Martha calls Linda who is home with the new baby.

"Stuart is trying to destroy me!"

To me, Linda commands, "Get Martha out of my hair!"

I take three sheets of blank letter paper, sign each at the bottom, and mail them to Martha with a note saying, as I recall, "My signatures herewith. Fill in as you please."

It's my second note. I'd torn up the first which said, "You have the morals of a waterfront whore," deciding it was defamatory, though not to Martha. When I next see her, she purrs, no reference to the blank signatures. My contract is upped to $450 with provision for 15 percent additional for the first three network airings. *Appalachian Spring* plays many times on public TV, but I never see another dime.

January 20, 1959

On Ruth St. Denis's eightieth birthday, Martha gives her a party. I arrive to see her installed in an armchair in Studio One, pillows and flowers at her feet. She's alone. Martha commandeers me to her presence, introduces me as a dancer in her company, and leaves.

On a pillow looking up, I say, "Miss Ruth, nine years ago, I sat beside you at a luncheon. You asked me a question I've been pondering ever since." She inclines toward me.

"You said, 'Young man, what are your dreams?' I said, within a year I wanted to be able to do four *pirouettes,* within two years, dance a role in Martha's company, within three, make my own dances and present them in a concert."

"Those weren't your dreams, were they?"

"Goals, maybe. Not dreams." Someone is now behind me but I have Miss Ruth's attention. "I still ask myself what my dreams are and I'm still not sure."

"Has that made you unhappy?"

"Oh no. I keep having wonderful new dreams. I want to thank you."

Miss Ruth still has her long queenly body, white hair coifed above a noble brow. When she was young, any beautiful nervy young woman could proclaim herself a dancer. Europe was full of young women who danced naked or almost, hoping for a rich sugar daddy. Most ended with less, and poor Margaretha Zelle, who was Dutch, apportioned herself among German, French, and English lovers, to be executed as Mata Hari, the spy.

Miss Ruth met an erstwhile divinity student and ballroom dancer, Ted Shawn, made him her partner and husband, created dances she deemed sacred, and the world agreed that they were. When faced by an intense young Martha Graham with distinctly unconventional beauty, she might have deemed it a kindness to discourage her from entering this pitiless arena. A nattily dressed young man bends over me and kisses Miss Ruth's hand. I vacate my pillow. Martha runs hither and thither directing traffic to Miss Ruth's throne.

July 1959, Opportunity Theater, Utah State University, Logan, Utah

Linda and I are hired for the summer. Most of the dance students are from New York City's High School of Performing Arts. We give technique daily, set dances for *Paint Your Wagon,* and I make a biblical ballet for the dance concert.

I request a conference with a Bible scholar, am referred to a USU professor, and when we meet he's smoking a cigarette so I know he's not a practicing Mormon. I ask why Moses had struck the rock at Meribah instead of praying before it as God had commanded. He asks what I think. I tell him it cannot be pride because the Bible describes Moses as slow of speech and humble before God. I relate the theory of a Catholic writer: that in the desert when the Israelites grumbled against God, it rankled the Almighty, who told Moses that He intended to destroy them and bring forth a new nation from Moses's loins. When Moses struck the rock, it was to turn God's wrath upon himself and thus save his people. This portended the sacrifice of Jesus who sacrificed Himself for all humankind. I hope for scholarly confirmation.

But the professor sees Moses as a Hebrew Oedipus who symbolically slays God the Father. Between Martha Graham and Erick Hawkins, I've had enough of Oedipus so stick with the other. The theater department builds me a huge papier-mâché rock and, when struck by Moses, out gushes a Heavenly stream.

In 1936, *New York Times* dance critic John Martin had taught at the Bennington Summer School of Dance. Martha, Doris Humphrey, Charles Weidman, and Hanya Holm were there. Martha said, "John came to breakfast one day with a sheaf of dance scenarios he'd written and handed them around. He expected us to use them."

John Martin was acting on a European view, that the essence of a ballet is a concept that can be written. Writers create scenarios and program credits read, "Ballet by X, Choreography by Y." When Lincoln Kirstein brought George Balanchine to the U.S.A., he proffered his own scenarios, one based on Custer's Last Stand. When I visited China in 1980, I learned that the scenario *is* the ballet. Once approved, it is handed to several choreographers. Each production may look entirely different, yet all are considered the same ballet. If America's number-one dance critic imagined that Martha Graham, Doris Humphrey, Charles Weidman, and Hanya Holm worked that way, he was clueless.

I met critic John Martin once. It was a dance gathering right after I'd done the Wild Horse on TV in *Annie Get Your Gun.* He mentioned seeing me. Before videotape, the East Coast saw Hollywood productions live when broadcast. Three hours later, the West Coast saw a kinescope (a movie made directly from the TV tube).

"I saw *Annie,* too."

"How did you like it?" asked Martin.

"Mary Martin was charming, but Ethel Merman is Annie Oakley to me."

"I meant, how did you like yourself as the Wild Horse?"

"Oh. Actually I hated myself."

"Why?"

"I have so many flaws."

"Was that the first time you ever saw yourself dance?"

"No. I saw myself in a film of *Diversion of Angels.* Hated that too."

"If it's any comfort to you, bad dancers always love themselves."

A genuine compliment, but it did not change my opinion of John Martin as a malign force in dance.

Louis Horst, in his journal, *Dance Observer,* put an extension of himself into print. Even after learning that Louis was unique, I believe that writing about dance can be done with honor and grace. Every performer wants to be "covered," and in the 1950s, New York City had nine newspapers plus the *Brooklyn Daily Eagle.*[3] But until Clive Barnes came on the scene, neither John Martin nor Walter Terry would cross the East River, even when Rudolf Nureyev played the Brooklyn Academy of Music. Broadway—the Main Stem—covered by all critics, was Martha's reason for insisting on playing a Broadway house.

After my ballet, *Abyss,* premiered in Cannes, France, Barnes, after questioning whether a modern dancer *ought* to choreograph a classical ballet, wrote a favorable review.

Martha read it. "Clive Barnes liked your dance. And he knows."

When Barnes arrived in New York City, he hosted a party for what seemed like every dancer in town and asked me, "Why are you the only modern dancer I know who doesn't have a dance company?"

Jokingly: "Because I have a family." I decided it was the simple truth.

I have a nodding acquaintance with Jennifer Dunning when we meet at performances, and Don McDonagh became a friend. Edwin Denby stopped being the *Herald Tribune's* dance critic in 1945, before I'd taken a dance lesson, but I've read enough of his 1965 *Dancers, Buildings, and People in the Streets,* to know I ought to read more. I also intend to hunt down and read his *Snoring in New York* (1974). For Christmas 1946, Martha gave me *Immortal Shadows: A Book of Dramatic Criticism* by Stark Young, including a piece on her. I read it dutifully. Next was *Mont-Saint-Michel and Chartres* by Henry Adams. Read that too. I think.

Shortly after *Ballet Review* published my essay "Lust for Lifts" (about my various dance partners), I ran into Jack Anderson who gave me a squinty stare and said, "Lust for *Lifts?*"

In 1988, I attended the American Dance Festival's International Critic's Conference, joining a dozen or so journalists to spend four weeks watching and writing about dance. The day I arrived, I ran into Paul Taylor, who said, "Have you become one of *them?*"

The best "notice" I ever got was from playwright Wendy Wasserstein in her book, *Shiksa Goddess.* She'd seen *I Thought You Were Dead* at Dance Theater Workshop: "I loved the Dancers Over 40. Especially a waltz danced by Stuart Hodes and Alice Teirstein. Hodes was Martha Graham's partner in the 1950s. His face is amazing, and his dancing was elegant and joyous. Nick and I want to cast him in our film."[4]

I hadn't met her, she's not a critic, has no axe to grind, so I can happily believe what she wrote. How I wish she'd been able to make her film.

No longer in Martha's troupe, I continue to teach in her school. One day several faculty and Martha were in the tiny lounge between the kitchen and Studio Three. Martha was sipping honeyed tea. Talk turned to a woman in the coaching class who had crippling tension.

"What does she do with her hands? They look like claws."

"So do her arms and elbows."

"Her shoulders are always up around her ears."

"She looks like she's having stomach cramps every time she does a Contraction."

"I can't get anything like a Contraction out of her."

"If you give a simple walk, she looks like she's going to break both legs"

I interrupt. "I think you're all terrible. She comes to class every day, never asks questions, never complains, takes every correction, does everything she's told, tries as hard as she can . . ." *Splatt!*

A pot of honey shatters against the wall a foot from my head. Martha had thrown it. "Oh, shut up, holier-than-thou."

Bethsabée de Rothschild holds Christmas parties for the troupe at her Manhattan town house. A decorated tree, superb food and wine, quiet conversation, and gifts. One year I spent days sticking sequins and beads into a Styrofoam ball. Bethsabée opened the package, smiled, showed it around, had it hung on her tree.

Martha and Bethsabée give personal but not too costly gifts, and, except for books, none are "practical." A proper gift is something you will admire but not buy: tiny carvings of stone or jasper; jewelry of jade, agate, or crystal; a framed square of antique brocade; an old print. One Christmas, Bethsabée gave each woman a beaded evening bag.

When Linda and I married, Martha gave us a jade carving of the Chinese ideograph for marriage—"double happiness"—and said that Bethsabée wanted to give us a dishwasher. Our kitchen had room for one appliance so our priority was a clothes washer. Too practical. Bethsabée gave us a signed Picasso lithograph.

Gifts for Martha could be antique curios, old prints, things found at Chait Galleries, where the proprietor, told that the Graham dancers are chipping in to buy a gift for Martha Graham, showed affordable treasures. Yuriko Kikuchi scored a hit with an ivory Buddha the size of a grape. One could also bake or sew a present. But except for tights knitted by Helen McGehee, I never recall anyone giving Martha a dance gift. After her death, Martha's entire gift collection, designer clothes, furniture, books, etc., were transferred to the minion she designated as her heir.

The Peking Opera Ballet, playing New York City, asked to see a class at the Martha Graham School. Martha decided to teach. Afterward, a catered luncheon in the garden. Thirty dancers arrived plus interpreters and officials. Francis Mason, chairman of Martha's board and the editor of *Ballet Review,* began, "Martha Graham is a revolutionary woman." He described her struggle to create American dance in a nation that had no traditional form of its own.

Martha also began with a speech. "We are washed by two oceans," and spoke of America's role as the inheritor of traditions from both West and East. "We cherish all our traditions, yet as Americans we must remain true to our differences." The smooth faces of the dancers hang on every word. "What I have done is called revolutionary, but it is built upon tradition. You will see much that is based upon classical ballet. We do not seek to destroy the work of 300 years."

Francis Mason had cast her as a revolutionary, while Martha took her stand as a conservator of tradition. Among the Chinese, two different groups were present: the lean rapt dancers and expressionless political cadres. Mason had addressed the dancers. Martha aimed her words directly at their keepers.

Martha's long-pending film of *Night Journey* was about to shoot. She wanted me to dance the Seer but with a pair of toddlers, I cannot afford to leave my musical, *Do Re Mi.* So I teach the role to Paul Taylor. Forty years later, when *Night Journey* is revived, dancers learn from the film. Martha, no longer dancing, pretty much ignores the Seer. In 2004, the reborn Martha Graham Company revived *Night Journey.* I was unhappy with the Seer and wrote a letter to directors Christine Dakin and Terese Capucilli:

January 29, 2003

I am disturbed by the role of the Seer. Gary danced well, but no performance could make up for what I view as loss of the Seer's essence. Although glad to see the Contractions gone that once followed each thump of the staff, the Seer's primary function is obscured. The three basic pillars:

1. Jocasta and Oedipus enact the tragedy.
2. The Chorus responds for us, with horror, helplessness, despair.
3. The Seer is Fate, implacable and inevitable.

Where the present choreography came from, I honestly don't know. Pearl thinks it came from Paul Taylor in the film. I've not seen the film but taught Paul the role and he did pretty much what

I taught. He certainly did not add the frills and furbelows (unless it was later) that presently clutter up the role.

Gary's Seer does not come across as blind because his head is constantly bobbing and swiveling, as though peering out through his blindfold. When I danced the Seer, he did not wear a blindfold. Blindness was evoked by the way the gaze was held, or rather withheld. Now, wearing a blindfold, the Seer no longer seems blind.

When he strode with his staff, the Seer always stood up straight, gaze lifted as if locked upon a past and future no one else can see. Now he lurches and flails, clinging to his staff with a rounded back. When he crawls upstage, his body is broken and twisted, as if wracked with pain. But Fate does not suffer pain. It is Jocasta and Oedipus who suffer Fate. With the Seer emoting all over the place, it renders the emotions of Jocasta and Oedipus less than central, and also competes with the cry of the Daughters of the Night. In show-biz terms, the Seer looks like he's trying to steal the scene.

The one-handed lift of the staff is out of context. The staff is a weighty and important object, a blind man's cane, a substitute for eyes. It is also a symbol of power and must be handled carefully, even reverently. When flung overhead in one hand, the staff loses both weight and importance, becoming a javelin, a drum major's baton, something less powerful.

I am genuinely perplexed by the loss of the trembling which once book-ended the Seer's dance of revelation.

To sum up, what I saw was not the image of the Seer I gained, first from Mark Ryder when he taught me the role, or from Martha, when she corrected and coached. Should you ever wish to explore any of its consequences (perhaps when the role is being taught to someone for the first time), I would be honored to participate.

Dakin and Capucilli invited me to work with David Zurak, new in the company. He's gifted but already knows the moves, so he'll have to unlearn. Although he is open and willing, I find myself constantly peeling away extraneous moves. Like trying to restore an antique house that's had many makeovers.

October 10, 1961

I'm dance captain of *Milk and Honey* and in the Society of Stage Directors and Choreographers (SSD&C), whose meetings feature celebrated guests. I'm asked to invite Martha Graham. Clive Barnes will introduce her. Martha agrees. The meeting is packed. Barnes and Philip Burton are at the head of the table, Martha on their left, me on Martha's left. Barnes begins: "When Martha Graham made the decision to become a dancer, it was a great loss to criticism."

The directors ask interesting questions, hang on Martha's words, and, as usual, she has them in the palm of her hand.

Among those present is a minor member of the cast of *Milk and Honey*, Juki Arkin's understudy, a European I'll call Krotchic. I'd not known he was a choreographer, much less a member of SSD&C. He keeps his elbow on the table when he puts up his hand. Martha nods. In a throaty foreign accent: "I think you are fake. People act like you genius, but you make ugliness. Everyone think this is wonderful, but I don't think so. I think ..." and croaks on in the astonished silence. I rise intending to strangle the little shit, but Martha's hand shoots out and presses me back down.

"I am not here to justify myself to you," she says quietly, and turns to Barnes and Burton. "I have heard such talk since the day I began."

"I assure you they do not represent the views of anyone else here," exclaims Burton. Barnes dismisses Krotchic as a relic, seconded by others as he rises and slinks out. All try to recapture the zest, but it's gone. The next day Martha dismisses my halting apology.

"I know I should never get involved in those things."

Next day, back at *Milk and Honey*, I tell Juki Arkin about the incident. He says, "Don't worry. I taking care of Krotchic."

"What do you mean?"

"I fucking his wife."

November 27, 1961

I'm startled by a telegram from Martha: DEAR STUART, ALL LOVE ON YOUR BIRTHDAY. IF I COULD I WOULD THANK YOUR MOTHER FOR YOUR LIFE. MARTHA.

Martha always made a birthday fuss over Bob and Bertram but sensed that I preferred to let mine pass unremarked. Is she reminding me she is still a presence in my life?

Summer, 1962, Connecticut College American Dance Festival

The Graham Company is in residence. I'm hired to teach Graham Technique. Martha invites me to watch a rehearsal of *Secular Games*. The men dance a section titled "Play with thought in a Socratic society." The women interrupt, thrusting and slapping their hips on each step. Martha rises and illustrates, vigorously slapping her own hip: "You *[slap]* love it You *[slap]* love it You *[slap]* love it And if you love it enough, maybe somebody else will love it."

1964

Linda and I are spending months apart. She assists director José Quintero in *Marco Millions* and for a time dances "Simon of Legree" in *The King and I*. She performs with Martha Graham, Paul Taylor, and Glen Tetley, tours Europe, Egypt, and Iron Curtain countries including Russia. In London she makes a ballet for Ballet Rambert, adapted from her duet *The Ringing Down,* made for me and Jack Moor. It becomes a trio, *The Act,* with herself as the ventriloquist's wife. I'm show-hopping, often out of town, and when we're both in New York, she rehearses days, I perform nights. We talk about divorce.

Me: "I couldn't live without the girls."

Linda: "They could live with you if you get someone nice to marry you, and I can have them sometimes."

"I'd want them to have you as much as possible."

It strikes me as a terrible failure yet inescapable. I call a family friend lawyer, who asks me for the name of Linda's lawyer.

"You."

"I can't be lawyer for both."

"Why not?"

"You're adversaries. I represent you. Someone else has to represent her."

"We are not adversaries. We both want this divorce."

"Lots of people say that but you'd be amazed what they fight about."

Elizabeth Hodes and Pooh. Photo by Stuart Hodes.

"We're done fighting. She wanted me to take the Picasso etching. I convinced her to."

In the summer of 1965, after choreographing the St. Louis Municipal Opera, I fly to Juarez, come back the next day with papers. Linda tells Martha Graham, who keeps it to herself. When mutual friends learn that Linda and I are no longer husband and wife, they resent not having been kept abreast of our personal lives and devise scenarios. Linda tells me someone said, "I hear it's because Stuart is a latent homosexual."

"What did you say?" I ask.

"If true, it would have made things easier."

The second part of this saga is Elizabeth. I'm no Daniel Petrie, who lives by the soldier-boy motto, "find 'em, fuck 'em, and forget 'em," and although acutely aware of Elizabeth, with whom I've been in three shows, I keep my distance. She had danced on the White House lawn to celebrate The Great Society, shook hands with President Lyndon Johnson, danced in an Off-Broadway hit, *Little Mary Sunshine,* and during the summer of my divorce, was dancing and singing in the Cleveland Musicarnival. I drive to Cleveland to propose. She says yes.

I go to work for Rebekah Harkness, about to open Harkness House for Ballet Arts. Elizabeth and I marry one day after its official opening. Catherine and Martha are flower girls. A year later, Linda marries Ehud Ben David in Israel, and for Christmas knits Elizabeth a pair of tights.

Harkness Ballet, 1965

Rebekah Harkness has a fortune from her deceased husband, William Hale Harkness, who'd been John D. Rockefeller's banker. She had bankrolled the Joffrey Ballet, now has her own troupe housed on East 77th Street in the luxurious Watson mansion. A glass case in the lobby exhibits a rotating sculpture by Salvador Dalí, a golden egg with wings that slowly open and close. It's for Rebekah's ashes.

After installing ballet studios, canteen, dressing rooms, massage therapy room, and a private eyrie for herself, Rebekah hosts two opening parties. The first is for dancers, the second, two days later, for the press and VIPs. I'm on staff, so attend both, and since there's food and liquor, many dancers who'd been invited to the first crash the second.

Elizabeth and I marry on the day between parties. We're on the buffet line next to Barbara Swisher and John Grigas, with whom we'd danced in *To Broadway With Love* and who'd been to the first Harkness party.

"Anything new since I saw you guys on Friday?" asks Barbara.

"We got married," I say.

Barbara grins. "Ah! So today you're being married."

"We *are* married."

Her grin widens. "Right."

Elizabeth softly. "We got married yesterday."

"You mean really?"

"Really."

"Not really?"

"Yes, really."

"Mister and missus?"

"Mister and missus."

"Omigod!"

John Grigas raises his glass. "What did you do with Linda? Throw her out the window?"

A request to Harkness comes from someone named Twyla Tharp, who invites me to the Judson Memorial Church. She, Sara Rudner, and Rose Marie Wright dance in a gym, floor cluttered with amber warning blinkers, the kind used at highway construction sites. The dancers do little more than *passé developpé* for twenty minutes, yet all have fierce charisma. I'm one of five in the audience and ask, "Do you have any men in your group?"

"No!" says Tharp. "If I need jumps, I can jump." She jumps up and down. "If I need someone picked up, I can pick her up." Grabs Rose Marie Wright and hauls her off the ground.

"Why do I need men?"

"Because men are in the world."

Two-second pause. "Martha Graham started without men. When I want a man, I'll get one."

I relate this to Jack Cole, who is making a dance at Harkness House. He nods: "She has a role model."

When Norman Singer, head of the Hunter College Concert Bureau, offers three performances for young audiences, the project is turned over to me, and in the next year I produce *Ballet Close-ups*, *Ballet Athletes*, and *Ballet Gallery*. George Skibine asks if I'd like to make a work for the Harkness Ballet, and I tell him my idea based on Andreyev's short story, "The Abyss."

"Has been done."

"Who by?"

Names some Russian. "Was not success."

"Mine will be."

I ask for a woman to work with, he gives me Lili Cockerille, who's seventeen and in a leotard looks fourteen. How can I create the climactic rape with this child? But ten minutes into the rehearsal she's re-engineering my lifts, and in record time we complete the duet and teach it to Lone Isakson and Lawrence Rhodes, who show it to Skibine and Rebekah. Skibine waits for her response.

"Interesting," she says, eyes like empty shot glasses. She hasn't the faintest idea what she's seen. Skibine convinces her to let me complete the ballet.

Rebekah Harkness invites Elizabeth and me to dinner in her Manhattan pied-à-terre at the Hotel Carlyle. Guests include Donald Saddler, composer Lee Hoiby, most of the younger ballet teachers and classroom musicians. There's noisy laughter, gossip, dishing, and campy jokes. Rebekah, the constant center of attention, seems desperately isolated. Her personal maid shows up with meds. When the maid turns away, Rebekah sticks out her tongue, eliciting shrieks. Dinner arrives wheeled in by waiters on carts. It's from Room Service. Elizabeth and I leave feeling sorry for this lonely, empty-headed, multimillionaire.

The Ballet Team, 1967–1969

After I'm fired from Harkness (don't ask) I start The Ballet Team, a troupe meant for young audiences, and ask a dancer from Holland what it was like to dance in a famed young-audience company, Scapino Ballet.

"Very good, as long as you don't mind getting up early."

Young audiences are great, and dancing at 9:00 a.m. not as bad as I'd feared, although I never relished getting up before dawn.

We opened with *Gymkhana,* a sports dance by me; then *Prayer Ritual,* an African dance by Percival Borde; *Karate,* by Gary Rambach; *Olé Olé,* by Vicente Nebrada; and closed with *Peter and the Wolf,* by Donald Saddler. When a gifted Harkness trainee, Sally Trammel, returns from study in India, she opens our show with Alarippu, a traditional dance in Bharatanatyam.

The school kids love Sally in her sari. They are gripped by Linda Hodes's *Curley's Wife,* based on Steinbeck's *Of Mice and Men.* A letter from a parent asks why I put violence on the stage when it is so terribly part of their children's lives. I answer every letter, explaining that street violence is destructive and mind-numbing, but on a stage as dance is deeply sensitizing.

At Hyattsville High, the principal hands an "H" to every one of us. "We have lots of teams, but no Ballet Team. We want you to be ours."

Ballet Team dancers go into major troupes. Clay Taliaferro becomes a José Limón star, Victor Vargas goes into Ballet Theater, Alan Tung becomes director of Maurice Béjart's school, Mudra. Going to Newark one morning, Nicholas Gunn mentions that Paul Taylor is holding an audition next day.

"I'll call Alex Kotimsky for tomorrow."

"I'm not going," says Nick.

"Why not?"

"My feet don't point, my legs don't straighten, and I have a barrel chest. What makes me think I can be a dancer?"

"You have something special," says Sally Trammel.

"Paul looks for people, not bodies," I say. "You have to go."

The next day Alex Kotimsky performs and when we arrive home, Nick is waiting.

"What happened?"

"Mr. Taylor told me I'm in the company, but I'm not sure."

"Why aren't you sure?"

"Because I can't believe it!"

Alex Kotimsky, who'd replaced Nick, emigrated from Hungary after the Russians sent in tanks, and wanting to become an American citizen quickly, joined the U.S. Army. A trained dancer, he'd heard that dancers were needed in Special Services and applied. But confusing Special Services with Special Forces, ended up a Green Beret. Now expert in martial arts, he gives our *Karate* dance fearsome power.

Booked into a grim Newark high school, we're escorted to a huge auditorium and told to stay onstage. The dancers change in student bathrooms, and the first show at 9:00 a.m. goes well. After the second show at 11, shy girls bring us sandwiches, an apple, orange drink, and hang around. The third show is at 2:00 p.m. and brings down the house. On the way back to Manhattan, I tell the dancers they'd performed brilliantly.

Armando Zetina: "Do you know why we danced so well?"

"What do you mean?"

"We were changing in the boy's bathroom when these guys came in and made a circle around us. They were really big. One said, 'Are you the dancers?' I said yes. He said, 'You *better* be good.'"

We give an adult show at Wagner College, Staten Island, another at Dance Theater Workshop, a third at Needle Trades High School, where I premiere a dance to Krzysztof Penderecki's Threnody to the Victims of Hiroshima, dancing in it myself. One of the dancers peeks through the curtain.

"I see Martha Graham!"

I look. There she is, coming down the aisle with Lee Leatherman. After the number she comes backstage saying she can't stay. I wait for her comment.

Stuart, Mariano Garcia, and Teresa Hill. Photo by Alfred Gescheidt.

"Your dancers dance beautifully."
(Oh, well.)

The Ballet Team plays Central Park's Delacorte Theater, Sunday, a kid's matinee. It's the day my daughters are returning from Israel. I wake early and while making coffee, hear the radio announce a multiple hijacking: El Al, Pan Am, Swissair, American, and TWA. My daughters are on the hijacked TWA flight. Nothing I can do, so go to the Delacorte Theater, do the show, afterward explain why I can't go to the party.

"You let us do the show without even mentioning that your daughters had been hijacked!" exclaims Armando Zetina.

On the El Al flight, sky marshals shoot one hijacker, capture the other, land at Heathrow. Pan Am lands in Egypt, the passengers debarked, the plane blown up. AA, Swissair, and TWA land in Jordan where they sit surrounded by armed men. Martha Graham calls to say that Bethsabée is willing to send me there but the U.S. State Department says that my girls' best defense is being children unconnected to wealth. Five days and nights I listen to news stations. The day after they're rescued, the Sunday *Times* runs a blurry photo of the interior of a bus, and I recognize Catherine. She's the *New York Times* quote of the week: "'All I want to do is thank God and have a bath.'"

I'm hugging them at Kennedy Airport when Catherine says, "Oh, Daddy, we were so worried about you."

In 2018, historian Martha Hodes gets a grant from the Guggenheim Memorial Foundation to write a book about the hijacking.

10

. . . .

A Presence Is Gone

Martha Graham graduated high school in 1913, editor-in-chief of her class yearbook, *Olive and Gold,* to which she contributed a poem:

> All nature seems to beckon forth my soul,
> And bind it to her by the fairy chains
> Of misty morrow mornings. 'Tis a call
> Sent inland 'cross life's gulf of mystic dream isles
> Sun-kist, and wafted by the breath of angels,
> Paint, illusive comes to me this call:
> 'Tis heard in liquid, rippling, soaring notes,
> From feathered throats of singing birds on high,
> It comes from Mountain's velvet shadows deep,
> Shrouded in the mystery, gleamed in hope;
> On, sweeping down from cloud-capped peak aloft,
> The breath of God, himself, hath touched my soul,
> And straightway turned it to His sacred lyre.
> And there be some in dreams have spanned this bridge
> Up which God leads us by His perfect love,
> Have caught in fancy's mesh the fleeting gleam,
> Imprison'd it in words—and lo 'tis there.
> But I must rest content to have heard the call,
> To have enter'd in the Land of heart's desire.

All her life, Martha thrilled to that "call sent inland 'cross life's gulf of mystic dream isles." It summoned when she saw Ruth St. Denis in Los Angeles, awoke the *Heretic* within her, inspired the warrior saint of *Seraphic Dialogue,* and all her heroes from Emily Dickinson to the Witch of Endor. She danced with ferocity and joy until she could dance no more. At eighty, her cry, "Old age is a pain in the neck," is not poetry.

1966

The telephone rings, "Hello, Martha." Elizabeth shoves a chair under me and we talk for an hour. If I could have said, "Martha, how about I drop over?" she'd have been delighted. But my family comes first.

1969

I interview for a job at the New York State Council on the Arts (NYSCA), but when offered it, decline because I intend to ask for a grant for The Ballet Team. I'm told that the job is half-time, hourly pay, no benefits, and that I will still be eligible. I sign on. My title: Dance Associate.

A letter from American Ballet Theater's general manager, Sherwin Goldman, puts NYSCA on notice that America's oldest and greatest ballet company expects to be served. In 1940 it had begun as *Ballet Theatre,* added *American* to its name in 1957, further Americanized when it changed *Theatre* to *Theater,* a nod to newly significant government funding. I draft a deferential reply.

My boss is French/Canadian, Richard d'Anjou, relaxed and folksy, with a genuine liking for arts people, plus a shrewd understanding of bureaucracies. Explaining my job: "We want to hitch a ride on your experience as an artist. But never forget that you're now a bureaucrat. Your job is tender loving care of every artist who comes calling. You are here to see that the bureaucracy does its job. Lots of wheels have to be turning before anything gets done."[1]

I call every dance company I can find in New York state asking them to write on letterheads so that when applications for "support" are ready, they'll get one. "Support" is the eleemosynary[2] word for money. Others in performing arts are Gina Shield, theater associate, and Brad Morrison, music associate. D'Anjou's assistant, Phil Hyde, greets us every morning with, "Okay team, let's move paper."

I soon realize that moving paper requires muscles I've not yet learned to use.

I turn in my hours each day, and on Ballet Team show days call a colleague, Larry Ross, who takes over. When it is certain that NYSCA will be making grants, there's a blizzard of ticket offers. I can't possibly see all of them, so engage "auditors." Eventually, d'Anjou gets a budget for tickets, saying that the very least NYSCA can do is pay for a couple of seats.

The eight-page application arrives, accompanied by a man from Albany, who explains that NYSCA does not "give grants," it "purchases services." This is excellent, giving artists the status of accountants, plumbers, state police, and other state employees whose services the state buys. Yet the Albany man manages to express his opinion of artists. The generic term for product is "widget," but the Albany man uses "toilet seats." He drones, "You fill in how many toilet seats the company produces, the cost of producing each toilet seat, the number of toilet seats sold, the loss per toilet seat, and the amount of state subsidy requested for each toilet seat." We are glad when this turd-eater returns to Albany.

But NYSCA can support only *incorporated* nonprofits, and most smaller dance troupes, even some famous ones, are neither. Charles Reinhart, who went from managing Paul Taylor and Alvin Ailey to setting up National Endowment for the Arts dance programs, suggests we allow "de facto" nonprofit status, determined by one question: Do you earn a profit? He also wants to allow, as an expense, the services of dancers who work *without pay,* terming it "deferred expenses."

Dancers in all modern companies, also smaller ballet troupes, rehearse without pay. By calculating, say, twelve dancers at five dollars an hour, twenty hours a week, forty weeks a year, $48,000 could be added to a deficit allowing $24,000 more support, little enough for dances whose value to American culture is beyond price.

NYSCA's accountants are dumbfounded. To them, something not paid for *doesn't exist.* I argue that dancing, including rehearsals, is a basic product, a stock-in-trade, and *must* be accounted for. As things stand, dancers are *endowing* the State of New York with their unpaid labor. I fire off a vitriolic memo to the accounting staff, copy to our boss, Eric Larrabee, for whom it is really intended, about a profession called "Accounting" that is unable to account for the basic product of an enterprise that the State of New York is *paying them* to account for.

Larrabee sides with Reinhart but stipulates that all unincorporated dance companies be informed that "de facto" nonprofit status is temporary, and they must become legal. He also allows "deferred expenses," causing the accountants to gnash their teeth.

I send an application to a choreographer who lives on a farm in bucolic Rensselaer County where NYSCA would be glad to put money. It comes back with a fat magic marker scrawl:

BEING ABLE TO FILL OUT THIS FORM IS A SIGN OF A HOTSHOT ADMINISTRATOR. IT HAS NOTHING TO DO WITH ART. I AM A CHOREOGRAPHER. I NEED $20,000.
   TWYLA THARP

I regret the lack of foresight that made me drop that note into a wastebasket. Dick d'Anjou has me send another application then get on the phone and help her through it line by line.

Meredith Monk demands to be considered by the theater panel, but theater associate Gina Shield fears that the panel will turn her down. I call Monk, saying that in a smarter world all the arts would be one but that dance is proud to claim her, and once she has the money she can make any kind of piece she wants.

When NYSCA's accountants get a dance application with a single mistake they bounce it to me until d'Anjou explains that it is *their* job to fix mistakes and fill in blanks.

The application of Erick Hawkins is perfect. I recall Martha saying, "I hate details. Erick loves details." Some college dance departments now offer Hawkins Technique. A few NYSCA dance panelists don't like his work but none question his integrity. They recommend $25,000, accepted by Council. Erick calls me at NYSCA.

"You have made possible a final flowering of my life's work. I have a big tour booked for next year, and we are working on a New York season. I want you to dance with me."

I'm taken aback. "Erick, I seldom get to class these days."

"That's good! Other techniques are *wrong*. You'll take all your classes with me, now."

I don't say no, although endless rehearsals, bus tours, irregular paychecks, and loss of family life—my girls are twelve and fourteen—rule it out. Concentrating on the family angle, I turn Erick down. For me, the life of a misty-minded modern dancer is over.

Erick invites me and Elizabeth to dinner at a tiny apartment on West

10th Street shared with Lucia Dlugoszewski, who writes many of his scores. She brings each dish to the table, including homemade strawberry ice cream. I'm struck by the profound change in Erick. Perhaps it is fulfillment as an artist, but Lucia is clearly a part. She adores him and her music is important to his work. He seems happy. Happiness is no small achievement for anyone but is astonishing in a creative artist. I feel sadly certain it is something Martha Graham will never know.

Agnes de Mille shows up at NYSCA. She has no troupe, doesn't want one, and since NYSCA can only fund organizations, isn't eligible. But her appearance triggers the de Mille Protocol: everyone stops what they are doing and stands up. Dick d'Anjou comes out of his office and says hello. I offer coffee and my undivided attention. She never gets a grant but never goes away mad.

Anna Sokolow shows up in full battle gear—black sheath, pearl choker, elbow-length black gloves, and sculpted hairdo pierced by a dagger. Not for the likes of me. I alert d'Anjou, who ushers her into his private office and shuts the door. In half an hour he walks her to the elevator, tells me that her manager will call.

My job includes assembling a dance advisory panel, putting each application before it with analysis, getting their recommendation, and passing it to Council, which has the final say. Council includes Alwin Nikolais, Dorothy Rodgers (wife of Richard Rodgers), James Petrillo, boss of Musician's Union Local 802, and other VIPs. Before Council's first meeting, Dorothy Rodgers shows up. "Can we put this money where it will do the most good, or do we have to spread it around?"

D'Anjou explains that the money comes from New York state taxpayers and must be spread around. Dance panelists include dancers, choreographers, academics, managers, scholars, teachers, critics, some from organizations who want grants. This is a conflict of interest, yet eliminating them would eliminate most experts, so when a panelist's organization comes up, he or she leaves the room, the request is decided on, and upon the panelist's return, no reference is made to what had transpired. Hardly perfect, but perfection is unattainable.

Clive Barnes had agreed to be a panelist but missed the first meeting and is half an hour late to the second. He arrives during a discussion of Paul Sanasardo. After five minutes, he rises to his feet, brandishing the list.

"I don't understand why we're discussing mediocrities. We should narrow it down to, say, three ballet companies and five modern dance companies. Spreading the money around may make you feel good, but it's not going to do dance one bit of good."

I break into the shocked silence. "You miss the first meeting entirely, arrive half an hour late to the second, listen for five minutes, and are now ready to tell us how to run the program."

"What do you think I should do?"

"Sit down in your seat and listen."

Barnes plops down and doesn't open his mouth again. In a few minutes, NYSCA's boss, Eric Larrabee, slips into the room. Word had reached him that I'm fighting with the dean of dance critics.

After the meeting, Barnes says, "I'm a critic. It's my job to criticize. That's not what's going on here." He quits the panel. Next day, a two-inch squib in the *New York Times*, to the effect that NYSCA's dance program would be better if it tried for less "democratic fairness."

I fire off a letter accusing him of slyly slipping into print against us, and that it is not "fairness" at issue, but an American tradition different from England's, where high art is simply what the king likes. My chauvinism is intentional. I do not mention that Council member Dorothy Rodgers is on his side, concluding, "Can a battleship defend itself against a million rowboats?"—meaning I have no idea what.

Two days later, Eric Larrabee tells me he'd called Barnes. "Do you think Stuart Hodes is the right one for this job?"

Barnes: "He's probably the only one for the job."

The dance panel is conflicted about Martha Graham. They agree she should be supported yet seem to believe that the once-vaunted leader of dance's avant-garde is now passé, a view also heard from June Arey, dance director at the National Endowment for the Arts (NEA) in Washington, D.C. She visits NYSCA and in d'Anjou's office, suggests that equal amounts for Eliot Feld, a hot new choreographer, and Martha Graham makes sense: "One's on the way up . . ."

"And the other's on the way down?" d'Anjou finishes, with a glance at me. I keep my mouth shut.

One day, d'Anjou hands me an application addressed directly to him. From the Martha Graham School, signed by LeRoy (Lee) Leatherman. "Notice anything wrong?"

One glance. "He's only asking for $18,000."

Other companies with roughly the same total operating expenses, or TOE (I like this acronym), but far less artistic chops routinely ask $50,000. Leatherman's application is for studio performances with fees to choreographers, composers, costume designer, rehearsal director, and administrator. *Nothing for dancers.* (Same old Lee.) Or had he added the cost of studio space, advertising, postage, and custodial, which applications routinely include.

"Do you know Leatherman?"

There are strict conflict-of-interest rules, but I've been out of the Graham Company for fourteen years. "I know him well. We never got along."

"Do you feel you can be fair to Graham's application?"

"Yes."

"Then you'll have to get along now. Give him a call."

I dial the Graham School, hear his voice, speak in a rush. "Hello Lee? This is Stuart. Stuart Hodes. I'm calling from NYSCA and wonder if you'd mind discussing your application?"

"What's there to discuss?"

"The feeling here is that you can ask for more."

"I asked for what we need."

"Is this the only project you need supported?"

"We have other projects."

"Richard d'Anjou thinks you can ask for, oh, $50,000. Not that you'll get that much, but . . ."

Snaps: "I know how the process works."

"Can I send you another application?"

"Certainly."

Two weeks later Leatherman calls describing a studio performance project that even pays the dancers. The request is for $35,000.

"It sounds good, Lee. What does Martha think?"

"She couldn't care less what we do."

"Will there be a Broadway season?"

"No season is planned."

"Is Martha starting a new dance?"

"We've seen nothing of Martha for months."

"Is she still in the hospital?"

"She's out of the hospital."

"Are you in touch with her?"

"I can't even reach her. She's living with some faggot in Westchester County."

I'm shocked by Leatherman's language. He goes on: "She thinks only about herself. She's a complete egoist. She cares nothing about the school, the company, or history."

Shortly thereafter, I get a call from Robin Howard, founder of The Place, home of the London School of Contemporary Dance. Without preamble: "We're worried about Martha. She may not make it and we don't want the company to disappear. I'm trying to set up something to make sure her dances will continue to be performed."

That Martha may be seriously ill is on everyone's mind. Howard outlines a plan to organize the company without her. "We'll build it around Bertram Ross and Mary Hinkson."

"What about Leatherman?"

"We'll find something for him but I don't think the troika can run the company. We'd like you to do that. Mary wants to dance so she should dance. Bertram wants to choreograph so he choreographs. You would work with the two of them."

"I don't think Lee would like that."

"Lee thinks of himself as a writer and there will be plenty to write about. It should keep him happy."

In Europe, I'd gotten the impression that Robin Howard didn't approve of me, and mention it. "Yes, I was a bit wary of you. You had these big fights with Martha."

"Who told you that?"

"You're famous for it. Didn't you once slap her?"

I gasp. "You think I *slapped* Martha Graham?"

"It's just something I heard."

"Who did you hear it from?"

"Oh, I don't know. And I don't know that I ever believed it."

The hell he hadn't!

"I'm appalled you even imagine I could strike Martha Graham."

"It's ironic. You had this reputation for being a wild man and turn out to be the most reasonable of the lot. So what do you say? Are you interested?"

"Well, Mr. Howard . . ."

"Robin."

"Robin. I'm sure that one day Martha will show up at the studio and just take over again. But if she doesn't, of course I'd be interested."

Robin Howard is not the only one thinking about the Graham troupe's future. Leatherman had said that American Ballet Theater proposed a "merger." Sherwin Goldman was willing to add the whole troupe, eighteen dancers, to his company of ninety, thereby getting a hundred of the greatest dances of the twentieth century. But after the feature stories and photo ops, ABT would slip its own stars into the leads, its *corps de ballet* into lesser roles, eventually dispensing with Graham-trained dancers, except for one or two as coaches. Stranded on ballet turf, how long would the dances look like Martha Graham's?

Another proposal comes from Juilliard offering to make Graham its resident professional troupe. But the notion of Martha Graham supervised by Martha Hill rule this out immediately.

I call Ross and Hinkson who are busy keeping classes going and the company in rehearsal. Bertram says, "One day Martha will walk in the front door and I'll say, 'Hello, Martha. When can I schedule rehearsal?'"

The NYSCA panel recommends $31,000 for Graham, Council approves, and Leatherman puts on an in-house "season," asking me to contribute a dance, which I am permitted to do if not paid. The Graham dancers are stunning, and for my lead, I use a breathtaking eighteen-year-old named Janet Eilber.

Juilliard's development director ("development," like "support," is another cozy euphemism for money) wants to take me to lunch. I ask Richard d'Anjou if lunch is permitted. Yes, if not expensive. The guy has a born-to-the-purple manner that likely goes over in corporate board rooms. In the Russian Tea Room, he asks how much is "allocated for education." I tell him that our tiny arts allocation, one million dollars, is for working artists. My killer line: "This money is for Juilliard students *after* they graduate."

He's unimpressed, says that "as a matter of principle," something should be allocated for education, no matter how little. I listen attentively and nod frequently, resolving that if up to me, not one dime of artist money will go to schools who pay fat salaries to people like him but not a dime to working artists.

A couple of months later I get a call from Leatherman. He's planning to resign and asks if I am interested in being his replacement. He'll be gone by spring. I ask if Martha knows. He is not in touch with her but says that Bertram Ross and Mary Hinkson are agreeable. I write a letter of acknowledgment to Lee, a memo to NYSCA files, and leave it at that. A few weeks later, Martha shows up and fires Lee, Craig Barton, and Bertram Ross. Mary Hinkson complains to no avail so walks out. If I'd been there in Lee's place, Martha would certainly have fired me.

Years later Bob Cohan tells me he'd been visiting Bertram on the day he was fired. The telephone rang, Bertram picked up, and Bob heard:

"Hello Martha."

"What?"

"What do you mean?"

"Why?"

"I don't understand."

"Who said that?"

"I demand to know who said those things."

Bertram's voice rises. Finally: "You can expect a call from my lawyer." Hangs up.

Bob asked what the call had been about.

"Martha says I am not to come to the studio anymore."

"Why did you say she should expect a call from your lawyer?"

"That's what they say in the movies."

Bertram's sad fate repeats a recurring pattern, Martha, convinced by one or another lying retainer that she is being betrayed. It happened to me when she believed a thuggish bus driver in Florida, again in Vienna, lied to by Lee Leatherman ("I know you were rude to Gert"), and now to Bertram by a factotum who sees Martha as a chance to succeed without really trying. Bertram has given his life to Martha. That she can so mindlessly dismiss him gives her weakness tragic scope. Yet it is clearly part of her nature. When I tried to remind Martha she'd said that if I got a leading role the world will fall, or that she'd once called me an oaf, she seemed not to remember. It's possible that she didn't.

If Robin Howard had heard about my fights with Martha, had others? Twenty years earlier, Martha Hill was organizing dance at Juilliard. She turned to Martha Graham, who supplied advice and temporary faculty, including me. Antony Tudor told me to ask Martha Hill to let me make a dance for the Juilliard ensemble.

Three times a week, I trekked to the old Juilliard School on West 123rd Street where I taught in a studio partitioned out of a recital hall with walls of flimsy sheet rock. Demonstrating a forceful move, I somehow put my hand right through a wall. If Martha Hill had heard that I fought with

Martha Graham, and also crashed through dance studio walls, she might well have decided I was a madman. After six months I asked her about my dance. She said, "I'm afraid that has fallen through the cracks."

She might just as well have said, "Piss on you."

Not much later we both sat on a panel to pick a recipient for a $25,000 prize for modern dance choreography. It was annual for playwrights but every two years also went to a choreographer. Martha Hill began by declaring that this year the award should go to a black choreographer, implying it hadn't before because we were all racists. All immediately agreed. She then proposed Arthur Mitchell. The panelists turned to me.

"There's others." I named Alvin Ailey, Talley Beatty, Katherine Dunham, Donald McKayle. The committee chose Alvin Ailey.

Martha Hill died in 1995. The Martha Hill Dance Fund put out its first newsletter in 2008, followed by contribution requests. I answered one with a letter, explaining why I could not. When I received a call from its president, Vernon Scott, I assumed it had to do with that. But he was asking if I would *accept* the award.

"Yes."

I'm still the guy who fought with Martha Graham and put his hand through a Juilliard wall. Today the Dance Fund is an organization of my peers whose award I was honored to receive.

I have lunch with the Joffrey Ballet's general manager, Omar Lerman. We go to a Central Park hot dog stand, order "franks with everything," pay for our own, and sit on a park bench discussing Joffrey's application.

Professor William Bales comes to NYSCA. A founder of the New Dance Group, he had headed dance at Bennington College, is now dean of dance at SUNY-Purchase. He wants money for a resident troupe.

The idea of symbiosis between a college and a resident professional dance troupe is popular. In theory, the troupe gets rehearsal space, performing space, and audiences, the college gets in-house professionals, a community resource, a magnet for students, job potential for graduates, and great PR. But the only example is Repertory Dance Theater of Utah, which began in 1966 with a $370,000 grant from the Rockefeller Foundation. NYSCA is not in the business of starting dance companies.

"When do you plan to start a professional company at Purchase?"

"We already have," says Bales heartily. "Four companies, freshman, sophomore, junior, and senior."

"You're talking about student companies."

"They're as good as any professional company."

"But dancers pay tuition to be in them."

"That's why we need your help. We want to pay *them*."

"And what about when they graduate?"

"What about it?"

"Do you know any professional company that kicks out its best dancers every June?"

Bales epitomizes the gulf that can grow between artists and academics, experienced again in 2001, when the Martha Graham School was renewing its accreditation with the National Association of Schools of Dance. One of the examiners, Daniel Lewis, dean of the New World School of the Arts, Miami, Florida, a Juilliard graduate, danced with José Limón for a decade. His report states that the Graham faculty appears to consist "almost entirely of adjuncts."

I conceal my shock, noting only that academe is not an appropriate model against which to measure a "Professional Studio School," the term NASD is supposed to use to define Alvin Ailey, Merce Cunningham, Martha Graham, Alwin Nikolais, and other schools not affiliated with colleges. Termed "non-degree-granting," they did not like being defined by what they were not, preferring "Professional Schools." Colleges objected on the grounds that they, too, were teaching to the profession. Martha Graham suggested "Professional *Studio* Schools," which NASD accepted. Twenty-five years later, "non-degree-granting" is back. NASD, now dominated by colleges, has forgotten its original raison d'être: to give professional studio schools benefits that accrue *automatically* to any college with dance courses. Professor William Bales, insulated from the artist world in which he began, asserts that a student company is professional, and Professor Daniel Lewis equates Graham's faculty of working professionals who also teach with adjunct professors.

Martha is making dances again, assisted in daily minutia by her new minion. Were he content with that, he'd be honored and esteemed, but he tries to insert himself artistically, is soon recognized as yet another commandeered personality, as she'd commandeered Erick Hawkins, Lee Leatherman, and Craig Barton, although no one doubted the sincere devotion of those three. The responsibility, however, is Martha's, who in a sense, commandeers everyone who makes her the center of their lives.

With the last NYSCA application submitted and the meeting about to end, Isadora Bennett says there is unfinished business, and asks me to leave. I'd forgotten that months earlier, d'Anjou had told me to fill out an application for my troupe, The Ballet Team. After about fifteen minutes, I'm called back; nothing said, except goodbyes.

NYSCA is over but Ballet Team still has twenty bookings. About six weeks later, I am informed that Ballet Team has been awarded $10,000, which allows us to reduce fees to New York State bookers from $245 to $165 a show. With this bargain, our agent, G. Conway Graml, gets forty more bookings, each for at least 500 kids. The $10,000 supplied by NYSCA bought a show for some 20,000 kids at fifty cents a head.

I get a call from Richard d'Anjou, asking if I am ready to consider "a change of lifestyle." The position of dance associate has been upgraded to full-time and is mine if I give up The Ballet Team. After a final show, I drive my VW minibus to my door in Manhattan where I sit for an hour before I can begin to unload costumes, props, and sound system. Ballet Team was great, but it's over.

1971

Applications for NYSCA's second round are piling in when I hear that Martha had appeared at 316 East 63rd Street and fired Lee Leatherman and Craig Barton. Shortly thereafter, my office gets a call from the Graham School. The caller is handling Graham's NYSCA application. We meet at a luncheonette near the school. He has a pale boyish face, short brown hair that looks like it had been washed and toweled but not brushed, and greets me with a shyly ingratiating smile. He speaks in a whispery voice, head down, to suddenly look up with his eyes.

He says, "Modern dance is America's only indigenous art form. Martha Graham is its most important choreographer. Critics consider her on a par with Stravinsky and Picasso."

Other souvenir-book statements follow. He's apparently unaware that I'd danced with Martha. I ask what Graham dances he'd seen.

"So far, only rehearsals, but Martha is teaching me."

"You're taking classes?"

"Oh, no. But she is explaining everything. She talks to me every day."

Ron Protas believes he is becoming a dance expert. Dance has always had non-dancing "experts." Lydia Joel, *Dance Magazine's* editor, had been a dancer in Hanya Holm's famed *Trend* and was teaching dance until the 1950s when she began writing and editing. She devoted a multi-issue series on a new "miracle method" of teaching ballet, which so bemused Rebekah Harkness that she hired the miracle-method teacher, who clashed with Patricia Wilde, resulting finally in the destruction of the Harkness School, Harkness Ballet, and what had briefly been the Harkness Theater.

In 1974, three years after I'd left NYSCA and was heading dance at NYU School of the Arts, I get a call from Lydia Joel, no longer editor of *Dance Magazine* but about to head up dance at New York City's High School of Performing Arts. The Board of Education says she needs a master's degree. She wants to do it at NYU, with me (no degree whatsoever) as her thesis advisor.[3]

Shortly thereafter, she called to say that the Board of Education is creating a new written exam for dance teachers and asks me to contribute questions. Recalling the feeble test I'd taken in the 1950s, I agree that a new written test is overdue. Joel says that the new test will replace all parts of the old test.

"Not the teaching and performance parts."

"Yes."

"Wait a minute. You're saying a written test without any performance tests?"

"That's right."

"It's not possible."

"The Board of Education thinks it is."

"They're wrong."

"Stuart, if you and I don't submit questions, they'll do it themselves."

"Let them. You should have nothing to do with such a loony idea."

"I don't agree with you."

"Lydia, if you were flying to California and learned that the pilot had gotten a perfect score on his written exam but had never flown an airplane, would you get aboard?"

"It's not the same."

"I'm a pilot. Do you know that?"

"You flew in World War II."

"Right. I'm a dancer and a pilot. I tell you it's the same."

I urge her to separate herself from the project. "Lydia, if you can test a person's dancing ability by having them learn the answers to questions, why not just teach them the answers?"

"We're not testing whether they can dance, but if they can teach dance."

"So you think a person can teach dance who can't dance?"

"Tanaquil LeClercq teaches from a wheelchair."

"But she was a dancer."

"Well, she can't dance now and she can still teach."

Joel had danced twenty years prior and is said to have taught, so I'm appalled she doesn't comprehend that to teach a complex physical skill the knowledge must reside in the muscles and cannot be reduced to words on paper. And that is why I was not too surprised that Martha's new factotum, a non-dancer, knows no better. Martha, of course, does, but that is a different matter.

I attend a meeting with the unlikely presence of Joseph Papp, Donald Saddler, James Waring, Lincoln Kirstein, and André Eglevsky. Eglevsky has a school on Long Island. When asked what he thought about joining the National Association for Regional Ballet, which required evaluation by Doris Hering and/or Lydia Joel, he says, "I don't want those women hanging around my school."

I am seated next to Lincoln Kirstein, who is silent until something is said about Martha Graham. He turns to me: "All Martha Graham's dances are about elimination. She dances about shit."

In 1952, I saw an orchestra rehearsal for Matti Haim at Juilliard. I have a penny postcard that lists the dances of a Haim concert dated October 14, 1949. Some titles: *Universal Heart, I Am the Mother of All Creation, I Balance the Earth on My Lap.* To be choreographed before the audience.

Does it not sound a little "New Age," which did not arise for some twenty more years? Merce Cunningham is said to have admired Matti Haim.

While the orchestra was tuning up, Haim sat cross-legged, downstage center. Finally the conductor said, "Ready to begin, Miss Haim." No reaction. "We're ready to begin Miss Haim." Still nothing. "Miss Haim? We're ready to begin."

She lifted her gaze, said softly. "But I've already begun. Concentric circles are descending around my body."

Matti Haim seemed to believe that her thoughts were visible. Soon

Penny postcard announcing Matti Haim performance.

after that, I noticed that Martha, in her technique classes, is emphasizing visibility.

"If it is not visible, it matters not at all what is in your mind." Clearly, Martha had heard about Matti Haim, and this was her answer.

Some believe Martha is now hopelessly out of date. She is uncompromisingly theatrical, believes that dance done in ignorance of underlying imagery loses coherence and refuses to let other companies perform her dances, infuriating artistic directors. She considers image without technique to be useless and struggles relentlessly to make her ideas manifest through rigorous experiment and grueling physical work.

Survival of Graham's repertory lies between the horns of a dilemma. If she restricts her dances to her own company, they're like the Snail Darter, endangered because it lives in one single cave in the whole world. If she gives her dances to the world to be danced without command of her technique, she fears they will fade away. In the hallucinogenic 1960s and '70s, she is a voice from the past, and worse, the recent past.

What others deem experiential she calls self-indulgent.

While they dismiss technique as irrelevant, she drives toward virtuosity.

Where they attempt to demystify art and themselves, she affirms mystery.

While they move in naive hope toward some vague nurturing principal, she makes doom-ridden dances that taunt human aspirations.

Where they strive to be angelic and unthreatening, Martha is demonic and threatening. *Threatening*. And how!

The mid-1960s to late 1970s, in addition to the evil madness of the Vietnam War, there was what critic Clive Barnes called a "dance explosion." It included experiment, daring, and also silliness. Martha called it, "Flutterings in the dovecote." In 1963, she rattled representatives Edna F. Kelly of Brooklyn and Peter Frelinghuysen of Morristown, New Jersey, with a scene in *Phaedra* where Bertram Ross, amply costumed, stood behind a screen flexing muscles, while Martha opened panels, exposing a thigh, an arm, a pectoral, etc. The two pols deemed it obscene, and it was. Martha intended to expose Phaedra's hopeless obsession. That the wages of sin led to Phaedra's death did not register with these self-righteous moralists, who convened a House Foreign Affairs subcommittee, where Kelly squawked that Martha should be dropped from a State Department tour because it would give the world a bad impression of the U.S.A. Other VIPs testified in favor of Martha, but Craig Barton made the most meaningful comment: "Evil lies in the eyes of the beholder."

A *NY Post* headline: "IS MARTHA TOO SEXY FOR EXPORT?"

1976

"Were all the men in the Graham Company in love with Martha?" John Gruen was interviewing me for an oral history project by Lincoln Center Dance Library. Before I could reply, he added, "Were *you* in love with Martha?"

"I love Martha, but I'm not sure what you mean by 'in love.'"

"Did you go to bed with Martha?"

"No."

He clicked off his tape recorder. "I want you to know that this record can be sealed for fifty years."

"You don't believe me?"

"Of course I believe you, but I want you to know that you do not have to reveal anything you'd rather not."

Tape recorder still off. "I never thought of Martha as a sex object. Most of the other woman in her company, sure, but not Martha. (Is *that* why we had fights?) You can turn your recorder back on now."

The above is not recorded because the recorder was off, but when the

Dance Library sent me the transcript, Gruen's leading questions were creepy. From the transcript:

Gruen: "Of course you were all in love with Martha. But did you want, in some way, to possess her more than anyone else?"

Hodes: "Did I want to go to bed with her? Never."

Gruen: "But the thing was, was there a kind of need to be the special one, the favored one, and perhaps . . . ?"

Why is Gruen trying so hard to get me to say that I wanted to screw Martha? It was no more my fantasy than screwing the Statue of Liberty.

After I gave Rebekah Harkness a few private modern dance lessons, she said she wanted to watch a class at the Martha Graham School. I passed her request to Martha, who bridled, then said she was willing to let her watch but would not teach the class herself. "That woman!"

"She is very rich."

"Yes, she is very rich, but she will never have what she wants. All that woman wants is to be a swan."

San Francisco, California, 1976

"Don't you think Martha Graham has created a theater of archetypes?" The question was posed by an urgent young woman at a reception for the NEA Dance Panel. She's a historian and she's right. Graham's theater is mostly of female archetypes.

Medea: wronged woman seeking vengeance
Circe: enslaving seductress
Clytemnestra: murderess, reborn
Every Soul Is a Circus: hopeless wannabe
Joan of Arc: warrior saint
Judith: warrior whore
Ariadne: courageous virgin

To create such larger-than-life characters, Graham needed a movement vocabulary that didn't exist, so she invented Graham Technique. Much pretentious verbiage is written about its "theory" and "principles,"[4] yet it does have some clear characteristics:

Moves tend to originate in the body's center and strike outward.

Moves engage several muscle groups, performed as though one single muscle.

Dramatic images animate moves, and where none is offered by the teacher, the Graham dancer creates her own.

Exercises follow a cycle of birth, growth, maturity, and death; they open clearly, build, reach a climax, and end. This is illustrated in her Exercise-on-Six, to m, the shortest dance masterpiece ever created.

Classroom moves are "performed," as if for an audience.

The technique is not "closed," and new moves are continually added.

Graham was ever alert for the unexpected, sometimes finding a new move in a dancer's "mistake." And she did not hesitate to use moves from other techniques. Today her technique can be taught as though closed, and some effective teachers teach it that way, although if all did, it would stop growing. If a day ever comes when one can rule out a move as "not Graham," the technique will have atrophied.

Martha knows that only individual muscles contract, yet her Contraction charges through the entire torso as if it were one muscle, giving her dances the dramatic power needed for a theater of archetypes.

Would Martha have achieved this if she'd studied classical ballet, or if Rudolf von Laban had been her teacher instead of Ruth St. Denis? Being Martha, I think she would. She had a messianic imperative, like Ruth St. Denis, and if she did not like being called a "high priestess," as she said, perhaps it was because her true calling was that of a messiah.

1977

I'm invited to the American Assembly, a think tank hosted by Columbia University at its bucolic Harriman Campus in Kingston, New York. Participants get transportation, accommodations, good food, interesting company, and a respite from everyday jobs. Our ponderous topic: "The Future of the Performing Arts."[5]

The invitation is to "Professor Stuart Hodes." I arrive wearing a vested tweed suit and meet Robert Lindgren, ex–Ballet Russe de Monte Carlo, now dean of dance at North Carolina School of the Arts.

He says, "You look like a professor."

"I'm wearing my professor costume."

At lunch, Arthur Mitchell bawls me out because Martha will not let him have *Diversion of Angels* for Dance Theater of Harlem. "What's the matter with her? We can do modern dance!"

On the second day, I'm handed a paper by Joseph H. Mazo, commissioned by W. McNeal Lowry, formerly of the Ford Foundation, who plans to publish a book about the performing arts. He asks for comments.

Joseph Mazo, dance critic for *Women's Wear Daily,* had written *Dance Is a Contact Sport.* (Such a sappy title, I can't crack it.) He'd stated that Pilobolus was founded by former college gymnasts. Not true. Startling, however, is his assertion that modern dance has *used up* its techniques. "Grants are needed, not merely for choreographers, but for teachers capable of working with contemporary dance-makers to develop new forms of technique."[6]

Can Mazo believe that dance techniques are made up by dance *teachers,* then used by choreographers to make dances, the way DuPont, say, develops new fabrics which fashion designers use to make dresses?

When I explain to Lowry that dance techniques are created not by teachers but by experimental choreographers seeking personal tools, he seems to think I am expressing dissent and rejects it with an irritable shake of his head, to leave Mazo's ludicrous assertion standing.

Martha is scheduled to address the plenary session on the last day. She and her factotum have a suite directly across the hall from mine. Passing, she shoots me a distracted smile. Later, I hear through the door. "You should never have accepted. You know how I hate these things."

Anyone would have leapt at a chance to dine with Martha, but she and the factotum sit at a table for two, inviting no one. At the plenary session, she took a proffered arm, mounted the dais, sat, leaned forward, and spoke about the artist and society. Of a vanished culture: "They had no poets, so they died." She described a tree that had taken root outside a chain-link fence surrounding the garden of her school. Seeking light, the tree had grown *through* the fence. "Its trunk is straight and strong, but you can trace the scars left by those links of steel to the very top of that tree. That tree is like the artist, growing through and beyond whatever obstacles and barriers life erects, offering shade and comfort to others, yet carrying still his scars."

Twenty years later, I read those words in *Blood Memory,* published after Martha's death.

Martha's Tree growing through the fence behind her studio on East 63rd St. Photo by Stuart Hodes.

The tree, an ailanthus, springs up in vacant lots, cracks in the sidewalk, on rooftops of old buildings. But even for an ailanthus, Martha's is unusual. Students often enter the garden and stand beneath its scarred trunk contemplating its struggle, its triumph, dreaming, perhaps, of their own.

I realize that Martha is talking about me, saying "my pilot." People look around, but I do not stir. She is still a spellbinder, finishes to warm applause, leaves the dais, and the American Assembly.

1979

Martha has an important patron, fashion designer Roy Halston Frowick. He gives money, designs elegant costumes, and adores Martha. At an NYU faculty cocktail party, critic Marcia Siegel complains, "He's glitzy and much too fancy. Graham should not be letting him design her costumes."

I did not argue with the strongly opinionated Siegel, whom I'd first met as a superior dance panelist for the New York State Council on the Arts. She knew about choreographers others hadn't heard of and was an early supporter of Twyla Tharp.

"These days her dancers have no idea what they're doing. They point their feet and lift their legs and think that's enough. I never saw your generation dance, but you can't tell me you danced like that." She took a gulp of her drink.

Me: "We laid on emotion because we didn't have enough technique."

Siegel shook her head. "The way Graham's dances are being danced, they will soon be unrecognizable. I think they should put them away for twenty years, then come back and start over."

"Are you saying, Marcia, that the dances would fare better if not danced at all?"

"The way they're being danced now, yes."

That night I decided to write. She was on NYU's faculty, but I addressed my letter to *Soho Weekly News,* where she wrote criticism:

> Can you truly want Martha's works denied to two generations of dancers? Can you believe that an archive of films and tapes is a substitute for a living repertory? Can you claim that from such an archive the works could ever be resurrected after twenty years, in a world which changes vastly in a quarter of that time, and using dancers who have never seen the works performed live? Can you believe that this would not, in fact, amount to extinction?

Her reply began by saying she didn't usually respond to "letters of this kind," lumping me, I guess, with those who complain about her reviews. But her next sentence, "Anyway, I was holding a drink in my hand," is as close to a retraction as I need from Marcia Siegel.

In any case, the problem was not Halston, but Martha. Consider the Husbandman in *Appalachian Spring.* Martha described him as a farmer in his Sunday best. Erick Hawkins had worn a loose jacket with sleeves a trifle short, off-white shirt, string tie, loose pants with no crease, and high-topped lace-up shoes.

That was my costume until the *Spring* film was made, when Martha gave herself a new costume and replaced the Husbandman's loose jacket with a tailored shirt, and in place of the lace-up high-tops gave him elegant suede boots. I tucked the pants into them. For the Asian tour, I got a fitted suede vest to go with the boots. It was snazzy, and I didn't much think about whether it was right for a farmer. But every costume is worn by two people, the performer and character being performed. I liked my nifty costume but the Husbandman grew uncomfortable, and when his voice finally broke through, all I could do was take the pants out of the boots so that they looked more like lace-up high-top shoes.

Fast forward thirty years. The Husbandman (danced by Tim Wengerd) wears *tights*. It put me in mind of a *Dance Magazine* cover of John Kriza parading through the White House costumed for Eugene Loring's *Billy the Kid,* bare-chested in tights, bandanna, and star-spangled chaps. I remember thinking that only classical ballet can turn a gun-toting desperado into a half-naked popinjay. Will the Husbandman be bare-chested one day?

1979

When Martha was approached about making dance videos, told she'd have to collaborate with a director, she said, "I do not collaborate." Eventually she did, with director, Merrill Brockway, who explained, "I think of myself as an accompanist, not a soloist."

The first time he called her about *Clytemnestra,* she said she didn't think TV audiences were ready. When she decided that they were, she called Brockway, saying, "I don't want long shots because they make all the dancers look like ants."

They began by watching a video of a live performance. Martha asked Brockway, "Do you think it's too long for television?"

Brockway: "I said yes, and she said 'How much?' I said about twenty minutes. She didn't flinch. I thought she'd take out scenes, but she took the twenty minutes out of little snippets. She sat on the piano bench with the composer [Halim El-Dabh], cut the music, and redid the dance to what she'd cut. I said, 'That was a very musical thing you did,' and she said, 'I'm not thought to be musical.'"

Linda Hodes, who was there, said, "Martha cut down the music by taking out musical phrases and repeats. She also added a role for Peggy Lyman. When she saw the video, she liked it so much, it became the stage version."

A telephone call from Reston, Virginia, a D.C. suburb, asking me to serve on a committee to evaluate the Merce Cunningham School. *Who in Reston presumes to evaluate Merce Cunningham?* I learn it is his own doing. American dance students can get financial aid to study Cunningham Technique in any accredited college that purports to teach it but not to study with the master in his own school.

Linda Hodes, now director of the Martha Graham School, told me that Graham is also part of the project to create an organization authorized to confer accreditation to private dance studios, so that their students are eligible for financial aid. In 1979, my NYU sabbatical year, I joined the process for the Martha Graham School.

I explained to Martha that accreditation would not limit her control, and a year later, accreditation assured, I told her that her American students will soon be eligible for financial aid, and, as a bonus, foreign students will be able to obtain visas to study with her.

"Does that mean I have to accept any students they send me?"

"No. You will always be in complete charge of everything."

In 1981, the Martha Graham School became a charter member of the newly formed National Association of Schools of Dance, or NASD, initials shared with the National Association of Securities Dealers.

October 1980

I receive an invitation to go to China as a member of the "First American Dance Study Team." It includes Laura Dean, Bella Lewitzky, Arthur Mitchell, Charles Reinhart, Suzanne Shelton, and Michael Smuin. A man from a Chinese-American friendship group tells us to take only casual clothes.

"You don't need a suit. The Chinese do not dress up."

He's hopelessly rumpled, wears falling-down argyle sox, and needs a haircut. I ignore this advice.

When we're in China, at lunch, I notice a small covered dish. "What's that?"

"Bugs," replies Bella Lewitzky. "We don't like seeing them."

"Look away, then." Resembling cockroaches, they have a spicy tang and crunch between my teeth.

At a banquet (one of many), each American has a personal hostess, who, wielding long chopsticks, reaches into each serving platter, identifies the food, and delivers it to one's plate. Holding a chunk of meat. "Bear. Bear paw."

I stop her arm. "No, thank you. I don't eat bear."

She seemed hurt. "But no shortage. Bear not endanger."

"I *like* bears."

Dance schools are the reason we are there. The Friendship Group man had said we were not *scheduled* to teach, but of course we are all asked. Students are brilliant.

We are also invited to watch classes. Most teachers are Chinese, plus a few aged Russians. Some smoke while teaching. Tea is served by retired dancers. After their dancing days are over, everyone gets a job of some kind with their own or another school or troupe.

After each observed class, a teacher will say, "And now we will be grateful to hear your criticisms so that we may learn from your expertise." Our criticisms are bland and laudatory until one day, after a *pointe* class for eight-year-olds, Arthur Mitchell and Michael Smuin want to tell it like it is.

"They're *asking* us to criticize," says Mitchell, whereupon he and Smuin point out that most of the children are not physically ready for *pointe* and could be hurt. The Chinese listen with bland smiles and offer polite thanks. Immediately afterward, our American translator says they'd been shocked and scandalized. Arthur Mitchell is annoyed. "Well, why do they ask for criticism if they don't want it?"

Officially, I represent NYU, but the dancers see me as an emissary from Martha Graham. Bidding farewell at the Beijing airport, a white-haired man takes my hand in both of his.

"Please, send us Martha Graham."

November 1984

"Stuart? This is Martha."

"Martha! It's wonderful to hear your voice." I have no idea why she is calling.

"I'm going to ask you to do me a favor. But first I want you to promise something."

"Anything, Martha."

"I want you to promise that if it's not convenient, you'll say no."

"Martha, I'd love to do you a favor."

"No, Stuart, I want you to promise first."

"All right. If it's not convenient, I promise."

"To say no."

"To say no."

"I'm working on a new dance, and we're using the *Song of Solomon*. Bert Terborg has been reading for rehearsals but his Dutch accent throws me. Can you read the poetry for rehearsals?"

The idea of being at Martha's rehearsals is thrilling and no way can I turn her down, but I play it through. "When are rehearsals?"

"Evenings. Two or maybe three times a week, from six to about ten."

"Martha, I'd love to.

"You're sure it's convenient?"

"I can't wait."

"Well, that's fine, then. I'll tell Linda to call you with the schedule."

Martha is eighty-nine and making a new dance. The last time I'd watched a rehearsal was twenty-two years ago in 1962.

The first rehearsal is Tuesday, November 27, 1984, my sixtieth birthday. Martha entered and walked to her chair as the dancers warmed up. Black gloves covered arthritic hands. Years earlier, when we'd found a quarter hour to chat in the lounge, Martha had removed the gloves and given me both hands, saying, "Massage them for a while." It took me back to theater rehearsals, when she'd beckon me over, touch a hand to her shoulder, I'd take the seat behind her, and massage her strong tense shoulder muscles, gradually feeling them soften, until she'd pat my hand, say "Good," and I'd stop. Massaging Martha's arthritic hands, I began to sense the pristine younger hands beneath the swellings, and realized that *that* is what she intended. A vital young Martha is there beneath the years.

She points to a Bible. I open it at the ribbon; "Solomon's Song." Sentences are highlighted. She tells the dancers where to begin, turns to me, and I read: *"Let him kiss me with the kisses of his mouth; for thy love is sweeter than wine."*

There are six couples, each woman's face covered by a filmy black veil. As they pass center stage, the man removes her veil. The first couple embrace, and as they separate, the man retains her veil. The next woman tilts back, supported by her partner, who leans over her and tenderly lifts the veil. Four more variations, each a tender riff on a first act of love. Martha gives directions, makes small changes, but the moves are set except for the lead couple, Thea Nerissa Barnes and Tom Smith.

Martha describes moves, expertly done by the pair. The process is much like what I remember from thirty years earlier, except that now Martha relies entirely on the dancers' bodies.

Thea and Tom pass front, she moving backward in a low glide supported by Tom. As they cross center, Martha directs Thea to stop, pivot on both feet, and do a back hinge into Tom's arm. He reaches over, catches the lower end of the veil and with a deft flip sends it high into the air over his head, to settle softly into the floor.

I think it is lovely. Not Martha. "Haven't you any idea how to undress a woman? *Gently.*"

Tom, furious, says nothing.

"Well, how can you know? These days no one undresses anybody. It's just throw off your clothes and jump into bed."

A few years later, at Southern Methodist University in Dallas, I remind Annie Carpenter, who'd been there, of Martha's remark. Annie smiles. "Oh, she was just jealous."

Martha's kinetic vocabulary has grown edgier, full of small quick moves of arms, legs, head, moves that I sense had been found by describing and suggesting, rather than getting up and demonstrating. She says, "I can't expect to create anything new, not now. But I demand integrity."

Her harangue was at least partly for me. I've become enough of an "outsider" that Martha felt obliged to put on a show. When I was with the troupe, her technique grew day to day and, contrary to her words, she is still driven to make it new. When *Song* premiered, the reader was English actor Jeremy Brett.

Rehearsal over, I approach and whisper, "Today's my birthday. I'm sixty years old."

"Darling. You aren't." She takes my face in her hands and kisses me. "Happy birthday."

When in the troupe, I'd never mentioned my birthday because I didn't want her to make a fuss. (Or maybe I was afraid she'd make less of a fuss over me than over Bertram or Bob.)

"*Song* is exhilarating."

A quick shake of her head. She doesn't want to hear about *Song*.

"I miss this," I said.

"What do you miss?"

"You. Being here. Everything from the days when I was an oaf."

"You were *never* an oaf."

Can Martha have forgotten Tallahassee? "It was great fun, Martha."

She too, is back in time. "I remember that temper of yours."

"Martha, I haven't lost my temper in twenty years."

Her expression hardens. *"Then it's time you lost it."*

How I wish I'd had the presence of mind to say, "But Martha, without you, there's been no one worth losing it for."

Celebration was premiered in 1934 by Martha's all-female troupe. Marjorie Mazia had told me that they'd jumped continuously for most of the dance. Martha herself helped revive it in 1987. Although joyous, it seemed light-hearted, even girlish, compared to dances like *Primitive Mysteries* and *Dark Meadow.*

Celebrating is not as weighty as religious ritual, or a plunge into the soul's depths, yet in the 1940s, modern dancers were serious about everything, even celebrating. Martha admitted that the new *Celebration* was less a revival than a re-creation.

1991

Martha Graham died a month short of her 98th birthday. Soon after, I encountered Paul Taylor. He said quietly: "A presence is gone."

I get a call from Richard Move inviting me to a performance titled, *Martha at Mother.* Mother is a nightclub in the wholesale meat district on the West Side of Manhattan. I arrive to be seated at a table with Bertram Ross.

Richard Move, six feet four inches tall, considers his evocation a tribute. Yet he receives a printed rebuke from critic Anna Kisselgoff, who deems his show disparaging. When Move asks me to be in one of his shows, Kisselgoff gets wind of it and calls me, saying that because Martha is gone, she's vulnerable. I'm surprised she doesn't realize that Martha is now a legend, and that legends are invulnerable.

Move is creative, inventive, and open to ideas. I bring him lyrics I want to sing to the tune of "Les Girls."

'Round the world I've been a dancer
From Beijing to Paris, France.
And if not a perfect prancer

I'm a guy whose eye is high on the dance.
I have polka'd in Poughkeepsie,
Suzy-Q'd in Syracuse.
But Contractions make me tipsy

(Richard Move as Martha appears.)

Cause Martha's my favorite danseuse.

Lyric:

Graham dance, Graham dance, there's no doubt about it,
I love Graham dance.
Graham dance, Graham dance, no wonder I shout it,
I dig Graham dance.
Clytemnestra is fine, and Medea's divine
In Dark Meadow I always wet my pants.
Appalachian Spring is just my thing.
Graham dance, Graham dance, Graham dance.

Sixteen bars of choreography:

I adore blood and gore, and the Witch of Endor
Fills my heart with the thrill of romance.
As for Ardent Song, it's where I belong
Graham dance (2—3—4), Graham dance (2—3—4).
Martha Graham dance

A nineteen-year-old from Belgium, Anne Teresa De Keersmaeker, joins my program at NYU. She wants to learn about the American avant-garde. I recommend a course by Professor Ron Argelander. A month later, we are walking on Second Avenue and I ask how her avant-garde course is going. "Very good."

I already know she's a huge talent, an obsessively hard worker, and adjusting for differences in eras, the closest I'll get to what Martha Graham might have been like at age nineteen.

She makes a fifteen-minute solo, shows it to me, and I manage to convince Patricia Kerr Ross, the SUNY dance festival director, to show it at the Purchase festival despite the rules (dances no longer than ten minutes and with a minimum of five dancers). Titled *FASE*, it astonishes audiences and critics. (You can see it on the internet right now by searching for Anne Teresa De Keersmaeker and *FASE*.) At semester's end Anne Teresa goes back to Belgium, founds a dance company, ROSAS, and a dance movement that spreads all over Europe and back to our shores when ROSAS plays Brooklyn Academy. As this is written, she is scheduled to make dances for a new Broadway production of *West Side Story*. (I have my ticket to the first preview performance, December 10, 2019.)

1996

Longtime Graham dancer David Wood observed: "Martha was completely different to every person with whom she dealt during the process of a day."[7] The Marthas I encountered can be discerned, I hope, in this book.

But an entirely different view is offered by Alma Guillermoprieto, author of *Dancing with Cuba* who first encountered Martha in 1965 when Guillermoprieto was a fifteen-year-old dance student from Mexico, taking classes at East 63rd Street.

> We, the students, would turn around to stare at the advancing monster, the scarlet mouth, the rolling, mascaraed eyes, the lacquered chopsticks plunged into her tied-up hair, the listing, weaving walk as she made her way toward the front of the big old mirrored studio.

Martha would have been frightening to an imaginative fifteen-year-old who'd never seen her. I took classes with Martha then and what Guillermoprieto saw as a "listing weaving walk" could have been the unsteadiness of an arthritic seventy-one-year-old picking her way through closely spaced bodies on a dance floor. Guillermoprieto also links Martha with Clytemnestra:

> Martha—Clytemnestra—trembling with mirth and hatred, flashed a blood-stained knife at Helen [of Troy]. It was Martha imagining the unimaginable. It was Martha—unspeakable, awful Martha—using two figures on an empty stage to rekindle a fury that first saw flames at the start of time. We left the theater filled with terror. She was the last tragedienne.[8]

It is tempting to seek connections between Martha's dances and her life. Someone will someday delve deep. Here are some that intrigue me but may be fancies, after all.

Heretic (1929). A metaphor for Martha's life—one against many—her role in the world, in dance, in her troupe, and likely, in her own family. The character was seen again fifty-five years later in *Rite of Spring* (1984), the Chosen One. Martha's lifelong theme was always a sacrificial commitment to some powerful entity.

American Document (1938). Martha's first dance using a man, Erick Hawkins. She put him at the center of her world, saying, "This is one man. This is one million men."

Every Soul Is a Circus (1939). A woman thinks of herself as the main event of the Big Top that is her life. She is wooed by the aerialist (Merce Cunningham) and takes her "star turn," only to be humiliated by the arrogant Ringmaster (Erick Hawkins), who cracks his whip and leaves her perched precariously on a seesaw. Was Martha having second thoughts about Erick?

Letter to the World (1940). Martha was drawn to Emily Dickinson, to her experience of the world, and the kinship she felt with the poet's rich inner life, despite physical isolation. Martha's love of Dickinson gave this shining masterpiece to the poet in a way that none of Martha's other dances belonged to anyone but Martha.

Punch and the Judy (1941). Amid a farrago of domestic discord, the Judy fantasizes about heroic lovers, while contending with Punch, her puffed-up blowhard of a husband. At the end, a light tap on Punch's chest collapses him like a pin-pricked balloon. Martha has had Erick around for three years. Has she uncovered his flaws?

Salem Shore (1943). A woman's lover goes to sea and does not return. Mad with grief, she lives on in the fantasy that one day he will come back and each day goes to the shore in her finest dress to be beautiful when he appears. Is it weeks, months, years? Has Martha recognized that hers will be a life in which no such lover will ever appear?

Deaths and Entrances (1943). The Brontë sisters, Charlotte, Emily, and Anne (like Graham sisters, Martha, Mary, and Georgia), live beset by repressed passions. Men stride in, stony, incomprehensible. She offers herself to the Dark Beloved, but when he tries to bend her to his will, she sends him packing. One sister (Martha) goes mad, and there's a battle royal—a game of chess—in which she makes a daring move that wins and also destroys the game. This dance takes us into the labyrinthian heart of Martha's overcharged inner world, posing questions, offering no answers.

Hérodiade (1944). A woman prepares for an ordeal (life?), assisted by a loving nurse who must finally leave her to face it alone. As a child, Martha had nurse Lizzie,[9] whom she loved and trusted more than she trusted her own family. All her life, if anyone in Martha's inner circle showed anything less than absolute devotion, she became the rejected infant whose mother had thrust her away. Rather than allow another such catastrophe, Martha struck first.

Errand into the Maze (1946). A metaphor for any shattering experience. The sexual dominates, however, and Martha's use of pounding jumps that go on and on and on more than hint at brutish lovers.

Cave of the Heart (1947). Martha admired witches as powerful female beings. Medea is daughter of the Sun. After destroying her rival in an orgy of fury, she eats a snake and vomits it up again. Martha would speak of Medea as if she were alive. "I have to arm myself against her. She is so powerful she can reach out and take possession. I must not allow her to do that when performing her role." When Martha flew into a rage, it was as if Medea had reached back and taken her. And when she directed her rage at me, that fury captured me too.

The Eye of Anguish (1949). Also titled *Lear,* one of Martha's less successful works, was created as a vehicle for Erick. I once thought that its didactic, program note had been written by him. Now I'd say it was not. It begins:

> Tragedy records, eventually, victory rather than defeat. The Eye of Anguish is the means by which the tragic protagonist achieves insight and self-knowledge, and in the end, redemption . . . Lear's tragic flaw is lack of imaginative insight. He errs in thinking that he can be king without a crown and in treating love as measurable. By introducing a spirit of calculation, he invests his evil daughters, Goneril and Regan, with power and banishes Cordelia whom he loves.

Not knowing who to trust was Martha's own tragic flaw. Lear gave away his crown. Martha gave artistic authority to those unequipped for it. The first was Erick Hawkins. The last was the minion she designated as her heir, who banished all who loved Martha and whom Martha, despite her blindness, loved.

> The two evil sisters, whose calculating minds become slaves to uncontrolled animal desire, are joined in a triangular passion with

Edmund, the Bastard. Opposite them are Edgar in the assumed madness of Poor Tom, the Fool, and Cordelia, joined in love and devotion to Lear.

For the scheming sisters, a scheming minion, for animal desire, venality; for Edmund, the Bastard, lawyers, for Mad Tom and the Fool, befuddled Graham trustees, for Cordelia, all whom Martha, in her blindness, betrayed, including audiences, students, her company, and especially Bertram Ross, Linda Hodes, Mary Hinkson, LeRoy Leatherman, and Craig Barton.

Judith (1950). The biblical heroine saved her people from a marauding general, first seducing then beheading him. Pearl Lang once said, "Martha had to make that dance so she could cut off Erick's head." *Judith* preceded the disastrous 1950 tour to Europe, which ended with Erick's defection, yet points, I think, to Martha's uncanny way of anticipating the big changes in her life.

Clytemnestra (1958). With Agamemnon, her husband, away at war, Clytemnestra contended with parasitic courtiers including "the womanish Aegisthus." When Agamemnon returned, she stabbed him in his bath, and when she died, went to Hades to walk "dishonored among the dead." Trapped in the underworld, the word "rebirth" resounds as Clytemnestra seeks redemption. Just as Clytemnestra was bereft of her warrior husband's strength, Martha in old age was bereft of the strength to dance. As Clytemnestra resisted, then accepted, Aegisthus, Martha resisted, then accepted, a scheming minion. Denied dance, she was trapped in a barren underworld. Martha had always known that one day she would no longer dance. Such foreknowledge lies at the heart of *Clytemnestra*, created fourteen years before she actually stopped. In 1969, Martha abandoned her school, her "Dancing-Ground," to stay away almost three years. She returned in 1971, thrust out her devoted partner, Bertram Ross, allowed her star dancer, Mary Hinkson, to leave, fired a hapless Craig Barton and the resentful yet longing-to-be-redeemed, LeRoy Leatherman. There was no rationality in these furiously self-destructive acts, and much lost, as when Medea murdered her innocent children. By betraying three who truly loved her, Martha sought revenge upon life itself. Aware of her betrayal and its dishonor, the keening cry, *"Rebirth Rebirth"* issued from Martha's soul. As Clytemnestra sought redemption in Hades, Martha sought it by making dances, twenty-four from 1973 through 1991.[10] And if none equaled her early masterpieces, *Acts of Light* has glory, and *Rag,* her last, is effervescent and wise.

Circe (1963). A bewitching woman ensnares every man she meets. This describes the mythological Circe and the living Martha Graham. When I saw *Circe,* I *envied* those enslaved minions and thought what a fool was Odysseus to reject so irresistible a siren. Under the dance's spell, I deemed myself a fool for having left Martha. And, oh, the rapturous music! Alan Hovhaness, aware that Martha had felt bullied by *Ardent Song,* gave her music that sounded like the echoing sighs of a hopeless passion.

Part Real-Part Dream (1965). Exposes Martha's inner life. Its sparkling choreography evokes a sun surrounded by planets, a black hole sucking in stars. It is life on Martha's event horizon, the magic of her dancing, dance itself. Any life not part real and part dream is incompletely lived.

Shadows (1977). An old couple remember their youth and the memory materializes—young lovers a-blaze with passion. And, we realize that *memory is the reality,* while the declining pair are the shadows. Martha is eighty-two years old. Can one imagine a more powerful revelation of her state of mind?

Two dancers, Tina Croll and Jamie Cunningham, create *From the Horse's Mouth,* bringing together dancers who dance and talk about their lives. It is such a success it takes over their careers. They produce one for ex–Martha Graham dancers. I offer the following "Martha's Rap":

There was a little lady named Martha Graham.
She could dance, wow! Dance, she could dance. She could slay 'em.
Ruth St. Denis said, "No! She's ugly."
Ted Shawn said, "But that doesn't bug me.
I need Martha Graham, you see,
Cause I must have a partner not as pretty as me."
So Martha danced her heart's desire,
And pretty darn soon she set the world on fire.
As "Chosen One" she wowed them all
At Radio City Music Hall.
But soon Martha wanted her own dance troupe,
So she left Denishawn and formed her group.
In her first recital, nineteen twenty-six,
She showed the world some brand new tricks.

With a guy named Erick, another named Merce,
She created a new dance universe.
The critics, poor slobs, were deeply dismayed.
"This is not dance!" they sobbed and brayed.
Lincoln Kirstein was mortified,
Saw "Lamentation," broke down and cried.
"Dark Meadow" left Antony Tudor annoyed.
He said, "Only I make dances based on Sigmund Freud."
Now Martha's in Heaven and as we speak
She is teaching a class in Graham Technique.
Agnes de Mille's Back Fall has grace.
Jerome Robbins's Triplets keep up the pace.
Nureyev's Prances are a wonder.
Eglevsky's Bison Jumps roar like thunder.
All the Angels are diverted.
Even Balanchine converted.
Now every day on celestial grass,
Heaven is taking Martha's class.

Martha's explosion when I told her I was taking more ballet than Graham classes, explained because she cared about me, had been instantly forgiven. Eventually I began to understand that Martha's wrath was a mix of jealousy, fear of desertion, drive for power, and—one more—the ecstasy of rage. How joyously she related having torn a telephone out of the wall after Ted Shawn called with a message she did not wish to hear. Eventually I realized that when I was overcome by temper, a strange sort of ecstasy captured me too.

Dancers spend their lives building the skills that give them exquisite control over their bodies, yet it is never enough. They are "control freaks," although the control they seek is over themselves. Only those who become choreographers need to control others.

Martha was driven to dominate, yet I never felt freer than when working with her. She explored her own ideas relentlessly and called upon her dancers to explore theirs. In most other places—from the Harkness Ballet in New York to the Guangdong Modern Dance Company in China—creative people zealously guard their ideas.

Martha said, "I am a thief but I only steal from the best," which is different, a cross-fertilizing in the ageless process through which art evolves. Martha spurred me, as she did so many, to explore my own ideas, and to make dances.

After a fight with Martha, one could feel intimidated, outraged, or deeply wronged, but never cheapened. She invested you with fearful strength when she cried, "You are trying to destroy me." And to Louis Horst, "You are breaking my very soul."[11]

Martha surrounded herself with trained, disciplined, hard-driving dancers, who put working with her before anything else in their lives. Paul Taylor wrote of being drawn to her dancing, yet he always kept a personal distance. "Our devotion as dancers went beyond devotion to an individual. We all saw Martha's faults and flaws every day," and, "Martha's grandeur was a little too grand for me."[12]

I'm certain that Martha saw through Paul's calculated simplicity of speech and manner to the genius beneath. But if he threatened her a little, it was not his genius, which she welcomed. It was simply that while she had Paul's admiration, even his love, she could never dominate him.

I shocked two young Graham adherents, dancer Jennifer Conley and musician Patrick Daugherty, when I said that in my opinion the greatest dance created in the twentieth century is Paul Taylor's *The Rehearsal*.

"Are you serious?" cried Patrick.

I had to explain that the greatest dance does not mean Taylor edges out Martha Graham as the century's most "important" choreographer. No one approaches Martha, who created a kinetic language, great dances, and a vision that the world embraced. She fulfilled the dream of all who joined her quest: *she changed the world*. Paul Taylor's dances, like Johann Sebastian Bach's music, are a priceless treasure, yet can one claim either changed art as did Martha?

Merce Cunningham changed dance too, although in an entirely different way. He offered no story or human setting in which one could imagine one's self. Watching his dances is like tracing fractal patterns, staring at cloud formations, where one's thoughts coalesce and are rearranged. One emerges pondering the universe, which is surely why the French, with their passion for abstruse thought, go mad for Cunningham, and why others can be stymied or outraged.

Martha is compared to two twentieth-century giants who changed their arts, Pablo Picasso and Igor Stravinsky. She deserves to be, yet my personal ardor is not generated by her effect upon dance but her explorations of the human soul. I think Martha is better compared to William Shakespeare.

Don McDonagh, first to write a biography of Martha,[13] was accosted by John Martin: "What makes you think you are the one to write Martha's biography?"

"Because neither you nor anyone else has written it," and shortly thereafter, to me, "There should be a whole shelf of books about Martha Graham." I offer this to that still underpopulated shelf.

I experienced transcendence when I first soloed an airplane, again when I flew one across the Atlantic Ocean, and in a conflicted way, on every combat mission. For a time I could "sign out" an airplane, fly to Rome, Pisa, Naples. But when I began to understand that all people have similar dreams and bewilderments, I lost the urge to fly hither and thither for brief stays.

Being at the controls of an airplane offers glimpses of a world hard to imagine on the earth's surface. (Being a passenger is nothing.) Dancing happens in the heart of a world of which non-dancers cannot even dream. During performance, as on a combat mission, thoughts are so tightly focused it feels like not thinking, but afterward one feels intensely alive.

No rational person would choose to live with demons that command every relationship, every thought. Martha's life chose her, and some were compelled to choose Martha. Amid the laughter and groans, revelations and furies, it was life in the eye of a storm, at the epicenter of an earthquake. Having flown and fought as a nineteen-year-old, I could live with nothing less.

Occasionally someone will ask, "What was it like to dance with Martha Graham?" The peaks were making dances, an adventure of the mind, imagination, and body into which Martha drew all who were there. In magical moments when she merged with my creative energy, I felt excitement, elation, and joy. Less exalted feelings faded, but the moments of illumination blazed with a fire that compelled me to keep ragged notes for some forty years and a dozen more putting them into comprehensible form.

Is this the book Martha wanted when she said, "Write it down?" Is it why she called me to her bedside after being injured in Paris? Would she have agreed that *Theater for a Voyage* was abandoned because the "fallacy" was the very idea of a dance based on actual relationships with Bertram

Ross, Bob Cohan, and me? Were we too close, part of the family, like the mother who had thrust her into the arms of Nurse Lizzie saying, "Here! Take her!" Martha's tragic flaw—not knowing who to trust—was hers to the end. Her life, was, nevertheless, one of prodigious achievement. If Martha had not lived, the world would be different, and, as I see it, a poorer place.

Martha was brilliant, irrational, flirting, rejecting, generous, vulnerable, impenetrable, isolated, surrounded, and, for me, impossible not to love. Looming over all were those transcendent moments in her rehearsals and on her stage. Working with Martha was like going into battle, physically demanding, emotionally charged, and fraught with danger. Martha Graham was the adventure of a lifetime.

Epilogue

My daughter Martha, visiting Germany, saw my paternal surname, Gescheidt, on a list of victims of Nazi genocide.

My maternal grandmother, Regina Lichtblau, lit candles and said her prayers. My parents did not inherit her religion or pass it to their children, yet I slowly developed a conviction that God is all of Creation.

My brother, Alfred, said he was afraid of dying. I don't think I am.

My first devastating love was Jenny (third grade), then Selma (college freshman), then Linda (young adult), and for the past fifty-three years, Elizabeth.

The first plotless *modern* dance I saw was by May O'Donnell. When Norman Walker made one, critic John Martin wrote that modern dance moves could not be used classically.

Laura Dean made *Circle Dance,* then made it again and again.

Trisha Brown claimed never to have made the same dance twice.

Merce Cunningham's dances originate somewhere beyond the scope of ordinary mortals. They evoke the mystery of, and may (who knows?) be linked to Dark Energy.

Paul Taylor and Alvin Ailey wanted their dances to last so had them notated and videoed. Yet a day will come when they're gone, other dances in their place.

Erick Hawkins did nothing to preserve his beguiling dances and distinctive technique.

Bob Cohan left the U.S.A. in 1969 to settle in London where he became founding director of London Contemporary Dance Theatre. Now he's been knighted. Bravo! *Sir Robert!*

Martha Graham, during the last fifteen years of her life, seemed to be trying to destroy her artistic legacy.

Louis Horst said that there is one great dance in everyone.

Writing, like dancing, can be all-consuming and can produce those instants of pure being that dancers call "magic time."

Life itself seems like a mighty dance in which I have a tiny yet absorbing role.

Acknowledgments

Gratitude to Ann and Stona Fitch of Concord Free Press who published an early electronic edition of this book seen by Robert Gottlieb, who sent me to Mindy Aloff, editor of *Dance in America,* which published an excerpt, and the University Press Florida, which published it all. I am grateful to Sandra Pallazone and Ann De Patto, who read the very first draft, to Francis Mason and Dalen Sciarra Cole, who read later drafts and made invaluable suggestions, to Helen McGehee, who supplied detailed answers to questions obscured by time, and to Barbara Bennion in the Martha Graham troupe; we shared some of the most interesting years. I am indebted to Norton Owen who provided photos from the Jacob's Pillow Archive, to my nephews, Jack and Andrew Gescheidt, who allowed me to use photos taken over the years by my brother Alfred. I am deeply grateful to the photo collections that supplied illustrations that so enrich the text: Ann Barzel Dance Research Collection, Houghton Library, Harvard University, Jerome Robbins Collection, NY Public Library, Philippe Halsman Archive and Irene Halsman, Magnes Collection of Jewish Art and Life, University of California, Berkeley, Anna Canoni granddaughter of Woody Guthrie and director of the Woody Guthrie Archive, photographer James H. Schriebl for photos of Lawrence Goldhuber, and the U.S. Library of Congress. Special thanks to Oliver Tobin of the Martha Graham Archive, and to Linda Hodes who read a later manuscript. I owe special thanks to Daphne Merkin, whose generous expertise improved sections of the text via a writing class at NYC's 92nd Street Y, , and to Sarah Cypher, whose meticulous reading showed me see things I had completely missed. I was ever encouraged by my daughters, Catherine and Martha, who first appear in the manuscript when they were born and grew up to read it and provide feedback, and to my wife, Elizabeth, who read the manuscript at several stages and never complained about time stolen from our fulfilling lives. Finally, my thanks to Meredith Babb, Linda Bathgate, Deirdre Murphy Ruffino, Marthe Walters, and Jenny Wilsen of the University Press of Florida.

Notes

Chapter 3. Dance Lessons

1. Some of those notes must still lie among old papers, historical treasures I hope will be unearthed one day.
2. David Zellmer, *The Spectator: A World War II Bomber Pilot's Journal of the Artist as Warrior* (Westport, CT: Praeger, 1999), pp. 41, 92–93.
3. Alma Guillermoprieto, *Dancing with Cuba: A Memoir of the Revolution* (New York: Pantheon, 2004), p. 46.
4. Letter to the author from Helen McGehee.
5. *The New York Times*, Aug. 14, 1948.
6. Agnes de Mille, *Martha: The Life and Work of Martha Graham; A Biography* (New York: Random House, 1991).
7. This was a two-month contest given by a radio show in which audiences had to guess who was the voice behind the whispered words of "Miss Hush." Martha agreed to participate; proceeds went to charity.

Chapter 4. The Green Tours

1. The Bicycle is conceptually simple: a big hop on one leg while rotating both through a complete circle, landing on the same leg, continuing leg to leg. I taught it in class.
2. Joan Skinner. Give her a Google.
3. LeRoy Leatherman, *The Caged Birds* (New York: Harcourt, Brace, 1950).
4. Agnes de Mille's biography has Martha and Erick sitting apart on a bus tour. (p. 284). I was on every one and this is no more true than that *The Eye of Anguish* was a "solo based on Lear" (p. 285).
5. Repertory: *Appalachian Spring, Cave of the Heart, Deaths and Entrances, Diversion of Angels* (first New York City performance) *Errand into the Maze, Eye of Anguish* (first New York City performance), *Every Soul Is a Circus, Gospel of Eve* (Martha's solo, world premiere), *Hérodiade, The Strangler* (first New York City performance).
6. Program: *Salem Shore, Diversion of Angels, Deaths and Entrances, Eye of Anguish, Every Soul Is a Circus.*
7. The Gila River Relocation Center.

Chapter 6. Drink the Sky

1. You can be let go during the first three days, making it an extended audition.
2. *The Art of Making Dances* (Princeton, N.J.:, Princeton Book Co., 1959).
3. See chapter 3, p. 47.
4. Ellen Graff, *Stepping Left: Dance and Politics in New York City, 1928–1942* (Durham, NC: Duke University Press, 1997), p. 9.
5. Ibid., p. 59.
6. His name appears in all advertising.
7. Ted Shawn had made a solo entitled *O Brother Sun and Sister Moon* depicting a moment in St. Francis's afternoon. Martha makes a duet between Ross, as Brother Sun, and Yuriko, as Sister Moon, wholly different.
8. Agnes de Mille, *Martha: The Life and Work of Martha Graham; A Biography* (New York: Random House, 1991).
9. A delightful dance by Valerie Hammer titled *Smile, Though Your Car Is Breaking.*
10. In Martha's *Blood Memory: An Autobiography* (New York: Doubleday, 1991), almost the same story is set in the home of Doris Duke in Newport, Rhode Island. Told to the company, it was the American South. Your choice.
11. Paul Taylor, *Private Domain* (New York: Knopf, 1987), p. 68.
12. Cited by Janet Soares in *Louis Horst: Musician in a Dancer's World* (Durham, NC: Duke University Press, 1992), p. 97.
13. *The Notebooks of Martha Graham* (New York: Harcourt Brace Jovanovich, 1973), p. 140.

Chapter 7. The Grand Tour

1. *Table Talk* by Pendennis, *The Observer.* (Clipping does not show date or page or name of paper.)
2. Don McDonagh, *Martha Graham* (New York: Praeger, 1973), p. 231.

Chapter 8. Asia

1. On its first show, December 27, 1932, along with Ray Bolger and the Flying Wallendas.
2. Paul Taylor, *Private Domain* (New York: Knopf, 1987), p. 33.
3. Leatherman extended the conflict by calling Bob Cohan in Boston, flying him to New York City for a rehearsal in which Paul taught him his role in *Phaedra*. Bob heard nothing more. The game of "chicken" was finally over.

Chapter 9. Dancing Fool

1. Music and lyric by Mary Rodgers.
2. *Dance Magazine,* January 1958, p. 9.
3. *Herald-Tribune, Journal-American, Mirror, News, PM, Post, Sun, Times, World-Telegram.*
4. Wendy Wasserstein, *Shiksa Goddess* (New York: Knopf, 2003), p. 57.

Chapter 10. A Presence Is Gone

1. This paragraph encapsulates several of the precepts Richard d'Anjou drilled into his theater, music, and dance "associates."
2. A jawbreaker commonly used at NYSCA; it means supported by charity.
3. At that time I had a total of one year of academic credits from Brooklyn College.
4. Two books that set down clear moves and associated ideas are Alice Helpern's *The Technique of Martha Graham* (Dobbs Ferry, N.Y.: Morgan & Morgan, 1994) and Robert Cohan's *The Dance Workshop* (Boston: Allen & Unwin, 1986).
5. Fifty-Third American Assembly, November 3–6, 1977, Arden House, Harriman, New York.
6. W. McNeil Lowry, ed., *The Performing Arts and American Society* (Englewood Cliffs, N.J.: Prentice-Hall, 1977), p. 88.
7. *On Angels & Devils & Stages Between* (Amsterdam: Harwood, 1999), p. 227.
8. "Sacred Monster: Martha Graham," *The New York Times Magazine*, November 24, 1996.
9. Lizzie Prendergast, whom Martha cherished all her life. In *Blood Memory*, Martha told of the day her mother, infant Martha in her arms, answered the door to see a young woman who said, "I am Lizzie. I have come to take care of the doctor and his family." Martha's mother thrust out the fretful infant, saying, "Here. Take her."
10. *Mendicants of Evening, Myth of a Voyage, Holy Jungle, Jacob's Dream, Lucifer, Adorations, Point of Crossing, Scarlet Letter, O Thou Desire Who Art About to Sing, Shadows, The Owl and the Pussycat, Equatorial, Flute of Pan, Frescoes, Acts of Light, Dances of the Golden Hall, Andromache's Lament, Phaedra's Dream, The Rite of Spring, Temptations of the Moon, Tangled Night, Persephone, Night Chant,* and *Maple Leaf Rag.*
11. Martha Graham, *Blood Memory* (New York: Doubleday, 1991), p. 53.
12. Ibid., pp. 239, 242.
13. Don McDonagh, *Martha Graham* (New York: Praeger, 1973).

Index

Page numbers in *italics* refer to illustrations.

New Dance Group (New York), 144, 261

New School, The (New York), 161–62

News of the World (London), 179

New World School of the Arts (Miami), 262

New York City Ballet, 126, 129, 155, 162

New York City Center, x, 49, 50, 232

New York City High School of Performing Arts, xi, 56, 191, 226, 231–32, 236, 264

New York Daily Mirror, 79, 294n3 (chap. 9)

New York Herald Tribune, 60, 61, 78–79, 221, 238, 294n3 (chap. 9)

New York Journal-American, 79, 294n3 (chap. 9)

New York Post, 79, 267, 294n3 (chap. 9)

New York State Council on the Arts (NYSCA), xi, 252–57, 259, 261–64, 272, 295n2 (chap. 10)

New York Times, 119, 137, 230, 250, 256, 294n3 (chap. 9); Atkinson, 232; Kisselgoff, 152, 161; Martin, 75, 78, 114, 161, 222, 231, 236

New York University School of the Arts (Tisch), 48, 137, 271–72; Hodes teaching at, xi, 7, 46–47, 158, 264, 274–75, 279

New York World-Telegram, 79, 294n3 (chap. 9)

Nichigeki Music Hall (Tokyo), 203

Nick (Wasserstein associate), 238

Night Journey (Graham), 72, 82, 152, 166; film of, 240–41; Hodes in, 114, 126, 185; making of, 27–31, 63; props, 28–31, *28,* 228–29, 241; reviews, 179; revival of, 240–41; score, 30, 31, 68

Night of the Living Dead (film), 7

Nikolais, Alwin, 51–52, 225, 255, 262

92nd Street Y (NYC), 52, 58, 78, 137, 140, 154; *At the Recital,* 63, 65; *Curley's Wife,* 54

Nirska, Mira, 196

Nixon, Richard, 63

Noguchi, Isamu, 165, 194; *Dark Meadow, 18,* 18–19, 59; *Errand into the Maze,* 112, *113; John Brown,* 65, 67; *Night Journey,* 28–30, *29,* 228, *229; El Penitente,* 65, 67; *Stephen Acrobat,* 60, 61, *62,* 66, 67–68; *Theater for a Voyage,* 166, *167*

Noh dance-drama, 203

Nordhoff, Paul, 66

North Carolina School of the Arts, 269

Nureyev, Rudolf, 78, 223, 237, 285

Nurit (Israeli soldier), 220

Oboukoff, Anatol, 34

Observer, The (London), 178, 181, 294n1 (chap. 7)

O'Connor, Donald, 223

O'Donnell, May, 23, 24, 89, 141, 169, 289

Oedipus myth, 27–30, 72, 75, 82, 179, 236, 240–41

O'Flanagan, Brendon, 50

Of Mice and Men (Steinbeck), 54, 247

Oklahoma (musical), 148

Once Upon a Mattress (musical), 136, 223

Osgood, Betty, 162

O'Sullivans (embassy couple), 208–9

Ouroussow, Eugenie, 33

Ouspensky, P. D., 172

Pajama Game, The (musical), 226

Pandor, Miriam, 81–82

Pantages, Alexander, 103

Paper Bag Players (New York), 106, 162

Papp, Joseph, 265

Partington, Arthur, 159

Pavlova, Anna, 35

Paxton, Steve, 99, 138

Payne, Carol, 194

P. B. (London reviewer), 179

Pearl Harbor, attack on, xv

Peck, Gregory, 105

Peking Opera Ballet, 165, 239–40

Pendennis (*Observer* column), 179

Penderecki, Krzysztof, 248; Threnody to the Victims of Hiroshima, 248

Pendleton, Moses, 138

Perse, Saint-John, 173; *Vents,* 173

Persichetti, Vincent, 88

Petrie, Daniel, 244

Petrillo, James, 255

Phillips, Wendell, 65

Piaf, Edith, 153

Picasso, Pablo, 239, 244, 263, 286

Piccadilly Theatre, 129, *130*

Pilobolus Dance Theater, 138, 270

Place, The (London), 258

Pond, Jonathan, 54

Stuart Hodes has danced for over seven decades—on Broadway, in TV, film, in recitals, and with his own troupe. His choreography has appeared at the Boston Ballet, Dallas Ballet, Harkness Ballet, Joffrey Ballet, San Francisco Ballet, and other troupes. He taught at the Martha Graham School, Neighborhood Playhouse, and NYC High School of Performing Arts and headed dance at NYU School of the Arts and Borough of Manhattan Community College. He was dance associate for the New York State Council on the Arts, dance panelist for the National Endowment for the Arts, president of the National Association of Schools of Dance, and a member of the First American Dance Study Team to China in 1980, returning in 1992 to teach the Guangzhou modern dance troupe.